Far Right Parties and Euroscepticism

Far Right Parties and Euroscepticism

Patterns of Opposition

Sofia Vasilopoulou

ecpr PRESS

ROWMAN &
LITTLEFIELD
INTERNATIONAL

London • New York

Published by Rowman & Littlefield International, Ltd.
6 Tinworth Street, London SE11 5AL, United Kingdom
www.rowmaninternational.com

Rowman & Littlefield International Ltd.is an affiliate of Rowman & Littlefield
4501 Forbes Boulevard, Suite 200, Lanham, Maryland 20706, USA
With additional offices in Boulder, New York, Toronto (Canada), and Plymouth (UK)
www.rowman.com

In Partnership with the European Consortium for Political Research
Harbour House, 6-8 Hythe Quay
Colchester, CO2 8JF United Kingdom
www.ecpr.eu

British Library Cataloguing in Publication Data
A catalogue record for this book is available from the British Library

ISBN: HB 978-1-78552-229-1
ISBN: PB 978-1-78661-304-2

Library of Congress Cataloging-in-Publication Data
Names: Vasilopoulou, Sofia, author.
Title: Far right parties and Euroscepticism: patterns of opposition / by Sofia
    Vasilopoulou.
Description: London; Lanham, Maryland: Rowman & Littlefield International, Ltd.,
    [2017] | Includes bibliographical references and index. |
Identifiers: LCCN 2017030057 (print) | LCCN 2017045658 (ebook) |
    ISBN 9781786605269 (Electronic) | ISBN 9781785522291 (hb : alk. paper) |
    ISBN 9781786605269 (ebook) | ISBN 9781786613042 (pb : alk. paper)
Subjects: LCSH: Political parties—European Union countries. | Right-wing extremists—
    European Union countries. | European Union—Public opinion. | Public opinion—
    European Union countries. | European Union—Membership. | European Union
    countries—Politics and government—21st century.
Classification: LCC JN50 (ebook) | LCC JN50 .V37 2017 (print) | DDC
    341.242/2—dc23
LC record available at https://lccn.loc.gov/2017030057

Contents

Contents

List of Abbreviations

AKEL	Progressive Party of Working People
AN	National Alliance
ECB	European Central Bank
ECU	European Currency Unit
EFDD	Europe of Freedom and Direct Democracy
EMU	European Monetary Union
EU	European Union
FI	Forza Italia
FN	National Front
FYROM	Former Yugoslav Republic of Macedonia
GAL/TAN	Green, Alternative and Libertarian/ Traditional, Authoritarian and Nationalist
LAOS	Greek Popular Orthodox Rally
MEP	Member of the European Parliament
MSI	Italian Social Movement
NATO	North Atlantic Treaty Organisation
ND	New Democracy
PASOK	Panhellenic Socialist Movement
PFN	Party of New Forces
RPR	Rally for the French Republic
TB-LNNK	National Alliance – For Fatherland and Freedom
TEU	Treaty of the European Union
UDF	Union for French Democracy

List of Tables

List of Figures

Acknowledgements

This book began as a doctoral dissertation at the London School of Economics. I am most grateful to Kevin Featherstone for challenging my ideas, and Jonathan Hopkin for supporting me throughout this period. The University of York has provided an excellent working environment that has facilitated the completion of this book.

This project has benefited from the guidance of many people. I would like to thank Michael Bruter, Willem Buiter, Liz Carter, Simon Hix, Bob Hancké, Kostas Gemenis, Simon Glendinning, Peter Mair, Paul Mitchell, Thomas Poguntke, Waltraud Schelkle, Tim Vlandas and the anonymous reviewer at ECPR Press. For research assistance, I thank Adriano Cozzolino, Nikoleta Kiapidou, Leyla Slama and Liisa Talving.

The research for this book was made possible by financial support from the Bodossakis Foundation, Greece. This book also benefited from a British Academy/Leverhulme Trust Small Research Grant entitled 'Radical right-wing parties and Euroscepticism: Issue salience in MEP speeches' (Ref: SG132583).

Material from Chapter 2 has been previously published in Vasilopoulou, S. (2011) 'European Integration and the Radical Right: Three Patterns of Opposition', *Government and Opposition*, Volume 46(2), 223–244. It is reproduced here with the kind permission of Cambridge University Press.

I am especially grateful to my friends and colleagues Katjana Gattermann and Daphne Halikiopoulou, who push me to think critically and have helped me develop into the researcher I am.

I thank my parents, George and Ria, and my aunt, Mosha, for believing in me and supporting my academic pursuits. My deepest thanks go to my husband, Matt, for his love, encouragement and unfailing support during this long journey. I dedicate this book to him and to the memory of my father.

Chapter 1

Introduction

The European Union (EU) is a major political and economic achievement in post–World War II Europe, created to guarantee the stability, growth and prosperity of its members. Over the past decades, it has expanded its jurisdictional authority over a number of key policy areas, including the single market, trade, the euro currency, justice, fundamental rights and citizenship. However, increased economic and political integration have produced growing party and public opposition. Euroscepticism, a term used to describe the disapproval of and opposition to closer European integration, has become an 'embedded' feature of both national and EU politics 'with the potential to cause irreparable damage to the EU's quest for legitimacy and stability' (Usherwood and Startin 2013: 2). The EU's failure to promptly resolve the Eurozone and migration crises has further eroded the project's credibility and has strengthened anti-EU sentiment among European citizens. Trust in the EU was at a record low at 33 per cent in 2016 compared to 57 per cent in 2007 (Eurobarometer 2016).

Within this ever-growing environment of 'constraining dissensus' (Hooghe and Marks 2009), the strongest advocates of Eurosceptic views may be found within the far right party family (Vasilopoulou 2011). Far right parties perceive the EU as posing a threat to nation-states' cultural homogeneity and national sovereignty. The EU's supranational decision-making structures, its global outlook and its promotion of cultural diversity go against the far right's mission of defending the nation (Halikiopoulou et al. 2012; see also Marks and Wilson 2000; Hooghe et al. 2002). Far right parties are also ideally placed to oppose the EU. Their marginal position in their domestic party systems provides them with additional incentives to criticise the EU (e.g. Taggart 1998; Sitter 2001). Indeed, Hainsworth (2008: 85) argues that '[these parties] are well placed to act as the voice of popular opposition and protest

1

against developments declared to be anti-national'. In short, by virtue of their nationalist ideology and marginal status, far right parties across Europe put forward similar Eurosceptic positions, i.e., they oppose the entire process of European integration. These parties are 'distinguished by their intense Europhobia' (Marks and Wilson 2000: 457).

This book questions this very premise. It argues and empirically substantiates that far right party Euroscepticism is by no means uniform. In fact, a comparison of these parties' positions on European integration reveals that they vary from complete rejection of the entire EU project to weak support for aspects of European integration. For example, despite a somewhat positive approach in the 1980s, the French National Front's EU position has crystallised into strong opposition to the EU. The party rejects the principle of multilateral co-operation at the EU level. It denounces all EU treaties as allegedly marking the end of nation-states' political sovereignty and economic prosperity. Marine Le Pen – President of the party since 2011 – has maintained her father's hard Eurosceptic position by calling for a referendum on France's EU membership. Following the party's historic victory during the May 2014 European Parliament (EP) elections, when it claimed first place in the polls, Marine Le Pen upheld this view by stating: 'I do not want this European Soviet Union' (Spiegel 2014). Other far right parties, such as the Greek Popular Orthodox Rally (LAOS), on the other hand, do not support their country's withdrawal from the EU. While LAOS opposes the creation of a European political union and is critical of various EU policies, it accepts the principle of European co-operation at a higher multilateral level. Interestingly, despite the fact that the Greek crisis presented an opportunity for the party to harden its EU stance, LAOS weakly supported the EU's economic adjustment programme for Greece. The – now dissolved – Italian National Alliance (successor of the neo-fascist Italian Social Movement) progressed from a critical position in the 1980s and early 1990s towards a more conciliatory view of European integration in the 2000s. The party accepted, by and large, EU policy integration and recognised the importance of EU institutions. Although it was unfavourable to various aspects of the EU project, its criticisms were mostly technical rather than substantive.

Comparative expert survey data also confirm this variation. Contrary to expectations, not all far right parties put forward extreme Eurosceptic positions. Rather, scores on the EU dimension range considerably with some far right parties strongly opposing the EU and others presenting relatively centrist or even pro-EU positions. On a scale from 1 to 7, where 1 indicates strong opposition to the EU and 7 strong support (Bakker et al. 2015), parties such as the French National Front, the British National Party and the Hungarian Jobbik have consistently positioned themselves very close to the Eurosceptic end of the dimension. Other far right parties, however, such as the Latvian For Fatherland and Freedom and the Italian National Alliance, have been supportive of various aspects of European integration, scoring between 4 and 5.75 on the same dimension. A third subset of far right parties, including the Greek LAOS, the Danish People's Party, the Northern League and the Bulgarian Attack, have adopted comparatively more moderate positions, scoring between 2 and 3 on the scale (Vasilopoulou 2018).

Why do ideologically similar parties oppose the EU to differing extents? The goal of this book is to conceptualise, analyse and explain patterns of far right Euroscepticism. In doing so, it focuses on party positions on the EU and the ways in which these parties may frame European integration. Starting from the assumption that far right parties are rational actors, the book argues that the way in which they may interpret structural incentives depends largely on their relationship with democracy, their attitude towards the polity, their target electorate/social basis and their behaviour towards competitors. Classification on these indicators leads to the identification of three far right party models, i.e., what this book terms anti-system, anti-liberal and normalised. Given that the EU is a core issue in far right parties' toolkit, it becomes a key policy in party competition. Anti-system far right parties tend to opt for a rejectionist position on the EU; anti-liberal far right parties tend to be conditional Eurosceptics; and normalised far right parties tend to adopt a compromising position on the EU. The specific Eurosceptic frame that parties may prioritise depends on the domestic political context and the ways in which they may perceive national identity. This book's findings are relevant in light of Europe's political and economic crises, and rising public support for Eurosceptic ideas and far right parties.

EXPLAINING FAR RIGHT EUROSCEPTICISM

The literature on party-based Euroscepticism has been structured in terms of party-level ideological (e.g. Marks and Wilson 2000; Hooghe et al. 2002; Marks and Steenbergen 2004) and national-level tactical (e.g. Taggart 1998; Sitter 2001; Szczerbiak and Taggart 2008a, 2008b) explanations. These have been summarised as the North Carolina and the Sussex 'schools' of Euroscepticism, respectively (Mudde 2011). The North Carolina school places emphasis on the role of cleavages and party ideology in predicting whether a party would oppose or support the EU. Issues related to European integration are assimilated into existing dimensions of political contestation. This relationship may be summarised as an inverted U-curve with parties situated on the extremes of the economic left-right dimension opposing EU integration and centrist parties supporting the EU project. The Sussex school, on the other hand, views parties as strategic actors whose EU position depends on nation-specific characteristics and party competition. These include the configuration of the party system, probability to access office and positions of major potential allies or competitors. Opposition parties and those with a marginal status in the system are more likely to oppose the EU in order to signal to voters their difference from the establishment.

This book does not treat these explanations as antithetical, and demonstrates that ideology and strategy are integral to party behaviour. In fact, they are 'mutually enforcing rather than mutually exclusive' (De Vries and Edwards 2009: 11; see also Halikiopoulou et al. 2012). On the one hand, centre-left and centre-right parties have regularly participated in government, and have been involved in EU decision-making. Given that the EU is the product of a carefully crafted compromise between centre-right market liberalisation and centre-left market regulation belief systems, centrist parties have limited incentives to criticise it. On the other hand, extremist parties view the EU project as antithetical to their core values. For parties of the far right, the EU is a super-structure seeking to dismantle the nation-state. For parties of the far left, EU policies go against the interests of the working class. At the same time, despite increasing success in the polls, these parties tend to operate in the margins of their respective party systems, and employ their EU stance as a way of distancing themselves from the mainstream.

Far right party Euroscepticism, which is the focus of this book, may be seen as the product of both ideological and strategic considerations. Values and beliefs serve as strong cognitive constraints in shaping actors' choices. This explains why far right parties broadly share a sovereignty-based criticism of the EU, arguing that it undermines cherished national sovereignty (Vasilopoulou 2011). Policy problems deriving from European integration may be resolved through a process by which the nation-state would regain a level of control in some or all EU policies. In the context of party competition, however, strategic considerations may condition the extent to which far right parties oppose the EU. Starting from the premise that far right parties are rational actors (e.g. see Wagner 2012), this book argues that their Euroscepticism is conditional upon the dynamics of domestic party competition and the parties' political agenda within their national party system. Each far right party crafts its unique EU policy niche in its domestic party system based on a careful balance between interest representation, electoral politics and party competition. Although far right parties share the core features of nationalism, authoritarianism and strong leadership, they tend to vary in terms of their relationship with democracy and the ways in which they view their position in the domestic party system, which is associated with their policy on European integration. Being true issue entrepreneurs, far right parties adopt and adjust their EU policy for electoral purposes.

How may we conceptualise far right party Euroscepticism? This book argues that far right parties may be categorised into three mutually exclusive and exhaustive (Gerring 2012: 144) patterns of opposition to European integration. These include the 'rejectionist', the 'conditional' and the 'compromising' patterns. This typology is constructed on the basis of four attributes, including the definition of Europe, the principle, the policy practice and the future building of European integration. Parties belonging to the rejectionist pattern of far right Euroscepticism are against the principle of member state co-operation within the EU framework, are intensely critical of the EU institutional and policy status quo and reject future EU political and economic integration altogether. Conditional Eurosceptics present a somewhat less monolithic position on the EU. They accept, by and large, the principle of member state co-operation at the EU multilateral level, but they voice criticisms of the EU policy practice and are averse to the extension of EU competence into new issue areas. The compromising Euroscepticism type comprises parties that support the principle of member state co-operation at the EU level, and view the EU's policy practice through a comparatively less critical lens.

These different Eurosceptic patterns are explained through a novel theoretical framework that refers to far right party models. Anti-system far right parties tend to adopt a rejectionist Eurosceptic position. These parties employ the EU in order to criticise what they frame as the domestic pro-EU consensus. Such an adversarial strategy serves to polarise the electorate and undermine the legitimacy of the political system. Anti-liberal far right parties tend to adopt policies that allow them to retain their core base while at the same time broadening their electoral appeal. These parties adopt a conditional Eurosceptic position. They avoid radicalising their discourse and seek to accommodate the European issue within debates that they perceive to be close to the convictions of the median voter. Normalised far right parties tend to opt for a compromising position on European integration. These parties employ the EU issue as a tool for political entrenchment in the domestic party system. By appearing closer to potential coalition partners of the right, they seek to improve their potential for collaboration with other domestic political forces.

Euroscepticism does not only relate to how parties position themselves on the EU dimension. Beyond adopting dissimilar positions on the EU, far right parties may also differ in the specificities of their Eurosceptic framing of the EU, and the ways in which they construct their argumentation. In addition to the general sovereignty-based critiques, which are common across the party family, these parties tend to link their Euroscepticism to nation-specific questions or societal problems. Given that the far right's nationalist ideology draws its resources from the national context more than any other party family, the specificities of far right Eurosceptic issue framing are associated to country-specific debates and may take a particularised tone and focus. This entails that Eurosceptic argumentation is sensitive to national contexts. Eurosceptic issue framing also becomes accommodated into party politics as an element of domestic party competition.

THE FAR RIGHT IN EUROPE

Authors have employed a number of designations to refer to this party family. The most popular labels include extreme right (e.g. Hainsworth 2000a; Hainsworth 2008; Mudde 2000; Carter 2005; Bruter and Harrison 2011), radical right (e.g. Kitschelt and McGann 1995; Minkenberg 2001; Norris 2005; Art 2011; Akkerman 2012; Immerzeel et al. 2015) and populist radical right (e.g. Mudde 2007; 2014; Dunn 2015). This book employs the term 'far right' as an umbrella term encompassing both the extreme and radical right variants of this party family (e.g. Cole 2005; Erk 2005; Ellinas 2010; Mudde 2010: 1169; Vasilopoulou and Halikiopoulou 2015; Halikiopoulou and Vlandas 2016). Although there is academic debate on the core characteristics that set far right parties apart from other party families, which in itself has been a subject of enquiry, this book suggests that these parties are defined by the core ideological doctrine of nationalism, authoritarian attitudes and strong leadership.

Mudde (2007) identifies a minimum and a maximum definition of this party family's ideology. The minimum definition suggests that nationalism is central to and constitutive of these parties' ideologies (see also Eatwell 2000; Rydgren 2007; Ellinas 2010: 29; Vasilopoulou and Halikiopoulou 2015). Far right parties tend to be proponents of exclusive and restrictive forms of nationalism. They make ethnocentric appeals, creating dichotomies between 'nationals' and those who they portray as the enemies of the nation. Their ideology is rooted in the defence of the national interest and draws upon the nationalist political doctrine, which holds that the political and national unit should be congruent (Gellner 1983). Their core mission is to protect national sovereignty from globalising forces, which they see as a threat to each nation-state's independence and right to self-determination. Although the Eurozone crisis has made the economy more salient in these parties' programmatic agenda, far right parties tend to primarily compete along the national identity axis.

According to the maximum definition, far right parties may also be defined by their authoritarianism (e.g. see Mudde 2007; Rydgren 2007; Hainsworth 2008). This often refers to a non-democratic form of government, and tends to be juxtaposed to totalitarianism (e.g. Linz 2000). In the context of attitudes and political ideologies, right-wing authoritarianism may be defined using Altemeyer's (1981) F-scale, i.e., conventionalism, authoritarian aggression and authoritarian submission. Authoritarians tend to believe that all members of the society should follow traditional norms and customs; seek to control behaviour through punishment; and are prone to accept established authorities, such as police, the government or a strong political leader. Authoritarians are predisposed to expressing intolerant and punitive attitudes under conditions of group threat (Dunn 2015: 368). Combined with exclusive nationalism, authoritarianism is associated with the support of strict law and order, the promotion of a return to the national/traditional way of life and opposition to immigration and policies promoting multiculturalism, which are seen as eroding national identity, culture and values.

Beyond nationalism and authoritarianism, the literature also points to populism as a key characteristic of the far right. Populist actors claim to speak on behalf of the 'common people,' differentiating them from the 'corrupt elites' (Mudde 2007). Those elites may vary from economic (multinational companies and banks), political (the establishment and the government) or cultural (intellectuals broadly defined, such as academics, journalists or writers). Some actors may go as far as presenting themselves and their movement as the embodiment of the people and its collective will, defending them against those perceived to be the enemies of the nation (Vasilopoulou and Halikiopoulou 2015). The centrality of populism to far right ideology has been contested, however, especially because there is no consensus on whether it constitutes an ideological feature (i.e., it defines a party's deep core values) or whether it refers to a political communication style (e.g. see Jagers and Walgrave 2007; Mudde 2007). Other scholars go beyond this distinction and view charisma and strong leadership as an essential feature of populism (e.g. Germani 1978, Betz 1998: 9, Taggart 2000: 102, Eatwell 2002, Pedahzur and Brichta 2002). The formal organisational structures of far right parties tend to be similarly controlled by a powerful leader who is relatively unconstrained by the rest of the party (e.g. Zaslove 2004). This may be seen in terms of the personalisation of politics, i.e., the leader becomes the epitome of the party and 'voters come to see parties [...] through a matrix of their leaders' (Eatwell 2002: 19).

In sum, nationalism forms the core ideological feature of this party family. Beyond nationalism, far right parties also share a common authoritarian vision with regard to how society should be structured and organised. Although there is no academic consensus on the role of populism in far right ideology, these parties tend to be characterised by top-down organisation and strong leadership.

RESEARCH DESIGN AND CASE SELECTION

This book seeks to conceptualise, analyse and explain patterns of far right Euroscepticism. To do so, it adopts a comparative research design, drawing upon literature in the fields of party politics, political behaviour and Euroscepticism. It combines the study of the wider universe of European far right parties with a controlled comparison of three parties in order to attain maximum analytical leverage. First, the three patterns of far right Eurosceptic opposition are examined through the empirical analysis of programmatic material of fourteen far right parties from eleven European democracies. Here, the focus is on the wider universe of far right parties in order to illustrate the empirical relevance of the three patterns. Subsequently, the book relies on a controlled comparison of three far right parties in order to construct a causal argument, linking types of Euroscepticism to far right party models. The controlled comparison follows the most similar systems design, in which ideologically similar parties exhibit variation in the dependent variable, namely that they belong to different patterns of Euroscepticism. This design allows for the detailed assessment of the dynamics that explain different party positions on European integration by ruling out competing explanations, and is able to generate both internal and external validity of the findings (Hancké 2009; Slater and Ziblatt 2013; see also Norris 2005: 36).

The controlled comparison consists of an analysis of the French National Front, the Greek Popular Orthodox Rally and the Italian National Alliance. The comparison starts from the premise that because the parties under investigation belong to the same party family, they share specific characteristics, including nationalism, authoritarianism and strong leadership. These party features are held constant in the comparison, i.e., are not considered as potential explanations for the variation in a far right party's position on the EU. Despite sharing these three key characteristics, the three far right parties display strong variation in the dependent variable. To illustrate the comparability of the three cases, Table 1.1 presents party scores from the Chapel Hill expert survey on a number of questions and policy fields (Bakker et al. 2015). All three parties are strong supporters of tough measures to fight crime, similarly oppose liberal policies on social lifestyle, strongly favour assimilation and advocate nationalism. There is some small variation with regard to their stance towards immigration policy and ethnic minorities, with the Italian party being slightly more lenient. In both questions, however, all parties score very high and significantly above the middle value. They also score very highly on the GAL/TAN dimension, where GAL stands for green, alternative and libertarian; and TAN stands for traditional, authoritarian and nationalist values. This suggests that they similarly value order, tradition and stability, and believe that the government should be a firm moral authority over social and cultural issues.

The French National Front and the Greek LAOS are similarly populist in the sense that they are anti-elitist (e.g. Mudde 2007; Tsiras 2012). The National Alliance has avoided anti-elitist appeals as part of its modernisation strategy

Table 1.1 Far right party positions on the GAL/TAN dimension and individual policy dimensions

	France FN	Greece LAOS	Italy AN
Civil liberties vs. law and order	9.67	8.57	9.15
Social lifestyle (e.g. homosexuality)	8.71	9.5	9.2
Immigration policy	8.57	9.75	7
Multiculturalism vs. assimilation	9.83	9.88	9.5
Cosmopolitanism vs. nationalism	9.83	9.89	9.4
Ethnic minorities	10	8.38	7.2
GAL/TAN Dimension	9.25	9.63	8.88
EU position	1	2.38	4.75

Source: Chapel Hill Expert survey (Bakker et al. 2015).
Note: EU position is measured as the overall orientation of the party leadership in each survey year, where
   1 denotes strongly opposed to 7 strongly in favour of European integration. Party scores on the remaining
   dimensions are measured on a scale ranging from 0 to 10, where larger values indicate traditional, authoritarian and nationalistic positions. Data from 2006 are presented because this year includes all three
   parties' scores on all relevant dimensions.

(Ruzza and Fella 2009: 166). This variation is incorporated in the explanatory framework. Specifically, the 'attitude towards the polity' indicator suggests that while some far right parties may strive for the complete delegitimisation of the system, others may seek to insert and establish themselves within that system. Crucially, all three parties are characterised by strong and personified leadership, which may be kept constant across the cases. The National Front's Jean-Marie and Marine Le Pen (Eatwell 2002; Hainsworth 2008), LAOS's Georgios Karatzaferis (Dinas 2008; Tsiras 2012: 110) and the National Alliance's Gianfranco Fini (Lee 2000: 372; Hainsworth 2008; Griffin 2011: 203) have all been strong leaders of their respective parties.

Note that the relationship between nationalism and Euroscepticism is what differentiates far right parties from the mainstream (Halikiopoulou et al. 2012). These parties' firm belief in the pursuit and maintenance of national self-determination links their nationalism to negative evaluations of European integration. The EU is viewed as a heterogeneous entity, which dilutes national sovereignty and seeks to assimilate European nation-states into a cultural melting pot, where each nation would lose its individuality. However, levels of nationalism do not vary enough within the party family in order to account for differences in the dependent variable, i.e., Euroscepticism. As shown in Table 1.1, whereas party scores on the cosmopolitanism versus nationalism question are all above 9 on an 11-point scale, scores on the EU dimension vary considerably. On a 7-point scale, they range from a strongly opposed 1 for the French National Front, to a comparatively less Eurosceptic 2.38 for the Greek LAOS, and a relatively pro-EU position for the Italian National Alliance at 4.75. Based on the typology of Euroscepticism proposed in this book, the French National Front may be categorised within the 'rejectionist' Eurosceptic pattern, the Popular Orthodox Rally displays a 'conditional' type of Euroscepticism and the Italian National Alliance has adopted a 'compromising' EU stance.

This book seeks to explain far right party positions on the EU by examining the characteristics of the parties themselves, which are theorised through the framework of party model. Nonetheless, it is acknowledged that party system incentives play a role in structuring party preferences. The three parties selected for the controlled comparison operate in countries that are dissimilar in many respects, but within the context of Western Europe they also share a number of important similarities. France, Greece and Italy are all 'old' Western EU member states, with fairly long lengths of EU membership. They similarly share a bipolar logic of party competition. This is defined based on Bartolini et al. (2004: 2), who suggest that 'a party system is bipolar if (a) there are two poles – made up by either parties or coalitions – that get most of the votes; (b) one of these wins the absolute majority of the seats and forms the cabinet. A corollary to this definition is the following: third poles, that is parties or coalitions offering candidates against those of the main coalitions, are systematically underrepresented and unable to play a pivotal role'.

A majoritarian as opposed to a consensual logic underpins the workings of these three political systems. The dynamics of party competition are bipolar (either two-party or two-block) rather than multipolar. This is reinforced by different electoral systems that all tend to favour polarisation, i.e., double ballot in France, winner bonus in Greece and thresholds incentivising pre-electoral alliances in Italy (e.g. see Gallagher and Mitchell 2005). In France, the centre-left and centre-right are the main competing party blocs within the political system. Although the National Front evolved into an important force from the 2000s onwards, the party was systematically underrepresented (Grunberga and Schweisguth 2003; Bornschier and Lachat 2009). In Greece, the system has been characterised as polarised pluralism, either 'limited' (Mavrogordatos 1984) or 'extreme' (Seferiades 1986). It has evolved into a two-and-a-half party system, where two major parties have been associated with the left and right, respectively, and an additional third small party has been associated with the radical left (Legg and Roberts 1997: 132). Despite the fact that the Greek party system experienced fragmentation in the 2012 elections (Vasilopoulou and Halikiopoulou 2013), the 2015 general elections showed significant signs of citizen realignment and a return towards the predominance of two main political forces (Tsatsanis and Teperoglou 2016). From the early 1990s onwards, Italy experienced a shift from consensual politics towards polarisation and strong political leadership. This marked the establishment of the Second Italian Republic, which is characterised by bipolar competition between two camps broadly associated with the 'left' and the 'right' (Fella 2006: 13–14; see also Bartolini et al. 2004; Fabbrini 2009).

This similarity is important because the bipolar logic of competition becomes a constraint to far right party electoral success. The three-party systems broadly provide similar incentives to far right parties. Nonetheless, these incentives are not fixed, and a specific institutional context may provide both centrifugal and centripetal incentives, depending on how specific actors interpret them. In line with the perspective that views parties as political agents themselves, this book takes this point forward by arguing that (1) we should take political context into consideration as it structures party competition; but (2) we should not be viewing institutional incentives as static, providing fixed incentives to political competitors; because (3) the way in which political entrepreneurs interpret institutional incentives depends on the far right party model. Table 1.2 summarises the similarities among the three case studies.[1]

It is worth mentioning that the Italian National Alliance has undergone dramatic transformation over the years. The party's fascist past suggests that it is a core member of the far right party family (e.g. Hainsworth 2008: 6; Bruter and Harrison 2011: 2). Although the fascist Italian Social Movement (MSI) reinvented itself in 1994/1995 as the National Alliance in order to integrate into the Second Republic, the party has had an 'incomplete and contested trajectory towards a post-fascist identity' (Hainsworth 2008: 11) with its ideology based on a nationalist platform opposing multiculturalism and immigration (Norris 2005: 64). The transformation resulted in a new ideological hybrid of 'democratic fascism' (Griffin 1996). At the 1995 Fiuggi Congress, the party officially changed its name into the 'National Alliance'. This was no more than a change in the name rather than a change in political personnel, organisation and ideology (Ignazi 2003; Tarchi 2003). The Theses of the Congress 'failed to acquire the status of a historic, path-breaking "manifesto" of the new party' (Ignazi 2005: 337). An overwhelming majority of the 1995 Congress participants continued to positively evaluate fascism (Baldini and Vignati 1996; Ignazi 2003: 46). The new party also presented elements of continuity with regards to its organisational structure (Morini 2007: 160; Ignazi, Bardi et al. 2010: 200). In the 2000s the National Alliance party participated in the House of Freedoms coalition governments led by

Table 1.2   Comparability of case selection

	National Front France	Popular Orthodox Rally Greece	National Alliance Italy
Nationalism	High	High	High
Authoritarianism	High	High	High
Leadership	Strong	Strong	Strong
Party system logic	Bi-polar	Bi-polar	Bi-polar

Silvio Berlusconi, and in 2009 the party disbanded, following an agreement to join forces under the banner of People of Freedom. Fini stepped down from party leadership in 2008 after being elected to the post of President of the Chamber of Deputies, and was succeeded by Ignazio La Russa. Following the party's dissolution, a significant number of National Alliance politicians remained within the People of Freedom. The value of this case study lies in understanding whether and how a party's ambivalent transformation may have an impact upon its Euroscepticism. The 'post-fascist' National Alliance (Mudde 2014: 221) provides an interesting contrast to the French and Greek cases, which have not shown a similar willingness to normalise.[2]

PLAN OF THE BOOK

This introductory chapter has defined the core puzzle of the book, presented the theoretical framework and outlined the research design. Chapter 2 maps far right party positions on European integration. Based on the empirical analysis of programmatic material of fourteen far right parties from eleven European democracies, it categorises far right parties into the 'rejectionist', 'conditional' and 'compromising' patterns of Euroscepticism. Chapter 3 develops the theoretical argument, and proposes a link between Euroscepticism and far right party model. It explains that differences in far right party positions on the EU may be understood with reference to a party's relationship with democracy, its attitude towards the polity, its evolving relationship with the electorate and its behaviour towards competitors. The following chapters (4, 5 and 6) proceed with a detailed examination of the three patterns of far right Euroscepticism through the controlled comparison of the French National Front, the Greek Popular Orthodox Rally and the Italian National Alliance. These three chapters follow a similar structure. They commence with a systematic analysis of each party's ideology and an in-depth examination of its Euroscepticism. They proceed by situating the party's Euroscepticism in the context of domestic institutional and electoral incentives. They finally examine Eurosceptic issue framing through the analysis of a wealth of party material and MEP speeches. The final chapter summarises the findings and revisits the book's central argument with reference to questions of internal and external validity. It discusses the wider relevance and broader contribution of this study, and assesses the implications of its findings for the future of European integration in light of developments related to Europe's political and economic crises.

The empirical analysis focuses primarily on the 1999–2014 period, which includes the EP's fifth, sixth and seventh EP terms. These fifteen years coincide with a large number of constitutional developments in the EU, including enlargement to Central and Eastern Europe, EU institutional and decision-making reform and the establishment of new supranational posts, such as a permanent President of the European Council and a new High Representative for Foreign Affairs. This period also covers the outbreak of the financial crisis, which has brought European solidarity into question and highlighted discussions over the stability and future of European integration. During these years, nationalist sentiment and opposition to the EU project have dramatically increased, and the far right has assumed a key role in fostering this Eurosceptic debate. A combination of empirical methods has been employed in order to collect and analyse data on far right party Euroscepticism. The study relies on elite interviews, expert surveys and the detailed analysis of party documents, voter data and content analysis of MEP speeches (see appendix for coding technique).

Chapter 2

Defining and Measuring Far Right Euroscepticism

'Euroscepticism' is a term employed to denote any type of opposition to, doubt or reservation about the EU project. Although as a phenomenon it has been prevalent since the early stages of European integration (Vasilopoulou 2013), the use of the term may be traced back to around the mid-1980s in the British press (Spiering 2004). The acceleration of the integration process from Maastricht onwards resulted in EU decision-making entering the world of electoral and party competition, with both European publics and elites opposing aspects of the European project. Over the years, Euroscepticism has become embedded at both national and EU levels, and has contributed to the growing contestation of European integration (Hooghe and Marks 2009; Usherwood and Startin 2013).

Far right political actors have been the main protagonists in the process of EU politicisation, some of them advocating their country's withdrawal from the EU. The aim of this chapter is to conceptualise and analyse the nature of far right Euroscepticism, and to show that, despite a number of ideological similarities, far right parties tend to oppose the EU to differing extents. Drawing upon the literature on Euroscepticism, the distinction between the policy and polity aspects of the EU and an attentive reading of the Maastricht and Lisbon Treaties, this chapter argues that far right party Euroscepticism may be categorised into the rejectionist, conditional and compromising patterns of opposition towards European integration. These are identified through the careful examination of party attitudes on four different aspects related to European integration and the EU. These include a cultural definition of Europe, the principle of co-operation at a European multilateral level, the EU's policy and institutional practice and the desire for building a future European polity.

The chapter is divided into three sections. It first discusses the key works in the literature on Euroscepticism, assessing the extent to which they apply to far right Euroscepticism. Second, it proposes the conceptualisation of far right attitudes to European integration in terms of three patterns of opposition. Third, it conducts analysis of party literature of fourteen far right parties from eleven European democracies, adding empirical substance to the theoretical reasoning of the chapter. The analysis demonstrates considerable qualitative differences within the far right, and establishes that far right Euroscepticism is significantly more complex than it is usually stated in the academic literature.

DEFINING OPPOSITION TO EUROPEAN INTEGRATION

'Euroscepticism' is a term widely employed to describe opposition to the EU project, including the nature and scope of its competences, institutional design and policies. Conceptualising and defining the various aspects of Euroscepticism, however, has not been straightforward. It is an elusive concept emerging from journalistic discourse, which has assumed different meanings across time and space. Its early uses can be understood as 'embedded within the specific British political and historical context' (Harmsen and Spiering 2004: 16). Indeed, the term was first employed in the British press during the mid-1980s, when there was a tendency to use the term 'Euro-sceptic' interchangeably with that of 'anti-Marketeer' (Spiering 2004: 128). This comes as no surprise due to the political climate of the mid- and late 1980s in which there were great tensions between the then UK Prime Minister, Margaret Thatcher, and the European Commission. The Thatcherite Discourse gave the term a connotation of extremism (Spiering 2004: 128), and in the British context Euroscepticism has come to refer to a position of hostility to and outright rejection of the UK's EU membership (George 2000: 15).

Although Euroscepticism has its historical roots in the United Kingdom, it progressively became established in other EU member states, especially since the process of ratification of the Maastricht Treaty (Taggart 1998). Mudde (2007: 159) also identifies 1992 as the 'turning point' for far right party Euroscepticism, both in terms of their position on European integration as well as in the salience of the issue in their agenda. However, given that Euroscepticism tends to be employed in distinct national contexts, it tends to assume a 'meaning which must be understood relative to the different national political traditions and experiences of European integration which frame those debates' (Harmsen and Spiering 2004: 17). In this sense,

'Euroscepticism' may be employed as a portmanteau for any type of opposition to or reservation about the European project.

Taggart (1998: 366), the first scholar to define Euroscepticism, suggested that it is 'the idea of contingent or qualified opposition, as well as incorporating outright and unqualified opposition to the process of European integration', and argued that Eurosceptic parties are more likely to stand outside the status quo. Over the years, Taggart and Szczerbiak have developed and refined this definition by suggesting the distinction between hard (principled) and soft (contingent) Euroscepticism (e.g. 2001, 2004). On the one hand, hard Euroscepticism indicates principled opposition to the entire EU project, including its political and economic aspects. Hard Eurosceptics advocate withdrawal of their country from the EU because they disagree with the conception of the project. This objection derives from a belief that the 'EU is counter to deeply held values or, more likely, is the embodiment of negative values' (Taggart and Szczerbiak 2001: 10). On the other hand, soft Euroscepticism does not represent a 'principled objection to European integration or EU membership but where concerns on one (or a number) of policy areas leads to the expression of qualified opposition to the EU' (Szczerbiak and Taggart 2008c: 2).

Szczerbiak and Taggart's definition of Euroscepticism is the most widely accepted in the literature for a number of reasons, not least because it successfully identifies Eurosceptic trends and tendencies within countries and party systems. If we apply this typology to far right parties, however, we are presented with a less clear picture of their attitudes and underlying argumentation. As far as the first type is concerned, Taggart and Szczerbiak argue that hard Eurosceptic parties view the EU as epitomising negative values. This assertion holds true in the case of the far right. Given that nationalism constitutes a core feature of far right ideology (Halikiopoulou et al. 2012), these parties perceive supranationalism as the archenemy of the nation-state. This, however, presents a conceptual problem, because not all far right parties are hard Eurosceptics. While some seek their country's EU withdrawal and reject European integration 'on principle', others are content to criticise the system from within. This hard-soft distinction is not able to capture the fact that some far right parties may not oppose their country's EU membership; rather they may disagree with the way in which the EU project is run. Additionally, the authors rightly argue that soft Eurosceptic parties articulate concerns over a number of policy areas. Far right parties, however, are not solely concerned with EU policies, but also over the type of EU decision-making and may present conditions under which they would support co-operation at a higher level. The definition of soft Euroscepticism does not capture the further distinction made between opposition to the policy (the nature of EU policies) and polity (the making of the EU political entity) and aspects of European integration (Bartolini 2005; Mair 2007; Braun et al. 2016). This distinction is particularly prominent in far right Euroscepticism and will be explained below.

Kopecky and Mudde (2002) have put forward an alternative categorisation of party-based Euroscepticism that differentiates between diffuse and specific support for European integration. Drawing upon Easton's (1965) seminal work on political regimes, the authors (2002: 300) define 'support for the general ideas of European integration that underlie the EU' as diffuse, while 'support for the general practice of European integration' as specific. This framework allows them to construct a two-by-two matrix of possible party positions on European integration structured along the Europhobe/Europhile and EU-optimist/EU-pessimist axes. These include the Euroenthusiasts, who support both the ideas and general practice of European integration; the Eurorejects, who do not accept either; the Eurosceptics, who support the idea of a united Europe but disagree with the general practice of integration; and the Europragmatists, who are against the general ideas of European integration underlying the EU, but are pragmatic in the sense that they support the EU project – most likely for utilitarian reasons. The authors argue that these categories – being ideal types – may serve for the qualitative analysis of party positions.

Mudde (2007: 161–165) has employed this typology to discuss the EU attitudes of European populist radical right parties. This typology is successful at describing far right positions on European integration to the extent that it has somewhat (albeit indirectly) incorporated the policy and polity aspect of the EU in the dimensions of diffuse and specific support. However, the four types that are distinguished on the basis of these two dimensions are not entirely relevant to the party family under investigation. The Euroreject category can be both theoretically and empirically applicable to this party family. The Eurosceptic category is also highly relevant, as it is empirically possible for far right parties to support the idea of co-operation at the EU level, but not in the shape of the EU. However, the Euroenthusiast category is not empirically observable, especially after the process of ratification of the Maastricht Treaty during the early 1990s. Simply put, there are no far right parties that are enthusiastic about both the ideas behind European integration and the practice of EU integration. The 'Europragmatist' type is also problematic in this regard, as principled opposition to the idea of European integration is unlikely to lead to favourable evaluations of the EU project. Mudde (2007: 162) accepts this, arguing that 'very few European political parties fall into this category'.

Another way of thinking about Euroscepticism is through Flood's (2002) six-point continuum. It commences from the rejectionist position at one end of the spectrum and ends with the maximalist position at the other end. The four intermediate positions include revisionist, minimalist, gradualist and reformist. Similarly, Conti (2003: 19) has suggested a typology of party attitudes to integration along a five-point continuum: hard Euroscepticism, soft Euroscepticism, no commitment, functional Europeanism and identity Europeanism. Conti's categorisation includes a middle/neutral point, whereas Flood's six-point continuum does not. Such categorisations seek to capture continuity into discrete categories. Their usefulness lies in their ability to map party attitudes across the entire dimension. Beyond problems associated with the hard-soft distinction explained above, it is also questionable whether they can capture in detail substantive differences within the far right Eurosceptic camp that relate to the polity-policy distinction, especially given that there are no clear boundaries between categories. Indeed, Flood (2002: 5) argues that the categories are rather broad and 'are not intended to convey any sugges-tion of a specific content to the positions which they describe, beyond basic stances towards the EU's development'.

Sørensen (2008) has identified four broad ideal types of Euroscepticism, including the economic, sovereignty, democracy and social types. Although the aim of her research has been to discuss public attitudes towards the EU, the 'sovereignty type' can be instructive in discussing far right Euroscepti-cism. Far right ideology is rooted in the defence of national interests and identity, drawing mostly upon the nationalist political doctrine that 'strives for the congruence of the cultural and the political unit, i.e. the nation and the state' (Mudde 2007: 16). As such, the issue of sovereignty is particularly salient within the far right and differentiates far right Euroscepticism from the Euroscepticism of other party families. Therefore, far right Euroscepti-cism belongs to the 'sovereignty type'. However, Sørensen's work does not help analyse different European positions of the far right party family that fall within the sovereignty type to which the chapter turns.

CONCEPTUALISING FAR RIGHT EUROSCEPTICISM: THREE PATTERNS OF OPPOSITION

Aiming to improve the conceptualisation of far right Euroscepticism, this section proposes the categorisation of their positions on European integra-tion into the rejectionist, conditional and compromising patterns. The three categories of far right party positions advanced here are deduced from party positions on four aspects of European integration, which derive from the liter-ature on Euroscepticism, the distinction between the policy and polity aspects of the EU and an attentive reading of the Maastricht and Lisbon Treaties. These include a cultural definition of Europe, the principle for co-operation at a European multilateral level, the EU policy and institutional practice and the future of the EU polity. They represent four fundamental aspects of the debate on European integration and provide the indicators on the basis of which the three patterns of far right Euroscepticism are identified.

Four Aspects of European Integration

The first aspect of European integration refers to a cultural 'definition' of Europe. The common identity of European peoples is defined as the feeling of cultural, religious and historical bonds among European nation-states. Mudde identifies this definition of Europe based on the Christian, Hellenistic and Roman traditions as present in far right party discourse. Europe is seen as a civilisation 'shared by the various different and independent European nations' (Mudde 2007: 169–70). This definition does not imply that Europe is considered to be above the nation. Rather, Europe – as a continent – encapsulates the common elements that bind European peoples together and serves to distinguish 'us' from 'them'. This cultural definition of Europe is closely related to a spatial/border definition, and becomes the prime justification for the exclusion of Turkey from Europe and, by extension, the EU. Because Christianity is one of the constitutive elements of Europe, its borders must stop at the Urals and the Mediterranean, excluding any non-Christian country to the east and south. If Europe accepted a religiously dissimilar country such as Turkey, then the European construction would lose one of its essential characteristics and would ultimately collapse.

The second aspect discussed here is the 'principle' of European integration. This is anchored on the preamble of the Treaty Establishing the European Union, which states that the member states are 'RESOLVED to mark a new stage in the process of European integration undertaken with the establishment of the European Communities' (European Union 2002: 9).[1] The 'principle' of European integration indicates a party's wish and willingness for co-operation at a higher multilateral level. This type of co-operation refers only to co-operation within the EU framework, even if the structures of the latter are criticised and reform is actively pursued. It does not signify bilateral or multilateral co-operation between selected European states on particular ad hoc policies, including, for instance, some aspects of trade. In this respect, co-operation under the European Free Trade Area does not imply support for the principle of European integration. The latter is an agreement providing only for trade, requiring no political commitment and taking place outside the EU framework. On the contrary, the principle of European integration refers to a multifaceted, multilateral agreement with a political character within the EU's structures, even if the reform of the latter is actively pursued. Thus, opposing the principle of European integration entails opposition against 'not only the government and its policies but also the whole system of governance'

(Mair 2007: 5). The principle of integration also features in Szczerbiak and Taggart's above-mentioned 'hard/principled' opposition to European integration, as well as Kopecky and Mudde's 'Euroreject' category.

The third and fourth aspects of European integration derive from Mair's discussion of political opposition in the EU context. They are deduced from the distinction between opposition to the policy and opposition to the polity aspects of the EU, and are respectively labelled as the 'practice' and 'future' of European integration (Mair 2007: 5; see also Bartolini 2005; Braun et al. 2016). The 'practice' indicator is also inferred from the stipulation in the Treaty on European Union (TEU), according to which 'the Union shall be served by a single institutional framework which shall ensure the consistency and the continuity of the activities carried out in order to attain its objectives while respecting and building upon the acquis communautaire' (European Union 2002: 11). The Lisbon Treaty has delineated the specific categories and areas of EU competence vis-à-vis the member states in articles 2 to 6 (European Union 2012: 4–6). The 'practice' of European integration comprises the overall body of EU law and institutional framework, which include the policies administered at the European level as well as the nature of decision-making. Opposition to the practice of European integration becomes opposition to the policy aspect of the EU.

The 'future' indicator of the EU refers to the member states' strong desire to promote European co-operation within the EU political framework, with the general aim of creating an ever-closer union. This aspect of integration features in the TEU, which specifies that 'this Treaty marks a new stage in the process of creating an ever closer union among the peoples of Europe' (European Union 2002: 10). According to the treaty, member states recall 'the historic importance of the ending of the division of the European continent and the need to create firm bases for the construction of the future Europe' (European Union 2002: 9). This is reiterated in the Lisbon Treaty 'DETER-MINED to lay the foundations of an ever closer union among the peoples of Europe' (European Union 2012: 2). Opposition to the future of European integration develops into opposition to the polity aspect of the EU. Note that this implies Euroscepticism because this is 'at odds with what is the dominant

Table 2.1   Conceptualising European integration

The four aspects of European integration	
Definition	The feeling of cultural, religious and historical bonds among the European peoples.
Principle	The wish and willingness for co-operation at a European multilateral level.
Practice	The EU institutional and policy status quo.
Future	The making of a European polity.

mode of ongoing integration' (Szczerbiak and Taggart 2008a: 8). Table 2.1 summarises these four aspects.

Three Patterns of Far Right Opposition

In defining the EU in terms of four fundamental features including the definition, principle, practice and future of integration, our understanding of the range of positions available for parties to adopt increases and the analysis becomes better specified. These four aspects of integration represent the principal point of reference of this chapter. They provide the analytical toolkit integral to the process of identification of potential far right EU positions. This section argues that far right Euroscepticism may be categorised into the rejectionist, conditional and compromising patterns.

'Rejectionist Euroscepticism' is a position that implies acceptance of the common cultural, historical and religious European roots. However, it also indicates strong opposition to the remaining three aspects of European integration. This includes rejection of the principle of co-operation within the EU framework, disagreement with the EU institutional and policy status quo and resistance to the future building of a European polity. National self-determination is the objective, i.e., all policies should be dealt with at the national level and withdrawal from the EU should occur at any cost. This position is generally associated with ardent anti-supranationalism as well as fierce criticism of the EU system as a whole. The general aim is to shift power back to the realm of domestic politics and restore the sovereignty and independence of the nation-state's institutions. This pattern overlaps with Szczerbiak and Taggart's hard Euroscepticism, as well as Kopecky and Mudde's 'Eurorejects'.

'Conditional Euroscepticism' entails acceptance of the common heritage of European peoples and approval of the principle of European co-operation, but hostility to the EU's policy and institutional practice to the future building of a European polity. Although the significance of nation-state co-operation at a European level is acknowledged, both the EU's institutional balance and policy status quo are unacceptable, because they are seen as compromising the nation-state's sovereignty. Consequently, closer unification of the European polity is not an appealing option. Conditional Eurosceptics accept, by and large, the principle of multilateral co-operation, but have objections to the policies and institutions of EU governance. This pattern is usually connected to a conditional wish for European co-operation to the extent that state sovereignty is not compromised by supranational decisions. A conditional position on Europe implies the rejection of decisions taken by supranational institutions and the endorsement of reform so that nation-state interests are guaranteed. Co-operation has already gone too far, and opposition to an ever-closer union is strong. Whereas both the practice of integration and the institutional balance of powers are dismissed, intergovernmental co-operation within the EU structures and in its policies deemed beneficial to the nation-state is supported. To be sure, there is great variation in which policies each conditional Eurosceptic may wish to see governed through an intergovernmental framework. Conditional Eurosceptics tend to favour the creation of a Europe administered by an institutional structure resembling a confederation, namely, intergovernmental co-operation without the presence or with limited power of supranational institutions. Given that a majority of decisions have been taken by supranational institutions and not by the member states, the EU project is not considered to be legitimate.

'Compromising Euroscepticism' comprises acceptance of a common European culture, as well as support for the principle and the practice of European integration, but entails opposition to the future building of a European polity. Compromising Eurosceptics admit that European integration is not necessarily a good thing. However, unlike rejectionist Eurosceptics, they propose that some of its aspects are beneficial to its member states. Transferring decision-making power to European institutions is particularly unattractive. However, a degree of integration is necessary for the general prosperity of the member states and their citizens, particularly in the economic domain. Partaking in the EU structures and institutions provides the possibility to (re-)negotiate change and radically reform the system from within the EU institutional structures. This implies a willingness to reluctantly co-operate, with a view to radically transforming the EU. This may be achieved, for example, by reinforcing the EU's intergovernmental structures and by strengthening member states' decision-making power, typically (but not necessarily) to the detriment of supranational institutions. An ever-closer union is not acceptable, however, because that would entail reinforcing federalism.

As seen in Table 2.2 below, a cultural definition of Europe is a point of agreement among the three patterns of far right Euroscepticism. Europe is seen as standing on a tripod comprised of ancient Greek democracy, Roman legal tradition and Christianity.[2] These three necessary, constituent elements provide the basis for a cultural as well as a spatial definition of Europe. They

Table 2.2   Patterns of far right opposition to European integration

	Aspects of European Integration			
Patterns of opposition	*Cultural definition*	*Principle of co-operation*	*Policy practice*	*Future EU polity*
Rejectionist	In favour	Against	Against	Against
Conditional	In favour	In favour	Against	Against
Compromising	In favour	In favour	In favour	Against

also generate the justification of the almost unanimous position of far right parties against Turkish EU accession. Furthermore, opposing the future building of a European polity under the auspices of the EU represents the lowest common denominator of far right negative attitudes on European integration.[3]

Given that, as mentioned above, far right attitudes on European integration are a case of 'sovereignty-based' Euroscepticism, the issue of sovereignty needs to be addressed. The question regarding the transfer of decision-making power to European institutions is prominent within all three types, but is viewed in a different manner in each. Both the rejectionist and conditional patterns entail strong opposition to supranationalism and any ceding of a member state's sovereignty to the benefit of European institutions. Any type of transfer of sovereignty to European institutions on any type of issue is unacceptable. However, conditional Eurosceptics differ from rejectionist Eurosceptics on three grounds. First, they recognise that particular issues cannot be resolved exclusively at the domestic level. Second, and as a result of the first, they are willing to accept that European countries must actively co-operate at a multilateral level. Third, they agree that co-operation can take place within the EU framework only if the latter is reformed. This entails taking power away from supranational institutions to the benefit of member states. This sometimes is articulated in a 'Europe of Nations' discourse, or in supporting the prospect of a European confederation. Conditional Eurosceptics usually suggest the creation of a confederation, whereby important issues would be dealt with at a higher level, while at the same time member states would fully retain national sovereignty. Rejectionist Eurosceptics only accept bilateral nation-state co-operation on a limited and case-by-case basis.

Compromising Eurosceptics do not support the transfer of sovereignty either. Nevertheless, they accept – albeit not without criticisms – the structures of European integration. A degree of European integration is desirable, because it brings important economic advantages and prosperity to the member states. The main difference between the conditional and the compromising patterns in terms of the issue of sovereignty lies in how the EU policy and institutional framework is treated. Whereas the first push for intergovernmental co-operation in all policy spheres advocating a framework without supranational institutions, the latter are willing to reluctantly act within the existing EU structures.

FAR RIGHT EUROSCEPTICISM: AN EMPIRICAL OVERVIEW

This section empirically tests the relevance of the above patterns though a qualitative analysis of party literature of fourteen far right parties from eleven European countries (see Table 2.3).[4] The analysis primarily relies on national

Table 2.3   Far right party positions on European integration

	Patterns of opposition to European integration		
	Rejectionist	*Conditional*	*Compromising*
Austria		Austrian Freedom Party	
Belgium		Flemish Interest	
Bulgaria		Attack	
Denmark		Danish People's Party	
France	National Front		
Greece	Golden Dawn	Popular Orthodox Rally	
Hungary	Jobbik		
Italy	Tricolour Flame	Northern League	National Alliance
Latvia			For Fatherland and Freedom/ National Alliance
Poland	League of Polish Families		
United Kingdom	British National Party		

manifestos, and is complemented by European manifestos and secondary literature where necessary. Party manifestos have been selected, as they are carefully crafted compromises representing the party as a whole and directed both externally to potential voters, as well as internally to party members.[5] The period of investigation ranges from the beginning of the 2000s until the mid-2010s. These years cover a number of important events in the development of the EU, including its enlargement to Central and Eastern Europe, the failed referendums on the European Constitution, the debates over the ratification of the Lisbon Treaty and the financial and migration crises. These developments have provoked strong nationalist sentiments across Europe and have contributed to the politicisation of European integration. A qualitative analysis of party manifestos is preferred in this chapter, as it helps to illuminate different party argumentation. It also enriches and adds substance to expert surveys' numerical evaluations of party positions.

The Rejectionist Pattern

The parties belonging to this pattern are the French National Front, the UK's British National Party, the Italian Tricolour Flame, the Greek Golden Dawn, the League of Polish Families and the Hungarian Jobbik. Such parties do not accept the principle that nations should co-operate at a higher European level. They advocate that policies must remain strictly national, and they push for their country's exit from the EU. While they make frequent appeals to a shared European culture, history and religion, they are against the principle of ceding national sovereignty to non-national institutions and oppose all European treaties. They tend to similarly oppose EU legislation and policies, such as immigration, enlargement, citizenship, borders and foreign and security policy. They also blame the EU for being one of the sources of their countries' domestic immigration and economic problems. These parties reject the EU policy and institutional practice and are fundamentally opposed to the future building of an EU polity, openly questioning the EU's political legitimacy.

The National Front has been a staunch critic of European integration. Although the party had an ambiguous stance towards European co-operation in the 1980s (Flood 1997: 131–32), it has maintained an anti-EU stance from the 1990s onwards. The party has made its position clear: France should 'exit the European Union' and 'establish French sovereignty' (National Front 2002a: 29; see also Hainsworth et al. 2004).[6] Over the years, the National Front has been less forthright in its support for France's withdrawal from the EU, but its rejectionist Euroscepticism is nevertheless extant. The party has denounced all EU treaties and has a firm view on the primacy of national law over EU legislation. Its 2007 national manifesto, which was drafted following the failed ratification of the European Constitution, suggested that France should have a plan for the radical renegotiation of EU treaties. If other EU member states did not support this plan, then the party advocated the organisation of a popular referendum on the question 'Should France regain its independence vis-à-vis the Europe of Brussels?' (National Front 2007: 61).[7] This indicates that the party is against the principle of co-operation at a multilateral level. The National Front supports the restoration of the French currency and the re-establishment of French internal border controls. It is against European citizenship, which it views as undermining national citizenship, and it opposes the European arrest warrant and any police co-operation through Europol. In 2004, Jean-Marie Le Pen argued, 'Let's liberate France' (National Front 2004);[8] and in 2009 that 'their Europe is not our Europe' (National Front 2009).[9] His successor, Marine Le Pen, has maintained the party's rejectionist position (see also Goodliffe 2015). Despite the party's attempt at modernisation (Shields 2013), the National Front's 2012 manifesto also committed to renegotiating all EU treaties in order to re-establish national sovereignty (National Front 2012b: 16). In a letter published on the party's website during the 2014 EP election campaign, Marine Le Pen (2014) explicitly urged voters to view those elections as a referendum on Europe.

Along similar lines, the British National Party manifesto (1999) had a clear message: 'Get Britain out'. The party is against the EU, which it views as a federal superstate run by a 'totalitarian' European Commission. It argues that the price of the UK's EU membership is 'astronomical' and that the country should reclaim its sovereignty. This is maintained in subsequent manifestos, in which the party argues that 'in place of the EU, we intend to aim towards greater national self-sufficiency' (British National Party 2001: 1), and that leaving the EU is the party's 'sine qua non' (British National Party 2005: 5). In fact, the question of Europe was the first topic in the party's 2005 national manifesto, which indicates the high salience of the EU issue, not only in EP but also in domestic elections. In the 2009 EP elections, the party argued that 'by voting for the BNP you will be voting to put the interests of Britain and British People FIRST. Our policy on the European Union is clear, straightforward and unambiguous: Britain would be better off out of the EU' (British National Party 2009: 2). Interestingly, in 2010 the party differentiated between Europe and the EU, arguing that 'the BNP loves Europe but hates the EU' (British National Party 2010: 27), implying a differentiation between Europe as a continent of peoples and the EU as a system of governance, which it portrays as an 'Orwellian superstate in formation'. The question of British democracy underpins this rejectionist position, as the EU essentially deprives British people of their 'inherited right to determine their affairs' (British National Party 2010: 27). Withdrawal from the EU would be 'the most important single foundation stone of our rebuilt British democracy' (British National Party 2005: 5). The party maintains its rejectionist position set forth in the 2010s, but the focus later tends to shift towards immigration, which is heavily prioritised in both its 2014 EP and 2015 general election campaigns. Exiting the EU is the key policy that will allow Britain to regain border control and thus stop mass immigration (British National Party 2014; 2015).

The Italian Tricolour Flame argues that Italy and the European states should restore political sovereignty, and that the EU is an elite construct artificially created in Maastricht without the will of the people (Tricolour Flame 2006; 2013).[10] The party 'dreams of' a Community of European Peoples as a Federation of all Nations based on the principle of self-determination that would also include Russia (Tricolour Flame 2006; 2013), echoing the fascist myth of Europe as a collection of peoples (Griffin 1994). In the same way, the Greek Golden Dawn maintains that Greece should withdraw from all international organisations that do not serve Greek national interests. The party supports a Europe of Nations rather than a Europe run by 'capital and loan sharks' (Golden Dawn 2012: 7).[11] It seeks a 'great, sovereign, and independent' Greece (Golden Dawn 2012: 12),[12] which is self-sufficient, having a national economy, a strong national army and a clearly demarcated territory (Golden Dawn 2015; see also Vasilopoulou and Halikiopoulou 2015). Similar to the Tricolour Flame, the Golden Dawn calls for a 'union of European peoples [...] from the Atlantic to the Urals and beyond'. This union of peoples with 'common origin' would respect the 'particularities of each nation,' while at the same time allowing 'Europeans to overcome old enmities and rivalries' (Lyris 2014).[13]

Rejectionist Eastern European far right parties have challenged their country's EU membership. The League of Polish Families views the EU as a 'supranational quasi State structure whose interests conflict with those of the individual nation-states'.[14] It is thought to overshadow national cultures[15] and to 'abolish the independence of individual countries' (League of Polish Families 2004: 29).[16] It was the only party in Poland opposing the accession agreement (Millard 2003; De Lange and Guerra 2009), maintaining that the country should not enter the EU (League of Polish Families 2005). The 2007 manifesto maintained the party's opposition to Polish EU membership and argued that 'we oppose the incorporation of Poland into the European Union and we will strive so that Polish people reject integration within the European Union in the national referendum' (League of Polish Families 2007).[17] Similarly, the Hungarian Jobbik also fiercely criticised Hungary's EU accession conditions, and associated EU membership with the loss of the country's self-determination (Pirro 2014). Both 2010 and 2014 national election manifestos stress the common cultural roots of European nations, i.e., 'Greek thought, Roman law and Christianity' (Jobbik 2010: 75; 2014: 80).[18] However, the party rejects the EU and supports a Europe of Nations based on national diversity and where national interests are not compromised (Jobbik 2010: 75; Jobbik 2014).[19] The EU is seen as a non-democratic organisation run by unelected bureaucrats and dominated by Western European interests at the expense of Central and Eastern European countries. Interestingly, party leader Gábor Vona stated in June 2016 that leaving the EU was no longer on his agenda and that the refugee crisis offered his party an opportunity to transform the EU (Kroet 2016). This marked a U-turn for the party, which had consistently campaigned in favour of Hungary's exit from the EU, but the leader has failed to clarify his vision of a transformed EU.

The Conditional Pattern

Far right parties adopting a conditional Eurosceptic position strongly differentiate themselves from the rejectionist pattern, because they do not oppose European integration and multilateral co-operation on principle. These include the Austrian Freedom Party, the Belgian Flemish Interest, the Italian Northern League, the Danish People's Party, the Greek Popular Orthodox Rally (LAOS) and the Bulgarian Attack. For these parties, the EU framework is clearly not the right platform for European multilateral co-operation. They refrain from supporting EU policies and institutional practices, as well as the future building of a European polity. In contrast to rejectionist Eurosceptics, however, they accept the principle that European peoples and states need and should co-operate.

The Austrian Freedom Party has a cultural conception of Europe, stating that Europe 'is grounded in the Western Christian community of values' (Austrian Freedom Party 2005: 8).[20] The party is against EU enlargement and against migration resulting from EU integration (Pelinka 2004). It is particularly sceptical towards enlargement to Turkey (Austrian Freedom Party 2004: 1; 2009: 2). It argues that Turkey is neither culturally nor geographically part of Europe, and as such, accession negotiations should be terminated (Austrian Freedom Party 2013: 279). It supports the radical reduction of EU bureaucracy (Austrian Freedom Party 2009: 1), and is against the primacy of EU law over national law (Austrian Freedom Party 2013). Adreas Mölzer, its only MEP during the legislative period of 2004 to 2009, argued that 'Europe of the Brussels syndicate has nothing in common with the conception of a Europe of free and sovereign states' (Mölzer 2007).[21] The Austrian Freedom Party 'is committed to a Europe of free and independent homelands as part of a confederation of sovereign Nation-states' (Austrian Freedom Party 2008: 5),[22] calling for the 'maintenance of Austria's sovereignty in a Europe of nations' (Austrian Freedom Party 2006).[23] While it does not openly support Austria's exit from the EU, it points towards the economic benefits of national currency reintroduction (Austrian Freedom Party 2013: 276–77). The Austrian Freedom Party argues that the future of Europe lies in the close co-operation of its peoples. The EU is only one part of the European reality and should not develop into a European federal state. While the party disagrees both with the EU policy practice and the building of a future European polity, it is committed to a Europe of self-determined peoples and fatherlands, and to European co operation according to the basic principles of subsidiarity and federalism. It supports the introduction of a European treaty that would delineate the rights and obligations of the EU and its member states. 'European integration can only be successful, if it happens without rush, on the basis of equal co-operation between the states and their citizens. This can only occur within a federation of states, which takes into account the historically entrenched diversity of our continent' (Austrian Freedom Party 2013: 277).[24] This support for an alternative framework for European co-operation suggests that the party accepts the principle of co-operation, but is critical of the EU's policy and institutional practice.

Similarly, the Flemish Interest criticises the EU for being increasingly bureaucratic, displaying 'totalitarian' tendencies[25] and encroaching the sovereignty of nation-states and their peoples (Flemish Interest 2014: 9). The party argues that the EU should not evolve into either a political union or a federation (Flemish Interest 2004: 27). It supports instead intergovernmental co-operation of sovereign states based on the principle of subsidiarity (Flemish Interest 2010: 29). 'The Flemish Interest supports a confederal Europe that respects national and self-determination. Not a European superstate, but an intergovernmental or confederal alliance of sovereign nations' (Flemish Interest 2009a).[26] The party said, 'Yes to Europe, No to an EU superstate [...] that gains more and more control over the internal affairs of the different member states; the nation-states have to remain the most important pillars of European co-operation' (Flemish Interest 2009b).[27] It argued that 'the creation of a federal Europe is impossible and undesirable because Europe is a mosaic of peoples, all having an ancient history, their own language and culture, tradition of law with specific collective goals. There does not exist a European identity in the same sense as an American identity. No one considers themselves primarily Europeans and then Italian or Swedish' (Flemish Interest 2009c: 6).[28] In its 2014 manifesto, the party goes as far as to argue in favour of the 'orderly dismantling of the EU and the Eurozone', but this is to be replaced with 'voluntary (intergovernmental) European co-operation' (Flemish Interest 2014: 9),[29] which suggests continuing support for the principle of European co-operation.

The Northern League has changed its position towards the EU over time, from supportive in the early 1990s, to a much more radical stance from the end of the 1990s onwards, consolidating its Euroscepticism over time (Conti 2003: 27; Quaglia 2003: 18). The party has criticised European institutions for not being close to European citizens and for failing to respect the traditions and cultures of European peoples (Caiani and Conti 2014: 189). It promotes the 'free association of European peoples' (Northern League 2004: 1),[30] but it is against the creation of a European federal state. It opposes a 'centralised superstate led by technocrats who are politically irresponsible for their actions' (Northern League 2004: 1).[31] It has argued that 'we must construct a Europe that is founded on the respect of national and territorial realities, giving the European Union only a limited degree of sovereignty, delimiting its competences and the fields of its intervention avoiding ambiguities' (Northern League 2006: 26).[32] For the Northern League, 'integration means pursuing our commonalities but also embracing our specificities' (Northern League 1999: 2).[33] The party is 'in favour of a confederal model in which the various member states maintain their sovereignty and where the regional and territorial specificities are recognised' (Northern League 2009: 61).[34] In line with its conditional Euroscepticism, it opposes any type of European Constitution and insists that European treaties should be ratified through the means of a referendum. In its 2013 manifesto, the Northern League asked for a 'Europe of the peoples and less bureaucracy', while at the same time it softens its position by supporting the direct election of the Commission President and the extension of the EP's legislative power (Northern League 2013: 3).[35]

Whereas the Danish People's Party is against European unification and suggests that the EU must not gain power over the member states, it sustains that particular policies may be dealt with at a European multilateral level.

In its 2002 programme, the party argued, 'The Danish People's Party wishes friendly and dynamic co-operation with all the democratic and freedom-loving peoples of the world, but we will not allow Denmark to surrender its sovereignty. As a consequence, the Danish People's Party opposes the European Union' (Danish People's Party 2002: 2).[36] Danish sovereignty is very important to the party, and as a result, 'nothing can be put above the Danish Constitution' (Danish People's Party 2002).[37] Whereas the party argues against European unification, suggesting that the EU must not gain power over the member states, it promotes particular policies that should be dealt with at a European multilateral level: 'We oppose the development of the EU which is going towards the United states of Europe'. The Danish People's Party wants a close and friendly co-operation in Europe (Danish People's Party 2004) but co-operation should be limited to areas such a 'trade policy, environmental policy and technical co-operation. We oppose the introduction of a European political union' (Danish People's Party 2002).[38] The party believes that the EU's functions 'must be limited to issues that great member state majorities wish to be addressed through the EU; where cross-border nature of issues calls for common solutions; and where economies of scale call for common solutions' (Danish People's Party 2007; 2009).[39] Whereas in 1999 the party was adamantly against the EP, accusing it of various scandals (Danish People's Party 1999), in the 2000s it agreed to an EP with controlled functions (Danish People's Party 2004; 2009: 62). The party supports co-operation in general, but it opposes the introduction of a European political union or a federal state (Danish People's Party 2004), supports the reduction of the EU budget (Danish People's Party 2009) and argues that Denmark should remain a sovereign state, especially as far as its borders are concerned (Danish People's Party 2011: 3).

The Greek LAOS maintains that the future of Greece is linked, to a great extent, to the EU. LAOS 'does not deny Greece's European identity' (LAOS 2003: 8).[40] However, co-operation should occur only 'within the context of a confederation and only under the condition that our national specificities would be protected' (LAOS 2003: 12).[41] The party envisages a 'Europe of nations' (LAOS 2004: 2)[42], whereby European nation-states would co-operate in matters of mutual interest while recognising and protecting their historic, cultural and ethnic roots (LAOS 2007: 23). LAOS has expressed strong criticisms against the EU's current and future trajectory. It is against a European superstate (LAOS 2012) and any type of European Constitution, arguing that it will 'destroy our national sovereignty and abolish the differences between peoples' (LAOS 2005: 1).[43] At the same time, it argues that the Greek crisis should be resolved within the context of a European political solution (LAOS 2015).

Lastly, the Bulgarian Attack has progressively become more Eurosceptic over time. The party does not dedicate much space in its electoral programme to the EU, indicating the relatively low importance of this issue in its agenda. In 2009, the EU is briefly discussed in the foreign policy section, in which the party argued that Bulgaria's foreign relations must be expanded to include not only the EU, but also other states (Attack 2009). This indicates that the party accepts the existence of the EU as a foreign policy actor. While the party does not have a consistent EU policy, over time Attack has deepened its anti-EU criticism by opposing Bulgaria's Eurozone membership while at the same time seeking closer ties with Russia. In 2016, Attack's leader, Volen Siderov, urged Bulgarian authorities to consider a referendum on the country's EU membership along the lines of the Brexit referendum (Novinite 2016). In its 2013 manifesto, however, the party sought to protect Bulgarian national interests by putting forward a series of demands to the EU, rather than seeking a referendum. These related to the closing down of the Kozluduy nuclear plant's reactors, higher agriculture subsidies and revisiting the validity of the Treaty of Neuilly-sur-Seine after the disintegration of Yugoslavia, with the possibility of returning the so-called Western territories to Bulgaria (Attack 2013).

The Compromising Pattern

The parties that may be categorised as compromising Eurosceptics include the Italian National Alliance and the Latvian For Fatherland and Freedom/ National Alliance[44]; these tend to agree with the principle of co-operation and the policy and institutional practice of European integration. They acknowledge that their country's economic prosperity is largely a result of co-operation within the EU framework. They maintain that the EU should be reformed from within, and they refrain from proposing an alternative framework for co-operation, such as the confederation argued by some of the parties belonging to the conditional pattern. Nevertheless, they do not actively support the deepening of European integration.

In his analysis of Italian party positions on European integration, Conti argues that the now-defunct Italian National Alliance attached particular importance to the nation. The party 'rejects the idea of a federal Europe and supports one of a looser union where the power of nation-states is preserved and the outcomes of European integration are systematically checked' (Conti 2003: 26). The National Alliance argued that national specificities constitute Europe's wealth and that the EU should not 'negate the nation-state, but rather constitute a confederation of nation-states; in this sense the states and their interests would contribute to rather than obstruct the formulation of the European interests and priorities' (National Alliance 2002: 6).[45] Italy should not entrust itself to Europe, but instead contribute to rebuilding Europe (National Alliance 2006a: 13). The party was against abandoning national sovereignty, arguing that 'the Right has always argued in favour of a Europe of nations rich by its identities and cultures that should be respected and cannot be reversed by a superstate' (National Alliance 2004: 6).[46] Nonetheless, the party supports a number of EU policies, including technology, energy and the Lisbon Agenda, as well as the reduction of the transatlantic technology gap, with particular focus on energy security, the liberalisation of the market, the completion of the Trans-European Energy networks and renewable energy. Without explicitly referring to Turkey, the party welcomed 'new countries from Europe, which grows geographically and politically starting with the immediate neighbours where the Italian projection is very important (Southeastern Europe and the Balkans)' (National Alliance 2006a: 9).[47] The Italian National Alliance felt that it was a European force, and intended to contribute to the process of EU reform. The party took a rational cost-benefit approach to its EU stance and sought to reinforce the Italian national interest through participating in European institutions (Conti 2003). This clearly indicates that the party had accepted that it should promote Italian interests within existing EU structures.

Likewise, the Latvian For Fatherland and Freedom/National Alliance argues that the EU must be strengthened only as an association of member states, and that Latvian politicians should work hard to achieve advantageous conditions for their country within the EU (For Fatherland and Freedom 2006). The party views Latvia as part of the Western European cultural and historical heritage. Taking into consideration Latvia's geopolitical location, on the border between East and West, the party seeks to strengthen ties with both the EU and NATO (For Fatherland and Freedom/National Alliance 2012). EU membership is considered as a means of stabilising the independence and democratic statehood of Latvia without, however, being a 'substitute for an independent foreign policy and long-term goals' (For Fatherland and Freedom/National Alliance 2012: 34).[48] As an EU member, Latvia should not diminish its national identity and cultural distinction, and should seek to maintain its national interest. 'We will strengthen member state national sovereignty', working together to achieve advantageous conditions for Latvia and Latvian citizens (For Fatherland and Freedom 2004: 1).[49] 'We support a Europe where the EU and the member states share accountability and responsibilities, rather than the creation of a federal Europe or a "superpower". The EU should have competence in issues where it can act more efficiently than individual member states' (For Fatherland and Freedom 2009: 1).[50] 'The European Parliament platform should not contribute to the erosion of Latvian and national sovereignty' (For Fatherland and Freedom 2009: 2).[51] According to the party, Latvia's EU aim should be not to delegate too much of its sovereignty, but instead it should achieve a union of free and equal nation-states in favour of the principle that member states can be the decision-makers in important policies, including foreign policy, defence, security and taxation (For Fatherland and Freedom 2004: 1). Both parties have thus accepted that they should promote and strengthen their country's position within the existing structures of the EU. In other words, they have accepted the idea of playing by the 'rules of the game'.

The above empirical analysis has resulted in the categorisation of six far right parties into the rejectionist pattern, six parties into the conditional pattern and two into the compromising pattern of Euroscepticism. To assess the validity of these qualitative estimates of party positions, it is worth comparing them with quantitative estimates of party positions derived from the Chapel Hill expert survey (Bakker et al. 2015). In this survey, country experts of political parties are invited to place the overall orientation of party leadership towards European integration on a 7-point scale, where 1 indicates strong opposition to and 7 strong support for the EU. The final estimate is the mean expert score on the question 'Overall orientation of the party leadership towards European integration', along with a standard deviation for each value. In Table 2.4 below, I report party positions on European integration in three survey years, including 1999, 2006 and 2014, covering a period of

Table 2.4 Chapel Hill party scores on the question 'Overall orientation of the party leadership towards European integration'

		EU position Chapel Hill Survey Year		
Pattern	Party name	1999	2006	2014
Rejectionist	British National Party	-	-	-
	League of Polish Families	-	1.38	-
	National Front	1.14	1	1.21
	Tricolour Flame	2.16	-	-
	Golden Dawn	-	-	1.11
	Jobbik	-	-	1.21
Conditional	Attack	-	2.46	1.5
	Austrian Freedom Party	2.59	1.75	1.9
	Danish People's Party	1.42	2.33	1.90
	Flemish Interest	2.22	2.5	2.59
	Northern League	3.16	1.5	1.14
	Popular Orthodox Rally	-	2.38	3.25
Compromising	For Fatherland and Freedom/National Alliance	-	4.75	5.69
	National Alliance	3.66	4.75	-

Source: Chapel Hill Expert Survey 1999-2014 trend file (Bakker et al. 2015).
Note: EU position is measured as the overall orientation of the party leadership in each survey year, where 1 denotes strongly opposed to and 7 strongly in favour of European integration. Not all parties are included in all survey years. Survey years: 1999, 2006 and 2014.

about fifteen years. In line with my findings, the National Front, the Golden Dawn, Jobbik, and the League of Polish Families score the lowest scores on the EU dimension. The opposite is true for the Italian National Alliance and the Latvian For Fatherland and Freedom. Six parties rank somewhere in the middle. Interestingly, the parties included in this analysis show stability in their Euroscepticism. This is true with the exception of the Italian Northern League, which appears to have become more Eurosceptic over time dropping from a fairly pro-EU 3.16 score in 1999 to 1.14 in 2014.

As shown above, far right parties exhibit great variation in their Eurosceptic positions. But is the EU issue important to these parties? Table 2.5 reports the relative salience of the EU issue, with 0 indicating that European integration is of no importance to the party, and 10 that European integration is the most important issue in the party's public stance. One key observation is that the EU issue is very important to most far right parties included in the sample. This indicates that far right parties engage in EU issue competition, i.e., view the EU issue as instrumental in vote gathering (see Vasilopoulou 2018; Guinaudeau and Persico 2014). In addition, the salience of the EU issue has increased over time. In fact, salience was fairly low in 1999 for most parties, except for the Danish People's Party and the French National Front. In 2014, most parties score above 5. Interestingly, the Greek Golden Dawn, which belongs to the rejectionist Eurosceptic pattern, exhibits the lowest salience score in 2014. Despite its rather extremist EU position,

Table 2.5 Far right party scores on EU salience

		EU issue salience Chapel Hill Expert Survey Year		
Pattern	Party	1999	2006	2014
Austria	Austrian Freedom Party	5.00	6.27	6.70
Belgium	Flemish Interest	1.94	3.67	4.60
Bulgaria	National Union Attack	-	5.47	4.59
Denmark	Danish People's Party	6.43	5.20	7.27
France	National Front	6.07	7.40	8.46
Greece	Popular Orthodox Rally	-	6.20	5.38
	Golden Dawn	-	-	4.44
Hungary	Jobbik	-	-	6.79
Italy	National Alliance	2.50	4.17	-
	Tricolor Flame Social Movement	1.25	-	-
	Northern League	2.08	6.67	8.86
Latvia	For Fatherland and Freedom/NA	-	4.17	6.80
Poland	League of Polish Families	-	7.10	-
UK	British National Party	-	-	-

Source: Chapel Hill Expert Survey 1999–2014 trend file (Bakker et al. 2015).
Note: The relative salience of European integration in the party's public stance is measured on a scale, where 0 denotes that European integration is of no importance, i.e., never mentioned, and 10 denotes that European integration is the most important issue.

it does not seem to prioritise it domestically, at least not as much as other parties, including the Italian Northern League, the French National Front, the Danish People's Party and the Austrian Freedom Party.

CONCLUSION

In an attempt to provide a bridge between the literature on far right parties and the study of Euroscepticism, this chapter has proposed the conceptualisation of far right opposition to European integration into the rejectionist, conditional and compromising patterns. It has presented four facets of European integration, including the definition of Europe, the principle, the policy practice and the future building of a European polity. It is on the basis of these four indicators that the three patterns have been identified. By building on our existing knowledge of these parties' EU positions from expert surveys, it has systematically mapped and analysed the nature of far right Euroscepticism through the qualitative analysis of party literature.

The identification of four fundamental aspects of European integration may become helpful in providing a solution to the wider problem of measuring the dependent variable, i.e., Euroscepticism. They can add precision and clarity when assessing a party's position on Europe, and they may be used to identify similar patterns within different party families. This, however, is true with a caveat. The definition of Europe may need to be refined in order to apply to other party families. The usefulness of this threefold conceptualisation of far right Euroscepticism lies in identifying the nuances of the phenomenon in descriptive terms. The three patterns have also an analytical purpose, because different patterns of Euroscepticism may be associated with different party behaviour at the domestic level.

The qualitative analysis of party literature demonstrates that, although these parties belong to the same party family, they display three utterly different patterns of opposition to European integration. This is a striking finding for a number of reasons. First, it demonstrates that far right parties not only differentiate themselves from other party families in that they adopt a 'sovereignty type' of Euroscepticism. They also seek to differentiate themselves from each other. Second, it demonstrates that – although highly nationalistic – far right parties do not present themselves as being anti-European in the wider sense of the term. They willingly accept the common aspects shared by European peoples, because these serve to distinguish 'us' from 'them'. Third, and perhaps contrary to common journalistic wisdom, not all far right parties oppose European integration to the extent of pushing for their country's EU withdrawal. It would be wrong to assume that all far right parties support leaving the EU. Instead, some far right parties are rather pragmatic in their approach to European integration. Fourth, there is a trend of the EU issue becoming increasingly salient, with some far right parties also placing the question of EU referendums on their agenda in light of the Eurozone and migration crises. This suggests that far right parties employ issue entrepreneurial strategies (see also Vasilopoulou 2018), signalling to voters that the EU is core to their programmatic agenda.

These findings have important implications in terms of possible explanations of party-based Euroscepticism. Arguably, the issue of European integration may be assimilated into preexisting ideologies that reflect long-standing commitments on fundamental domestic issues. Traditional cleavage theory may account for general party response to European integration (Marks and Wilson 2000). However, the findings of this chapter demonstrate that traditional cleavage theory is less able to explain the extent of opposition to the EU, or to predict different types of Eurosceptic argumentation within a given party family. Other predictors of party-based Euroscepticism, including the national context and party strategic objectives within the domestic party system, may also have explanatory power. This is especially true for far right parties. Given that nationalism is core to their ideology, their European position may be largely influenced by the national context. A comparison of far right party policies and preferences across Europe 'can tell us a great deal about the boundedness of the various party families' (Treschel and Mair 2009: 2). It can offer great insights into how an issue may be emphasised in different political settings and provide some hints regarding the association between the issue of Europe and the dynamics of party competition in EU member states. To this aim, Chapters 4, 5 and 6 proceed with a controlled comparison of far right party Euroscepticism by focusing on the French National Front, the Greek LAOS and the Italian National Alliance respectively. Before doing so, Chapter 3 puts forward the theoretical framework of this book.

Chapter 3

A Theory of Far Right Euroscepticism

Why do parties that belong to the same party family address the EU question differently? Starting from the assumption that parties are rational actors, this chapter develops a theoretical framework to account for different patterns of far right party Euroscepticism. The chapter constructs a causal argument, which suggests that the way in which far right parties position themselves on the question of Europe depends on the party model to which they adhere. Party models are developed with reference to the party's relationship with democracy, its attitude towards the polity, its target electorate and its behaviour towards competitors. Classification on these indicators leads to the identification of the 'anti-system', 'anti-liberal' and 'normalised' far right party models.

The EU is a core issue in far right parties' programmatic agenda and has become a key policy tool in party competition. However, the specific way in which the EU may be employed for party political and electoral purposes depends on the far right party model. Anti-system far right parties tend to opt for a rejectionist position on the EU. They adopt adversarial and confrontational tactics, employing their Euroscepticism in order to differentiate themselves from the domestic party system. Anti-liberal far right parties tend to be conditional Eurosceptics. While they put forward an anti-EU agenda, they tend to under-emphasise their ideological differences, and carefully select their specific criticisms. Normalised far right parties tend to adopt a compromising position on the EU. Where they oppose aspects of the EU, they put forward qualified criticisms, which allow them to enhance their coalition potential with other mainstream parties. In addition, far right parties may choose to prioritise different Eurosceptic frames. Far right parties tend to frame the EU and its policies with reference to national identity and the domestic political context. This allows them to associate the EU with other policies that may appear to have domestic relevance, thus increasing the resonance of the EU issue in the national electorate.

The chapter commences with a discussion of the literature on party-based Euroscepticism, showing that ideology and strategy should not necessarily be considered as two separate and separable explanations. It subsequently constructs the three far right party types, on the basis of which it models far right preferences and behaviour. These allow us to understand why parties that belong to the same party family may interpret interest representation, electoral politics and party competition in a different manner. It finally develops a theory for explaining different far right party positions on European integration, and examines the role of national identity and the domestic context in Eurosceptic EU issue framing.

PARTY-BASED EUROSCEPTICISM

How may we explain why parties take the positions they do? Literature on party-based Euroscepticism identifies two broad explanations. The first relates to party ideological characteristics, and posits that parties oppose the EU because it is antithetical to their deeply entrenched ideological values and beliefs (e.g. Marks and Wilson 2000; Hooghe et al. 2002; Marks and Steenbergen 2004). The second refers to partisan- and national-level characteristics, and suggests that party competition, coalition dynamics and the positions of major potential allies or competitors may act as catalysts in the formulation of a party's Eurosceptic position (e.g. Taggart 1998; Sitter 2001; Szczerbiak and Taggart 2008a, 2008b).

The fundamental basis for understanding party positions on European integration as primarily the product of party ideology draws upon the seminal work of Lipset and Rokkan (1967). The cleavage theory of party competition views political conflict as rooted in socio-structural transformations triggered by macro-historical processes, including nation-building, industrialisation and – more recently – postindustrialisation (Bornschier 2009). Political parties are agents of these deep and long-lasting societal divisions. Their political survival lies in maintaining and perpetuating existing structures of political conflict. When a new issue arises in the political arena, mainstream parties are incentivised to maintain existing patterns of competition, not least in order to minimise internal divisions and avoid reputational costs (e.g. Hix and Lord 1997; Hix 1999; Whitefield and Rohrschneider 2015). Party positions on new issues, such as European integration, are thus conditioned and filtered by historical processes ingrained in the fundamental left-right structure of party competition in Europe. Political parties have historically rooted ideologies that guide the way in which they may respond to such new issues to the extent that European integration may be 'assimilated into pre-existing ideologies' (Marks and Wilson 2000: 433).

However, there is no simple linear relationship between where a party stands on the economic component of the left-right dimension and its position on the EU (Hooghe et al. 2002). Instead, we may observe an inverted-U curve relationship between party positions on the two dimensions. Parties that are positioned towards the centre of the economic left-right scale tend to support European integration, whereas those situated on the extremes of this dimension tend to express Eurosceptic positions. This may be explained through a focus on both party ideology and strategy. Ideologically, the EU is the product of centrist, rather than extremist, party policies. At the same time, when adopting positions on new issues, successful centrist parties have little incentive to 'rock the boat', whereas smaller, peripheral parties are less constrained by existing cleavage structures and have more incentives to emphasise extreme positions (see also Wagner 2012). Rather than a question of more or less government regulation of the market, party positions on European integration should be seen as a reflection of a new cleavage in European politics. This may be conceptualised as the new politics GAL-TAN dimension, which ranges from Green/Alternative/Libertarian positions to Traditional/Authoritarian/Nationalist positions (Hooghe et al. 2002). This value dimension refers to non-economic matters, such as law and order, immigration, the role of authority in society and the trade-off between exclusive and inclusive structures of the community. Parties close to the TAN pole, such as the far right, insist on nation-state independence and react against perceived threats such as immigration, cosmopolitanism and globalisation. They thus oppose European integration as a project that embodies these threats and undermines national sovereignty.

Progressing through the 2000s and the Eurozone and migration crises, conflict over European integration has become a durable dimension of contestation in European politics. Politicisation of the integration process has transformed not only the structural basis of European integration, but also European domestic politics (see De Wilde et al. 2016). Conflicts over sovereignty, identity and transnational solidarity have contributed to the restructuring of political conflict in Western Europe and the emergence of a new transnational 'demarcation-integration' cleavage between the so-called losers and winners from globalisation (Kriesi et al. 2006, 2008; Hutter et al. 2016). In such a context, we observe the fusion between cultural values and economic interests (Hooghe and Marks 2016). On the one hand, the winners from globalisation and European integration include cosmopolitan citizens and educated individuals who benefit from transnationalism and international competition, and thus support European integration. On the other hand, the losers from such processes include less educated and low-skilled individuals working in traditionally protected sectors who strongly identify with the national community, and insist on the maintenance of national boundaries. Far right parties, which justify all their policies on the basis of the nation, appeal to those individuals who feel threatened by international competition, who are concerned by the outsourcing of production and immigration and consider themselves losers of globalisation.

This framework suggests that far right parties tend to oppose European integration both for ideological and sociological reasons. Far right parties 'oppose supranationalism because of the erosion of national power and the threat to national identity this entails, as well as the danger to economic well-being' (Aspinwall 2002: 87). It also hints to the importance of strategy and vote-maximisation, as mainstream parties are perceived not to cater for the interests of the so-called losers of globalisation. Despite socio-economic changes associated with globalisation and Europeanisation, mainstream political parties have displayed remarkable stability in their position towards the EU, and have continued to subsume new issues such as globalisation, immigration and European integration into existing dimensions of contestation (Hooghe and Marks 2016). Challenger parties that do not ordinarily participate in government, such as those belonging to the far right party family, politicise specific issue dimensions that mainstream actors are programmatically constrained to respond to (e.g. van de Wardt et al. 2014; Hobolt and Tilley 2016).

This points to the relevance of a second set of explanations that view party positions on European integration as primarily a function of party strategy and domestic electoral and institutional incentives. Parties are not isolated organisations. They are constrained by party system dynamics, which may compel them to amend and adjust their values, policies and beliefs. A party's strategic position in the domestic party system may also affect its specific policy orientation towards European integration. Taking this perspective, Taggart (1998: 368) conceptualised Euroscepticism as a 'touchstone of domestic dissent', arguing that it may be manifest 'in different forms and can be used in different ways', most likely to be observed in single-issue and protest-based parties. Parties peripheral to their domestic party systems are more inclined to employ Europe as a mobilising issue, compared to parties that occupy a central position in national politics. For single-issue anti-EU parties, opposition to European integration constitutes their sole raison d'être. For protest-based parties, Euroscepticism may be seen as an appendage to their general opposition to the functioning of political systems. These parties adopt a Eurosceptic stance 'as a deliberate means of differentiating themselves from the political mainstream' (Szczerbiak and Taggart 2000: 7).

Patterns of competition at the domestic level may shape the ways in which the European issue becomes translated into party politics. Party positioning on European integration is also a function of government-opposition dynamics (Sitter 2001). On the one hand, catch-all or cartel parties tend to downplay ideology in order to increase their chances of accessing office. For this reason, they are unlikely to publically adopt strong Eurosceptic positions. Their Euroscepticism will more likely become manifested in the form of internal dissent. On the other hand, the anti-cartel and protest-based character of the old hard left, far right and populist parties incentivises them to oppose European integration. This dissent-driven Euroscepticism is the result of their peripheral – almost excluded – position in the party system. Taking this perspective, Batory and Sitter (2004) have shown that variation in agrarian parties' Euroscepticism may be understood through a combination of reasons driven by party long-term goals linked to identity, and party short-term goals linked to their position in the party system and electoral strategies. Similarly, communist party varied responses to European integration has been attributed to vote- and coalition-seeking opportunities (Benedetto and Quaglia 2007). Johansson and Raunio (2001) also stress the role of strategic considerations in party responses to European integration, arguing that whereas in Finland party competition and leadership may explain party EU attitudes, in Sweden public opinion and factionalism are stronger predictors. This strategy-based model is dynamic and can account for policy change. It suggests that when Eurosceptic parties aspire to participate in a governing coalition, they tend to modify their Euroscepticism in order to become more attractive partners (see also Taggart and Szczerbiak 2013).

Studies that focus on the role of party strategies and party system dynamics do not discard the role of political ideology. Party strategy and ideology are closely intertwined and integral to party behaviour (see also De Vries and Edwards 2009; Halikiopoulou et al. 2012). While ideology is key in determining broad underlying positions on European integration, parties may employ the EU issue as an element of party competition (Kopecky and Mudde 2002; Szczerbiak and Taggart 2003). Batory and Sitter (2004: 525) argue that 'if a party assesses European integration as a threat to both its (voters') economic interests and its values or ideology, it is expected to adopt a hard Eurosceptic stance.[...] However, if these two conditions do not hold, electoral strategy and coalition tactics shape a party's incentives regarding Euroscepticism'. Along similar lines, the comparative analysis of the varied socialist party response to Europe in the 1970s and 1980s reveals a diverse pattern of influences, including factors internal to the parties, determinants related to party system dynamics and country-specific historical experiences, which primarily point to the 'importance of the national dimension in policy making' (Featherstone 1988: 302).

In sum, long-standing structures of conflict serve as cognitive and ideological constraints shaping actors' choices. Far right parties are Eurosceptic due to

their nationalist ideology, which insists on cultural and economic protectionism. However, the 'degree to which ideology serves as a constraint depends
partly on the party's position in the party system and so it is necessary to also
consider the relative positions of parties within their respective party system'
(Taggart 1998: 379). When examining variation within a party family regarding EU positions, domestic party strategies and party system dynamics must
also be considered, especially if one expects that parties have to carefully balance between interest representation, policy promotion and electoral politics.
In line with De Vries and Edwards (2009: 11), who argue that ideology and
strategy may be seen as 'mutually enforcing rather than mutually exclusive',
the following section constructs three ideal models of far right parties that
allow us to categorise and predict far right party policy on the EU.

THREE MODELS OF FAR RIGHT PARTY BEHAVIOUR

Political parties are complex organisations. Their behaviour is a function of a
number of internal and external constraints, including their ideological predis-
position, programmatic commitments, their internal organisational structures,
their social basis of representation, their relationship with civil society and
the state and the positions of their domestic political competitors. Parties
exist in a variety of different forms, and political scientists have developed a
number of models and typologies in order to capture the prominent features
that characterise them. Prominent classifications include Duverger's (1954)
distinction between cadre and mass political parties, Neumann's (1956)
distinction between parties of individual representation and parties of democratic mass integration, Kirchheimer's (1966) catch-all party, Panebianco's
(1988) electoral-professional party and Katz and Mair's (1995) cartel party
(see also Gunther et al. 2002; Gunther and Diamond 2003).

   In contrast to the cadre party's loose structures, the mass party type is
organisationally thick. It tends to be associated with left-wing ideologies,
as these parties have – at least historically – mobilised well-defined social
groups, which formed their membership. While Duverger paid most attention
to party organisational structures, Neumann primarily emphasised parties'
integrative functions. Building on Neumann's mass integration party, Kirchheimer's catch-all party variant has an overwhelmingly electoral orientation,
and responds to the law of the political market by actively downplaying ideology and emphasising the qualities of the party leader (Gunther and Diamond
2003; Krouwel 2003: 26). Panebianco adds an organisational dimension to
the catch-all party through the development of the electoral-professional party
type, which is characterised by the central role of professionals and weak
ties to its membership (Wolinetz 2002). Lastly, Katz and Mair's cartel party

is defined by its relation to the state. Cartel parties are no longer brokers between civil society and the state. They are dependent on state subsidies and have ultimately become agents of the state.

These typologies posit a broad transformation from cadre to mass to catch-all/electoral-professional to cartel parties. They have primarily been used in order to account for party change over time, and tend to pay systematically more attention to mainstream well-established parties and parties of the left (Wolinetz 2002). These models, however, do not adequately capture the full range of variation in party types within less established party families, such as the far right. Whereas these parties are increasingly employing entrepreneurial and leader-centred strategies, they are not as professionalised as catch-all parties. Although some far right parties have altered their discourse to prioritise ideological rather than biological justifications of national belonging, they have certainly not downplayed or abandoned their nationalist ideology, and they continue to justify all their policies on the basis of the nation (Halikiopoulou et al. 2012; Vasilopoulou and Halikiopoulou 2015). In addition, given that – unlike the cartel party – they do not ordinarily participate in government, they have limited access to state and government subsidies.

Another way of thinking about party types relates to the distinction between policy, votes and office (e.g. Strom 1990; Wolinetz 2002). Policy-seeking parties seek to primarily maximise their impact on policy, vote-seekers prioritise winning elections over other goals and office-seeking parties pursue control of the executive branch either by holding power alone, in coalitions or by acting as a stabiliser within a multiparty system. However, pure policy-, vote- or office-seeking parties are unlikely to exist (Strom 1990: 570). Parties prioritise goals depending on a combination of electoral, institutional and partisan constraints, which structure political opportunities in any given political environment. Goal prioritisation may entail compromise, as 'maximising one goal may entail merely satisfying another, or even fully-blown trade-offs' (Bakke and Sitter 2005: 244). In line with other literature that views parties as rational actors (e.g. Downs 1957; Muller and Strom 1999; Wagner 2012; Meyer 2013), a core assumption of this book is that far right parties and their leaders tend to be primarily vote-seeking actors, choosing their policy positions strategically. Whereas the prioritisation of office or policy becomes constantly recalibrated depending on domestic electoral dynamics, vote maximisation takes place for instrumental purposes, i.e., as the most promising way to ensure either access to office, policy impact or even survival.

Building on literature in the fields of party politics, political behaviour and Euroscepticism, this book theorises the preferences and behaviour of far right parties in modern European democracies, and argues that the way in which they interpret electoral and structural incentives depends to a large extent on party model. This is constructed on the basis of four indicators, i.e., (1) relationship with democracy, (2) attitude towards the polity, (3) target electorate/social basis and (4) behaviour towards competitors. Classification on these indicators leads to the identification of three far right party models, i.e. 'anti-system', 'anti-liberal' and 'normalised'. This categorisation allows us to understand how parties belonging to the same party family may interpret interest representation, policy promotion, electoral politics and party competition in a different manner.

Before delving into the analysis of the three far right party models, it is worth explaining the characteristics that far right parties share, which allow us to categorise them within the same party family in the first place (see Table 3.1). As mentioned in the introductory chapter of this book, nationalism is core to far right party ideology (e.g. Eatwell 2000; Vasilopoulou and Halikiopoulou 2015). Far right parties strive for the congruence of the nation and the state. They make ethnocentric appeals and attack most forms of internationalism. These parties present themselves as true defenders of the nation, seeking its protection and independence from foreign intervention and globalising forces. They advocate exclusionary forms of identity, and justify all their policies on the basis of the nation. Far right parties are culturally protectionistic. They view foreign cultures as eroding national identity, and seek to limit their effect on national traditions and the national way of life. Their economic policies have transformed from primarily neo-liberal up until the 1990s (Kitschelt and McGann 1995), to mostly economically protectionistic, putting natives first when it comes to access to jobs and welfare. Although the Eurozone crisis has made the economy relatively more salient in these parties' agenda, far right parties tend to primarily compete on the national

Table 3.1   Three far right party models

	Anti-system	Anti-liberal	Normalised
Core ideological feature	Nationalism	Nationalism	Nationalism
How society should be organised	Authoritarianism	Authoritarianism	Authoritarianism
Leadership	Strong	Strong	Strong
Relationship with democracy	Ambivalent towards procedural; rejects liberal democracy	Does not reject procedural; but is openly critical of liberal democracy	Does not reject procedural; but is ambivalent towards aspects of liberal democracy
Attitude towards the polity	De-legitimisation of the system	Radical change within the system	Part of the system
Target electorate	Niche	Mixed	Conservative
Behaviour towards competitors	Confrontation	Accommodation	Co-optation

identity axis, and provide cultural justifications for economic protectionism (e.g. Ellinas 2010).

Far right parties have also a similar vision with regard to how society should be structured and organised. They tend to be defined by their authoritarianism, which refers to a cluster of values that focus on 'high levels of respect for authority, loyalty and dutifulness, obedience and resignation to one's inherited station in life, order and social control' (Flanagan and Lee 2003: 238). Right-wing authoritarians tend to believe in a strictly ordered society and value tradition and stability. They accept established authorities at the expense of personal freedoms. They view the state as the firm moral authority on society, and support strict law and order. Far right parties tend to present society as fragmented and threatened by a number of internal and external enemies, whom they seek to punish severely. Their policies tend to promote a return to the national/traditional way of life, including reviving traditional family structures and boosting the national birth rate. They are proponents of a strong justice system, they are in favour of building more prisons, and they have a zero-tolerance approach to criminality. The combination of exclusive nationalism and right-wing authoritarianism leads these parties to oppose policies promoting multiculturalism, and to believe that immigrants, whom they view as alien out-groups, are responsible for societal fragmentation and the erosion of national identity.

Although there have been instances of poorly led and divided far right parties (Carter 2005), these parties have developed into leader-centred organisations characterised by a top-down approach to party organisation (see Art 2011 regarding variations in far right party activists). The formal organisational structures of far right parties tend to be controlled by a powerful leader who is relatively unconstrained by the rest of the party (e.g. Pedahzur and Brichta 2002; Zaslove 2004). Far right leaders tend to be polarising personalities, often perceived as charismatic. They tend to portray themselves not as 'elites', but rather as 'ordinary' individuals fighting for the rights of ordinary men and women. This development is partly a reflection of new forms of electoral competition in Europe that rely on personalisation of leadership and personification of politics, with the party leader becoming the epitome of the party (e.g. Poguntke and Webb 2005).

However, far right parties display variation in terms of a number of other characteristics, including their relationship with democracy, their attitude towards the polity, their target electorate and the goals that they prioritise. This variation allows us to construct three far right party models. Far right parties vary in their rejection/ambivalence towards the principles and values of the democratic political system. Democracy may be thought of as an institutional arrangement for elite competition for power (Schumpeter 1950). This system of government may be defined through a focus on procedure, i.e., the rules and arrangements needed for the system to endure. Dahl's (1989) 'procedural minimal' conditions for the existence of democracy include institutional guarantees, such as free and fair elections; the freedom to form and join organisations; freedom of expression; and the rights to vote, run for office and seek alternative sources of information. Whereas procedural democracy is ultimately based on the fundamental notion of political equality, the liberal understanding of democracy prioritises the quality of outcomes and substantive goods over political procedure. The primary focus is the limiting condition of democracy, i.e., the protection of minority rights regardless of the preferences of the majorities. Constitutionalism and separation of powers protect citizens' liberty, while at the same time they set a limit on unbridled popular sovereignty (Riker 1982; Bollen 1993).

Far right parties have different degrees of ideological opposition towards democracy. This may be conceptualised as a spectrum of ideological resistance, which ranges from wholesale opposition to a degree of co-optation and normalisation. To the extent that far right parties participate in the electoral process by fielding candidates in elections, they may not be considered as fully rejecting procedural democracy. Some of them, however, oppose procedural democracy in that they do not support equal political liberty and often seek to undermine free and fair elections by obstructing the process and/or questioning electoral outcomes. Other far right parties may accept procedural democracy as a necessary rule of the game, but they may remain critical or ambivalent towards aspects of liberal democracy, including pluralism, political diversity, inclusivity, toleration and the constitutional protection of minorities. These parties' strong commitment to authoritarianism is fundamentally at odds with liberal democracy, which they associate with cosmopolitianism and universalism. For far right parties, order and submission to authority is the fundamental basis of freedom as opposed to pluralism, checks and balances and constitutionalism. Minority rights may only be respected if supported by the majority (Mudde 2007), but while some parties are involved in outright human rights violations, others have sought to undermine constitutionally protected liberal rights of minorities, including the Roma, religious minorities and immigrants.

A party's relationship with democracy also allows us to derive its attitude towards the polity. This relates to how a party views the existing regime, i.e., whether it seeks to 'preserve, amend, uproot or rebuild a given social order' (Seliger 1976: 14). Far right parties that are ambivalent or critical towards the procedural aspects of democracy tend to seek the complete delegitimisation of the system. Those far right parties that may accept aspects of procedural democracy but are openly illiberal may choose not to fully overthrow the system, and to pursue instead radical change within the system. Far right parties that are ambivalent towards aspects of liberal democracy without being openly illiberal may seek to rebuild the social order by becoming part of the system.

Another very important characteristic that may vary across far right parties is their target electorate. Far right voters tend to be individuals adversely affected from socio-structural change, including modernisation, globalisation and denationalisation (e.g. Betz 1994; Kriesi et al. 2008). In terms of socio-demographic characteristics, they tend to be male individuals with low levels of education working in low-paid low-skilled professions. Far right voters are also distinguished by their attitudes, including their negativity towards immigration, authoritarianism, political mistrust, opposition to income redistribution and anti-establishment sentiment (e.g. Van der Brug et al. 2013; Zhirkov 2014; Dunn 2015). However, for party political and electoral purposes, far right parties may choose to widen their appeal by targeting different electorates. Some far right parties may choose to put forward a policy-specific agenda focusing on the needs of a clearly defined electoral clientele, and in this sense create their own electoral niche in the system. Other far right parties may seek to target voters who do not only belong to the far right's niche clientele, in an effort to attract voters with a variety of different profiles. It is also conceivable that other far right parties may seek to appeal to voters with less extreme attitudes or those with a more traditional conservative profile and outlook.

Related to a party's electoral strategy, a last area of potential divergence among far right parties is their behaviour towards competitors at the domestic level. Party competition in multiparty systems entails that political parties have a number of strategies at their disposal in order to manipulate their electoral fortunes (e.g. Downs 1957). Some far right parties may seek to create an image of strong differentiation, and opt for full confrontation with their adversaries in order to increase policy divergence. Other far right parties may seek to widen their appeal, and thus choose to under-emphasise their ideological differences in order to portray themselves as a non-extremist force in domestic politics. Lastly, another set of far right parties may conceivably seek to branch out to competitors and thus opt for a strategy of co-optation vis-à-vis specific parties (see also Meguid 2008). Categorising far right parties on these indicators allows us to identify three discernible far right party models, i.e., what this book terms 'anti-system', 'anti-liberal' and 'normalised' types (see Table 3.1).

Anti-system far right parties do not share the values of the regime and seek change incompatible with the constitutional structures of the polity. They represent ideas that are at odds with procedural democracy and directly oppose liberal democracy. They seek to replace the existing pluralistic democracy with a regime 'uniformly committed to the achievement of their programmatic objectives' (Gunther and Diamond 2003: 171). They seek to amplify popular discontent and undermine the legitimacy of the political system (e.g. Scarrow 1996; Capoccia 2002). To a large extent, their opposition may be thought of as an 'opposition of principle' (Sartori 2005), with a view to creating a crisis of legitimacy in the political system. Such parties tend to engage in adversarial politics and take diametrically opposed positions to other parties in the system in those issues where they have a comparative advantage. These may include immigration, globalisation and European integration. The ultimate goal is to differentiate themselves from other parties and create an image that they represent a niche and clearly defined electorate. Such parties opt for full confrontation with their domestic political adversaries, which allows them not only to achieve policy differentiation, but also to undermine the legitimacy of the system.

While anti-system far right parties are ambivalent towards procedural democracy and essentially reject all aspects of liberal democracy, the anti-liberal far right party model does not reject procedural democracy; instead, it is openly critical of liberal democracy. Such parties do not accept the limits that liberalism places on citizens and elites. They are against pluralism, constitutionalism and checks and balances. Their exclusive understanding of belonging to the nation entails that they seek to restrict the demos into only one group, i.e., the 'nationals'. They are against the constitutional protection of minority rights and often target minority groups, including religious, ethnic and linguistic minorities in their domestic systems. These parties seek the radical change of the system, which they pursue within the confines of the existing regime. Although they continue to appeal to core far right constituencies, they seek to broaden their electoral appeal and attract support from a wider variety of societal groups. While these parties are clearly illiberal, they actively de-emphasise their radicalism, and they choose issues and policies that appear to be consistent with domestic public opinion. Although they criticise their competitors, they broadly adopt an accommodative stance towards them in order to portray an image of relative moderation.

Lastly, the normalised far right party does not fully reject liberal democracy. Rather, it tends to be ambivalent towards aspects of it. Normalised far right parties have different incentives. They seek institutional entrenchment, i.e., to become part of the political system, and they wish to mitigate the consequences of party competition. These parties portray an image of de-radicalisation, which includes avoiding controversial statements, extremist policies and anti-democratic references. They also seek normalisation and legitimacy through coalition formation with larger political groups of the right, and ultimately access to political power. Given that they actively pursue coalition formation, their target electorate is one with policy preferences close to its major potential governmental allies. As such, they are less likely to accommodate the extremist policy preferences of a niche electoral clientele. To the extent that they seek to prove that they are capable of holding a governmental portfolio, they tend to carefully avoid the adoption of controversial policies and the pursuit of drastic change. Their priority is to consolidate their position in the domestic party system while at the same time preserving nationalism as their core ideological feature and authoritarianism as their main principle of how society should be organised.

In sum, each party model tends to operate differently on a number of indicators, and as such may interpret party competition and electoral incentives differently. The anti-system party's confrontation relates to the exaggeration of ideological differences vis-à-vis its competitors in the system; the anti-liberal model's accommodation refers to the under-emphasis of such ideological differences; and the normalised model's co-optation relates to the pursuit of convergence with other parties. This theoretical framework allows us to understand why far right parties take different positions on European integration, which is explained in detail below.

A THEORY OF FAR RIGHT EUROSCEPTICISM

Far right party Euroscepticism has often been conceptualised as a question of 'issue ownership' (e.g. De Vries and Hobolt 2012; Vasilopoulou 2018). Theories of party competition posit that there are two sides of issue competition, including issue conflict and issue salience (Guinaudeau and Persico 2014). According to this approach, small and less-established parties tend to emphasise extreme positions in order to carve their own niche in the system (e.g. Wagner 2012; see also Adams et al. 2006; Lefevere et al. 2015). This also applies to the question of Europe. Mainstream parties have historically had few incentives to politicise the EU (e.g. Hooghe et al. 2002; Hooghe and Marks 2016), which has opened political opportunities for 'issue entrepreneurs' (De Vries and Hobolt 2012), such as parties belonging to the far right party family, to employ the EU in domestic party competition. This book provides an important qualifier to this approach by showing that, although Euroscepticism comes at no ideological cost to far right parties, the specific way in which the EU may be used for party political and electoral purposes depends on the far right party model. In other words, different levels of Euroscepticism, as well as the dissimilar ways in which parties may frame the issue of European integration, are a careful balance between a party's relationship with democracy, its attitude towards the polity, its interest representation, party competition and electoral politics.

Anti-system far right parties express distrust vis-à-vis the system, seek to appeal to a specific social niche and have no interest in collaborating with other domestic actors. They utterly reject European integration in order to differentiate themselves from the political establishment. Such an adversarial strategy enables them to emphasise their ideological differences, distance themselves from the rest of the party system and signify strong policy divergence. The adoption of a rejectionist Eurosceptic policy is in line with their ideological rejection of liberal democracy, while at the same time it becomes an opportunity to undermine the legitimacy of both their national political system as well as the EU. These parties' anti-EU argumentation is likely to be antagonistic, articulated in a manner that appears unique to their own worldview and dissimilar from all other parties in the political system. Their rejectionist position on European integration allows them not only to attack the dominant pro-EU discourse in the domestic party system, but also to supply a clearly defined and potentially unique policy to the electorate. Therefore, if a far right party adheres to the anti-system party model, it is likely to adopt a rejectionist Eurosceptic position distinct from its competitors in the party system.

Anti-liberal far right parties, however, tend to adopt a qualitatively different position on European integration. These parties seek to broaden their electoral appeal outside the far right's core social base, which constrains their policy options. Anti-liberal far right parties are faced with a dilemma: They must appear less extreme in order to reach out to different pools of voters, while at the same time they should retain their radicalism, as this is what makes them unique in the system. This incentivises them to adopt a conditional position on European integration. Their Euroscepticism allows them to criticise the mainstream pro-EU consensus and respond to the needs of their core far right supporters. The conditional qualification to their EU policy enables them to appeal to wider sections of the electorate that may view the EU critically but not wish for their country's full withdrawal from the EU. This stance also ensures that the party's EU position is not so extreme as to thwart potential future collaborations. These parties tend to avoid radical statements, and they select their specific anti-EU criticisms on the basis of what they perceive to be representative of domestic public opinion. As such, anti-liberal far right parties are likely to adopt a conditional Eurosceptic position and a much more nuanced approach to the question of Europe.

Normalised far right parties are expected to modify Euroscepticism because of its potential electoral cost. These parties seek to improve their collaboration potential with other domestic political forces, by appearing closer to their potential coalition partners. 'To the extent that these parties oppose European integration their co-operation with pro-integration catch-all parties of the right is problematic, if not jeopardised' (Sitter 2001: 26). A strong Eurosceptic position constrains probabilities to acquire office, hold portfolios and become central in government coalitions. As such, they adopt a compromising position on the EU and are more likely to criticise the EU in a constructive manner. Tactical dilemmas become important to the extent that these parties aspire to become part of the governing cartel. Therefore, normalised far right parties are likely to adopt a compromising position on European integration and avoid the adoption of controversial policies.

This theory is introduced with two caveats. First, while the theory of issue competition focuses on both issue position and issue salience, this book primarily concentrates upon EU position. As shown in the previous chapter, a comparison of far right party Euroscepticism reveals instances of rejectionist Eurosceptics that choose to attach strong emphasis on the EU (e.g. the French National Front) and others that do not emphasise their Euroscepticism to the same extent (e.g. the Greek Golden Dawn). This could mean two things: either that there is no strong correlation between position and salience, or – most likely – that salience should be primarily analysed with reference to the party system rather than the party family. Second, the categories proposed here are not fixed. Parties are open to change and may move from one model to another (see also Meyer and Wagner 2013). Changing electoral incentives and vote-seeking considerations are likely to affect how they position themselves on the question of Europe.

FAR RIGHT EUROSCEPTIC ISSUE FRAMING

The question of Europe carries with it an inherent contradiction for the far right party family. On the one hand, politicising European integration may promise high electoral gains to far right issue entrepreneurs. Europe is an issue that has long remained in the margins of political discussions, especially because mainstream parties have avoided its politicisation, despite the fact that European citizens have increasingly been expressing Eurosceptic views. By focusing on European integration, far right parties are likely to marshal support from those citizens who might feel that their views remain unrepresented. On the other hand, far right parties tend to conceptualise the question of Europe as an international issue. Despite the fact that the boundaries between the 'domestic' and the 'international' are blurred when it comes to European integration (Risse-Kappen 1996), far right parties view the EU as an external organisation imposed on the nation-state. As a result, annexing what they perceive to be a non-domestic issue to their policy toolkit may sit uncomfortably with their nationalist ideology, which prioritises questions related to the national polity.

To justify this apparently contradictory focus on an international issue and increase the resonance of the EU issue in the domestic electorate, far right parties tend to frame the EU and its policies with reference to other policies that might have more obvious domestic relevance. Framing is defined following Entman's (1993: 52) definition: 'to frame is to select some aspects of a perceived reality and make them more salient in a communicating text, in such a way as to promote a particular problem definition, causal interpretation, moral evaluation, and/or treatment recommendation'. Far right parties tend to employ nationalism as their master frame. They propose 'nationalist' solutions to all societal problems (see Vasilopoulou and Halikiopoulou 2015; Halikiopoulou et al. 2016). This explains why they tend to criticise the EU from a predominantly sovereignty-based perspective (Vasilopoulou 2011; 2018). Far right parties broadly share a common justification of why they oppose European integration; namely, they view the EU as a project undermining cherished national sovereignty. Policy problems deriving from European integration may be resolved through a process by which the nation-state would regain a level of control in some or all EU policies.

Beyond the sovereignty justification, however, each far right party may choose different frames to problematise and discuss European integration. For example, some far right elites may prioritise a Eurosceptic frame that views the EU as posing a security concern to the nation-state. Other far right elites may frame the EU in terms of placing strain on public resources or promoting free trade. In other words they may emphasise different subsets of 'potentially relevant considerations' (Druckman and Nelson 2003: 730) that relate to the specific issue of the EU. In the context of electoral competition, this is important, because issue framing is a means of elite influence on public opinion (Slothuus and De Vreese 2010). Far right parties' specific anti-EU framing may vary depending on the interests they traditionally defend at the national level and the specificities of the domestic political context (see also Helbling et al. 2010). The domestic context constrains the ways in which far right party elites may choose to debate and politicise European integration. This is especially relevant to such elites, as by virtue of their nationalist ideology, their discursive toolkit draws largely upon national identity and the particularities of the national context, which naturally vary from one European country to another (Smith 1991; Zimmer 2003; Halikiopoulou et al. 2013). Far right parties tend to associate the EU issue with other issues of domestic relevance in order to improve their chances of influencing domestic public opinion. This explains why, despite the fact that far right parties tend to share similar levels of nationalism, they may employ different nationalist frames when discussing European integration. It also suggests that Eurosceptic argumentation is sensitive to national contexts. The articulation of specific anti-EU frames is therefore structured with reference to the particularities of the nation and national identity, and the ways in which a given far right party will perceive national identity and draw upon available cultural reservoirs.

In short, this book suggests that far right party positions on the EU are the product of a party's careful balancing of interest representation, electoral politics and party competition. The precise EU issue framing, however, is influenced by the national context and may be linked to other issues of domestic relevance considered to be core to the party's political agenda. More broadly, it argues that Euroscepticism becomes an element of domestic party competition, as far right parties tend to capitalise on the EU question for party political purposes relevant to their domestic strategic agenda.

CONCLUSION

This chapter has critically reviewed the literature on party-based Euroscepticism, showing that to understand variation in party EU positions, we need to take into consideration both ideological and strategic considerations. It has continued by constructing three models of far right party behaviour, i.e., anti-system, anti-liberal and normalised far right parties, with reference to the reinforcing role of ideology and strategy in electoral politics and party competition. It has shown that, despite sharing the core features of nationalism, authoritarianism and strong leadership, far right parties may vary in terms of their relationship with democracy, their attitude towards the polity and their behaviour towards party competition. The chapter has put forward an explanatory framework of far right party Euroscepticism, which proposes a link between party model and position on the EU. It has suggested that anti-system parties are likely to put forward a rejectionist position on European integration; anti-liberal parties are likely to be conditional Eurosceptics; and normalised far right parties are likely to express a compromising Eurosceptic position. It has finally examined the role of the domestic context in far right EU issue framing, by showing that Euroscepticism is also sensitive to national contexts.

The book employs a standard research design whereby an independent variable is identified as explaining a dependent variable. Far right party positions on European integration (dependent variable) are contingent upon its party model (independent variable). The explanatory framework complies with the criterion of falsifiability (Popper 1968), whereby one 'should construct theories so that they can be shown to be wrong as easily and quickly as possible' (King et al. 1994: 100). If future research identifies a case exhibiting that a systematic association between party model and its position on the EU does not exist, the argument of the book could be falsified. Examples that may lead to the argument's falsifiability could include an anti-system far right party adopting a pro-EU position albeit its generic aim to delegitimise the system. Other examples include a far right party seeking to achieve change within the system, but nonetheless espousing a rejectionist EU stance; or a party seeking to assume a leading role within a governmental coalition but strongly opposing the EU. Until such evidence is produced, however, this book will treat the party model as the main independent variable of far right party Euroscepticism.

The following chapters proceed by testing the utility of this analytical framework to the study of far right party Euroscepticism in three EU member states. The controlled comparison starts from the premise that the French National Front, the Greek LAOS and the Italian National Alliance belong to the same party family, and thus share the core characteristics of nationalism, authoritarianism and strong leadership, but that they display variation in terms of their Euroscepticism.

Chapter 4

Rejectionist Euroscepticism

The French National Front

On a dans la cœur les choses qu'on défend.
C'est un credo, des valeurs morales, comme une religion.

We cherish what we stand for.
It is a belief, a moral value, a type of religion.

—Lydia Scénardi, former National Front MEP, 2009

This chapter studies the first pattern of far right Euroscepticism, namely, the rejectionist Eurosceptic stance on European integration. Far right parties that belong to this pattern utterly reject the principle of co-operation at a European multilateral level. They are opponents of the EU institutional and policy practice, and they fully discard the future building of an EU polity. The first and foremost goal of these parties is the attainment and maintenance of national sovereignty, which may be achieved only through the complete repatriation of competences from all external organisations to the nation-state. To further analyse this type of far right Euroscepticism, this chapter proceeds with a detailed examination of the 'anti-system' French National Front. The party's position on European integration has radically transformed over the years. In the 1980s, the National Front supported aspects of co-operation. However, as European integration deepened, the party's vision of Europe clashed with the development of the European project. Since the end of the 1990s, its position has crystallised into a complete rejection of the EU and any co-operation within the EU framework. Despite the fact that the National Front accepts that Europeans share a common heritage and civilisation based on Greek philosophy, Roman law, Christianity and the Enlightenment, the party evokes precisely these values as forming the basis of the European states' national self-determination. It opposes the EU as a project going against the fundamental principle that each nation-state should be able to be independent from external interference and free to govern its clearly demarcated territory. The EU does not promote the principles of community or national preference that the party holds dear. It is a neoliberal organisation, which is seen as the root for all social, cultural and economic problems facing European nation-states, including high levels of immigration, low purchasing power, crime, precariousness, delocalisation and outsourcing of production.

Commencing with an analysis of the party's electoral fortunes since its establishment in the early 1970s, the chapter shows that despite increasing success in the polls, the party has failed to achieve substantive parliamentary representation domestically. Similar to many other European far right parties, the National Front is characterised by the key features of nationalism, authoritarianism and strong leadership. The party draws upon the doctrine of national preference, prioritises polices that would preserve traditional lifestyles and is a champion of law and order. However, its effective isolation from the political system has incentivised it to engage in adversarial and confrontational politics. The National Front is an arch critic of liberal democracy, it is staunchly anti-establishment, and it seeks to undermine the legitimacy of the political system by calling for its radical transformation. On most issues, the party holds diametrically opposed views compared to other parties in the system. Its rejectionist EU position may be placed in the context of this domestic strategy of differentiation and its attempt to further polarise the political debate. This rejectionist Euroscepticism has a two-fold effect. It allows the party to differentiate itself from its immediate competitors in terms of policy, while at the same time it preserves its anti-party and anti-establishment status. The National Front's rejectionist Euroscepticism is ultimately linked to its master frame, i.e., opposition to globalisation. Contrary to some literature that would expect far right parties to prioritise cultural frames, the National Front has also highlighted what it sees as the negative economic and social consequences of France's EU membership, blaming the EU for failing to mitigate the adverse effects of market liberalisation and economic globalisation. This Eurosceptic frame is in line with the party's strategy to attract support from a niche electorate that perceive themselves as losers from economic liberalisation. Adopting a rejectionist Eurosceptic position has allowed the National Front to portray its policy divergence within the political system, and present itself as providing a unique – yet extremist – niche in the French political system.

THE 'ANTI-SYSTEM' FRENCH NATIONAL FRONT

The National Front was established in 1972. The party first participated in French elections in 1973, when it gained approximately 0.5 per cent of the vote. Its leader, Jean-Marie Le Pen, first ran for president in 1974, and his electoral results were equally poor. Due to lack of funds and a series of disagreements with the Party of New Forces (PFN), the National Front's domestic far right rival, the party did not run in the 1979 EP elections. Jean-Marie Le Pen was also not able to run for the presidency in 1981, as his candidacy did not win the 500 signatures required for eligibility (Shields 2007: 182). In both elections, Le Pen's strategy was to call for abstention. During the parliamentary elections of the same year, the party received very low support, confirming its status as a marginal party in the system during the 1970s (see Table 4.1).

The 1980s marked a turn in the National Front's electoral fortunes. The party experienced its first electoral success in 1983, when the general secretary, Jean-Pierre Stirbois, gained 16.7 per cent of the vote in a local by-election in Dreux. Following a deal concluded with the Rally for the French Republic (RPR) and the Union for French Democracy (UDF), the joint RPR-UDF-FN list won the second round and Jean-Pierre Stirbois became the Deputy Mayor. The party scored approximately 10 per cent in two further by-elections held in 1983, which attracted media attention and paved the way towards its electoral breakthrough in the 1984 EP elections. Campaigning under the list 'Front of national opposition in favour of a Europe of nations' (Mayer 1998: 13),[1] the party received 11 per cent of the French vote, which translated into ten out of eighty-one seats in the EP. Its performance in the 1986 legislative elections was equally strong, gaining 9.8 per cent of the vote and securing thirty-five seats in the National Assembly. This was facilitated by a reform of the electoral code of 1985, which introduced party-list proportional representation. Following the 1986 elections, however, the government reintroduced single-member districts with a two-round system. This change in the electoral system resulted in the party's 9.8 per cent in the subsequent 1988 elections translating into only one seat. During the presidential elections held in the same year, Jean-Marie Le Pen received 14.4 per cent of the vote in the first round – an inconceivable result for a far right candidate – marking a political 'earthquake' in the French political system (Shields 2007: 224). Presenting itself as the champion of 'Europe of the Nation-States', the National Front sustained its electoral scores in the 1989 EP elections with 11.7 per cent of the vote.

The National Front further solidified its electoral base in local, municipal and national elections during the 1990s. During both 1993 and 1997 legislative elections, the party gained over 10 per cent of the vote in the

Table 4.1   The National Front's election results (National and European)

Year	Election	Percentage	Votes	Seats
1973	National Assembly	0.5	108,616	0
1974	Presidential	0.7	190,921	-
1978	National Assembly	0.3	82,743	0
1979	European	-	-	-
1981	Presidential	-	-	-
1981	National Assembly	0.18	90,422	0
1984	European	11	2,210,334	10
1986	National Assembly	9.8	2,701,701	35
1988	Presidential	14.4	4,376,742	-
1988	National Assembly	9.8	2,353,466	0
1988 (2nd)	National Assembly	1.07	216,704	1
1989	European	11.7	2,129,668	10
1993	National Assembly	12.4	3,159,477	0
1993 (2nd)	National Assembly	5.9	1,168,160	0
1994	European	10.5	2,050,086	11
1995	Presidential	15	4,570,838	-
1997	National Assembly	15	3,800,785	0
1997 (2nd)	National Assembly	5.6	1,434,854	1
1999	European	5.7	1,005,285	5
2002	Presidential	16.9	4,804,772	-
2002 (2nd)	Presidential	17.8	5,525,034	-
2002	National Assembly	11.1	2,873,556	0
2002 (2nd)	National Assembly	1.85	393,205	0
2004	European	9.8	1,684,859	7
2007	Presidential	10.4	3,834,530	-
2007	National Assembly	4.3	1,116,136	0
2007 (2nd)	National Assembly	0.08	17,107	0
2009	European	6.3	1,091,691	3
2012	Presidential	17.9	6,421,426	-
2012	National Assembly	13.6	3,528,663	0
2012 (2nd)	National Assembly	3.66	842,684	2
2014	European	24.9	4,712,461	24

Sources: http://www.france-politique.fr/chronologie-fn.htm; http://www.parlgov.org/; http://www.election-resources.org/
Note: First round reported in presidential and national assembly elections unless otherwise noted. In 1981, the far right jointly gained about 0.4 per cent of the vote. MPs: 1988 Yann Piat; 1997 Jean-Marie Le Chevallier; 2012 Gilbert Collard and Marion Maréchal-Le Pen.

first round, and contested the second ballot in some constituencies, confirming its status as a powerful actor of the French right. Due to the two-round electoral system, however, which penalises small parties that do not run in coalitions, there was a great disparity between the strength of support for the National Front and the seats it gained in the National Assembly; specifically, in 1997, 15 per cent of the vote in the first round translated into only one seat in parliament. Jean-Marie Le Pen's performance was equally high at 15 per cent of the vote during the 1995 presidential elections. It was not until 2002, however, that the party literally shook the French system. Jean-Marie Le Pen overtook the socialist Lionel Jospin in the first round of presidential elections, and qualified to run in the second round, competing with the right-wing candidate, Jacques Chirac. With over 5.5 million votes (17.8 per cent) in the second round, the National Front became firmly the third electoral pole in French politics. This trend continued following the replacement of Jean-Marie Le Pen by his daughter, Marine Le Pen, as President of the party in January 2011. Although Marine Le Pen did not qualify for the run-off between the final two candidates in the 2012 presidential elections, she came third in the first round with 17.9 per cent of the vote, gaining approximately 900,000 more votes than her father's 2002 result in the second round. Finally, for the first time in French history, the party came in first during the 2014 EP elections with 24.9 per cent of the vote, translating into twenty-four seats out of seventy-four.[2] This electoral success provoked a 'eurosceptic earthquake', not only within France, but also across Europe (Halikiopoulou and Vasilopoulou 2014). As of the time of writing, the party is in full pre-electoral mode in the run-up to the 2017 elections, with its leader predicted to qualify for the second round.

In terms of its ideology, the National Front has often been thought to be the archetypal far right party. In the 1970s and 1980s, it attracted a number of intellectuals from different extreme right ideological factions, including 'French Algeria die-hards, revolutionary nationalists, wartime Vichyites, Holocaust revisionists, neo-fascists, neo-Nazis, monarchists, Catholic fundamentalists [...] and so on' (Hainsworth 2000b: 18; see also McCulloch 2006). This resulted in a degree of internal division and ideological blurring. Personified by its charismatic leader, Jean-Marie Le Pen (Eatwell 2002), the National Front was by the 1990s a key player in French politics, with an ideology and a discourse promoting forms of solidarity that went beyond social class and were based on identity and the nation (Flood 1997; Davies 1999; Swyngedouw and Ivaldi 2001). The party's ethnocentric worldview suggested that humanity was separated between in-groups and out-groups. The doctrine of national preference – the defence of French culture and identity over other cultures – is key to this distinction (McCulloch 2006: 167), and it may be summarised by the party's well-known slogan, 'La France d'abord' [France first]. The right of the French nation to be different from other nations became crucial in the party's ideological evolution, replacing earlier references to cultural superiority and biological differences reminiscent of fascism (McCulloch 2006: 176). The doctrine of national preference entails hostility to multiculturalism, internationalism and communism, which explains the further differentiation of in-groups between, on the one hand, 'nationals', and 'anti-nationals/cosmopolitans/communists' on the other. Within the in-group, the community takes precedence over the individual and is led by those nationalist-committed elites who have higher moral values and are 'capable of abnegation' (Swyngedouw and Ivaldi 2001: 5–6).

The doctrine of national preference and a fear of French decline also justify the party's dislike of immigrants, who are seen as culturally different (Hainsworth 2000b: 25), and its support for a restrictive immigration policy. Key personalities of the National Front, however, have sought to normalise the party's anti-immigration rhetoric by acknowledging that 'we have the obligation to help the poor countries. But the French should come first' (de Saint-Just 2010),[3] and that 'we want to help Africa. But we want to do so in their own country. Not in Europe' (Schénardi 2009).[4] National preference also accounts for the party's support for the international promotion of France and the Francophonie, its progressive turn towards economic protectionism (Ivaldi 2015), its rejection of the 'New World Order', its focus on national defence policy, its support for a strong military and its criticism of the United States and international organisations such as the World Trade Organisation and the EU (Bastow 1997). The principle of national sovereignty underpins the party's discourse against globalisation and European integration.

The party insists that modern society is in decline and has degenerated into a system of social and moral decay. As a solution, the National Front expresses strong support for a strong state, respect for authority and a national demographic policy that puts emphasis on population growth of the 'nationals' as opposed to immigration. The party views the family as the core institution structuring the social and moral values of French society. It promotes public policies that would preserve traditional lifestyles, revive the traditional family, boost the French birth rate, reduce French abortion rates and ban same-sex marriages (National Front 2004; 2007; 2012a). Moreover, the National Front presents itself as a champion of law and order, fighting for the rights of respectable French citizens who are violated by criminals (Flood 1997: 121). It advocates a stronger justice system with increased numbers of magistrates, the re-establishment of the death penalty, the deportation of foreign criminals, the building of more prisons and a zero-tolerance approach to a number of crimes, including illegal immigration, organised attacks against the police and all forms of trafficking (National Front 2004; 2007; 2012a; 2017).

The National Front's 'utopia' consists of a rejection of all aspects of the status quo (Swyngedouw and Ivaldi 2001). The party claims that French society is undergoing a crisis at all levels – cultural, economic and social. The crisis has hit the family, the educational system and employment, among other areas. It has impoverished the French household, the French economy and the French State (National Front, 2007 preface by Jean-Marie Le Pen), and it has 'accelerated the decomposition of the French social tissue and solidarity' (National Front 2004: 151).[5] The National Front is calling for the radical transformation of the socio-political system, i.e., the 'liberation of France', and it argues that the French regime is totalitarianism with a 'democratic mask' (National Front 2004: 1). It is staunchly anti-elite and anti-establishment. It undermines ideological and policy differences between political parties, and it presents the political universe in terms of dichotomies (Flood 1997; Swyngedouw and Ivaldi 2001). The party supports plebiscitary politics on issues that relate to the 'future of our Nation' (National Front 2004), as a way of delegitimising the system.

The change of party leadership in 2011 marked a change of party strategy. Marine Le Pen has attempted to soften the party's message and increase its credibility in a range of policies beyond immigration, with a view to broadening its electoral appeal (Mayer 2013a; Shields 2013). The new President avoids terms such as 'extreme' or 'radical' right, as well as anti-Semitic and Holocaust revisionist statements. She labels the National Front a 'republican' party, and she embeds her rhetoric within republican concepts such as laïcité and sovereignty (National Front 2012a; 2012b; 2017). This intends to signal that – unlike under the presidency of Jean-Marie Le Pen – the National Front respects the institutions of the Fifth Republic (Stockemer 2015). However, this strategy of de-demonisation (*dédiabolisation*) has not necessarily received unanimous support within the party. Since Marine Le Pen assumed the presidency of the National Front, there have been many defections of newly recruited members and numerous public disagreements, most notably with her father, Jean-Marie Le Pen, and her niece, Marion Maréchal-Le Pen. The focus on national preference continues, now described as 'national priority' (Mayer 2013b). In addition, despite this attempted top-down modernisation, party members and supporters are consistently more ethnocentric and xenophobic compared to the voters of other French parties (Mayer 2015). In what follows, the analysis of the party's Euroscepticism will take into consideration Marine Le Pen's attempt to strategically reposition the party, and will highlight areas of continuity and change.

THE NATIONAL FRONT'S REJECTIONIST EUROSCEPTICISM

The National Front's position towards European integration has undergone radical transformation over the years, to ultimately crystallise into an utter rejection of the EU system. In the 1980s, the party flaunted that 'we are first and foremost Europeans', and it supported a European project that would include 'a common European defence and nuclear strategy, a common foreign and security policy, common immigration controls and a "European Preference"' (Hainsworth et al. 2004: 45). Echoing the fascist myth of Europe as a collection of peoples (Griffin 1994), the party called for

'European patriotism', whereby the fusion between French and European identity could be achieved with a vision of jointly confronting a common enemy: 'What strikes at Europe strikes at France, and what strikes at France strikes at Europe' (Le Pen 1984: 164). As EU powers increased from the early 1990s onwards, the party hardened its Eurosceptic position. The French referendum over the ratification of the Maastricht Treaty in 1992 provided a platform for the National Front to further differentiate itself from the mainstream French right, by denouncing the treaty as a 'conspiracy against the peoples and nations in Europe' (quoted in Fieschi et al. 1996: 248), and it led the party to progressively abandon its European patriotism arguments.

From the end of the 1990s onwards, the National Front's EU position may be categorised within the rejectionist pattern of Euroscepticim. Similar to other far right parties in Europe, it defined Europe in cultural terms, i.e., as a continent with a common cultural heritage and western values, as well as a common European identity (de la Tocnaye 2010). The party claimed to 'stand for a European Europe, just as it does for a French France' (Flood 1997: 131). European tradition is based on four essential elements, namely, 'Greek philosophy, Roman Law, Judeo-Christian values and the Enlightenment' (Gollnisch 2007).[6] Europe should remain faithful to its moral and spiritual values, including its cultural and legal traditions deriving from Ancient Greece and Rome, as well as its Christian origins. Europe is not only a cultural reality, but also a human and geographical one (National Front 2009: 4). Despite European wars throughout the centuries, a long common history has created strong ties between the European peoples (Martin 2010). The conception of common religious values as essential to European identity is manifested in the party's criticism of the European Constitution for not including a reference to Christianity (Le Pen 2005).

However, the National Front's definition of Europe took an exclusionist and insular form. This common European history 'has invented the freedom and equality of Nations, self-governing without external interference, which is a unique model unparalleled elsewhere' (National Front 2009: 4).[7] A common cultural heritage serves as a justification for both nation-state self-determination and European independence from external intervention. It is only 'free, strong and sovereign nations that can make European civilisation shine in the world' (National Front 2002a: 28; 2004: 72).[8] This idea is put forward with the implicit acceptance that France would serve as a model for other European nations (National Front 2002a; 2004).

It is precisely this European conception that is reflected in the National Front's opposition to Turkey's EU accession (National Front 2007: 60). Europe is a 'club' of equal and sovereign nation-states, and there is no space for a country that is considered 'Asian' in geographical, cultural, historical and demographic terms (Gollnisch 2006b). Instead, the National Front is motivated by the 'hope that Europe as a whole, West and East, would at last discover its strength and forge a new collective role in the world' (Flood 1997: 131). Europeans should maintain strong and privileged links to Russia, which, contrary to Turkey, 'is a great European nation' (Le Pen 2007),[9] that 'belongs culturally, spiritually, geographically to the European space' (Gollnisch 2009b).[10] The National Front supports a 'European Europe, without Turkey but linked to Russia' (National Front 2008; see also 2012a; 2012b).[11]

Despite insisting on Europe's cultural links, the party is a staunch critic of integration. The National Front rejects the principle of European integration. It opposes any type of co-operation at a European multilateral level. The post-Maastricht EU does not bear any resemblance to its ideal model for European collaboration, which includes either bi- or tri-lateral co-operation of nation-states in specific policies of mutual interest governed exclusively by national institutions rather than supranational authorities. This justifies the party's support for France's withdrawal from the EU, and its rejection of all European treaties that are seen as 'linking France to the Europe of Brussels (Rome, Single Act, Schengen, Maastricht, and Amsterdam)' (National Front 2002a: 26; 2004: 70).[12] According to the National Front, the EU is a neoliberal organisation promoting globalisation, which is ultimately responsible for the destruction of public services, outsourcing, unemployment and precariousness (National Front 2012a). EU membership heralds the end of political sovereignty, economic prosperity, food independence, and social protection – and ultimately the end of France (National Front 2002b; 2004).

As a solution to those problems stemming from EU membership, the National Front proposes to re-establish French sovereignty in all policy spheres (National Front 2002a; 2002b; 2004; 2017). In its 2007 manifesto, the party suggests a tour of European capitals in order to renegotiate all European treaties with other member states. If this renegotiation tour failed to bear fruit, the National Front would organise a national referendum asking 'Should France regain its independence vis-à-vis the Europe of Brussels?' (National Front 2007: 61).[13] In its 2012 manifesto, this renegotiation was envisaged in the context of Article 50 of the EU. Interestingly neither manifesto stipulates which specific policies the party would seek to renegotiate, illustrating that its main aim was to leave the EU irrespective of the outcome. Marine Le Pen (2016a) became clearer following the Brexit vote: [If elected as French President], 'I would go to the European institutions, I would demand for the French people four sovereignties: territorial—our borders; monetary and budgetary; economic; and legislative. Either the European Union says yes to me, or they would say no, and I would say to the French, there is no other solution but to leave the EU'. The party's insistence on French withdrawal from the EU is consistent with its vision for France as a global force in international relations. This can only be achieved if it is a sovereign country whose international co-operation goes beyond what it calls the 'Euro-Atlantic' alliance (National Front 2012a: 51; 2017).

The party seeks to construct a 'Europe of Nations' (National Front 2008; 2017). In the 1990s, this new Europe was envisaged as 'French dominated, Catholic and White' (Benoit 1998: 21), operating on the basis of the principle of community preference, which would 'assure the prosperity of our peoples and the international influence of European nations' (National Front 2008). This should take place outside the EU framework on a case-by-case basis. The party argues that projects work much better outside the EU. Examples include the aircraft manufacturer Airbus, the satellites company ARIANE and the European Organisation for Nuclear Research (National Front 2009: 2; see also 2012a: 49). These projects provide a yardstick for comparison, because they are thought to work very well (or even better) outside the EU political framework. The party supports the creation of a pan-European union of sovereign countries (National Front 2012a): 'Co-operation should be undertaken on a project-by-project basis following a cost-benefit analysis managed by a secretary general without political forces' (Gollnisch 2009a). Areas with no political character, such as research and technology, would be given priority. Economic or industrial co-operation should only take place at a bilateral or trilateral level (Reveau 2010). Marine Le Pen (2016a) confirms this view, arguing that 'we will work together in work groups on projects. [...] It will be what I call a Europe of co-operation. Some people will find a project and circulate it, and some will say, I like this project, others will say I don't like it, I don't want to participate'. Some party cadres have toyed with the idea of a common European army independent from the North Atlantic Alliance and the United States of America (Schénardi 2009; de Saint-Just 2010). However, following the EU's enlargement to Central and Eastern Europe, accord among member states was thought to be difficult to achieve, which ultimately made this project unfeasible (de Saint-Just 2010).

Because the National Front is adamantly opposed to the principle of European integration, it is hardly surprising that it opposes the EU's policy and institutional practice. The party disputes the primacy of EU over national law, argues that the EU executive is unaccountable and pursues the empowerment of national legislative bodies. It seeks to re-establish political authority and sovereignty in all policy domains ranging from monetary and fiscal policy, agriculture, food and commercial policy and the single market, to border control, immigration and citizenship. The National Front is a staunch critic of the EMU. The euro is seen as a failure and associated with high unemployment and low economic growth (National Front 2012a). It is thought to 'create economic disparities and promote unfair competition among European countries' (de Saint-Just 2010).[14] The European Central Bank (ECB) is held responsible for speeding up the effects of the financial crisis in Europe by keeping the euro-currency parity stable and by not varying the interest rate of lending money. Instead of focusing on ensuring full employment, the ECB's main objective was to reduce inflation (National Front 2012a: 47). Its powers should, therefore, be limited, including its authority to administer the Eurozone's monetary policy (de Danne 2010). Far from strengthening the French economy, the euro currency 'accelerates the process of globalisation, namely structural instabilities' (National Front 2004: 112).[15] France should regain its monetary sovereignty in order to allow competitive devaluations and flexible exchange rages (de la Tocnaye 2010; National Front 2008; 2012a: 48). Rather than addressing the Eurozone crisis through further integration, national governments should have authority over their own monetary policy: 'EU Member states should be able to manage the financial crisis by themselves' by setting their own exchange rates (de la Tocnaye 2010).[16] Jean-Marie Le Pen has maintained that 'we have to recover our national currency in order to guarantee the purchasing power of our compatriots' (Au Front 2008: 4).[17] It is acknowledged, however, that an outright exit from the Eurozone might be very risky. The party's strategy has been first to seek reform of the ECB, and then proceed with exiting the Eurozone if the proposed reforms fail (de Danne 2010). During the 2017 electoral campaign, Marine Le Pen's vision for France leaving the Eurozone consists of the return to a basket of recognised national currencies, linked through a common currency system similar to the European Currency Unit (ECU) (Horobin 2017).

The Common Agricultural Policy is seen as subjugated to the ultra-liberal principles of the EU and the World Trade Organisation, which has resulted in high levels of unemployment in rural areas (Martinez 2006a; Martinez 2006c). The National Front criticises the European Commission for gradually decreasing the budget for agriculture and destroying this European industry to the benefit of countries outside the EU, such as Brazil (Martinez 2006b). Jean-Marie Le Pen (2005b: 3) has argued that 'European agriculture is dead'.[18] The EU's commercial policy is condemned on a similar basis, namely, that it promotes an ultra-liberal agenda, which has dismantled traditional European industries such as textile, leather, farming, fishing and home appliances (Martinez 2006a), and it has failed to protect European industries to the benefit of countries outside Europe, such as China (Jean-Marie Le Pen 2005a). For these reasons, unless the EU's commercial policy promotes protectionism, it continues to be a 'suicide' (Le Pen 2005a: 3).

The National Front is against the European single market, which involves the free movement of goods, services, capital and labour. Although the party accepts that Europe's internal market may lead to development and prosperity, it maintains that it does not ensure the protection of European workers from worldwide competition (Gollnisch 2009a). The single market is seen as the cause of the de-industrialisation of France and the outsourcing of French companies (de Saint-Just 2010). The gradual phasing-out of internal physical and economic borders constitutes a form of betrayal to the party's core principles (Gollnisch 2009a), which also accounts for the National Front's staunch opposition to the Schengen accords. Immigration and citizenship constitute the party's prime concerns and should be dealt with only at the national level in order to ensure the defence of French culture and identity. Open borders are thought to have encouraged increased levels of immigration, both from within and from outside the EU (Le Pen 2009: 3). Moreover, the National Front is against European citizenship, arguing that 'the only possible access to citizenship is nationality' (Gollnisch 2006a; see also National Front 2004: 71).[19] As a result, the party opposes any European competence on immigration policy, is against Schengen and favours the re-establishment of control over French borders (National Front 2002a; 2004; 2012a: 49; 2017: 6).

Beyond simply criticising the EU policy and institutional practice, the National Front opposes the future building of a European polity. The values and principles upon which the EU has been built are antithetical to the party's ideology and general raison d'être. The party envisages 'a Europe of Nations founded on state sovereignty, community preference, and borders protecting the nation-states from immigration and outsourcing' (National Front 2008).[20] Europe becomes stronger only when the European nation-states remain sovereign, independent, strong, prosperous and respected (National Front 2009: 1), not when supranational institutions govern them. The EU does not promote the principles of community or national preference, and for this reason it is seen as the root for all social, cultural and economic problems facing European nation-states, including high levels of immigration, low purchasing power, crime, delocalisation and the outsourcing of production.

The National Front presents Europe in a dichotomous manner, i.e., 'their' Europe – a bureaucratic superstate with political powers used against European citizens – as opposed to 'our' Europe – a geographical continent of sovereign and independent nation-states (National Front 2009; 2012a). The EU is perceived to be advocating ultra-liberal, free-market economics, which contravene the National Front's ideas of economic patriotism (see Ivaldi 2015). The European model has assumed power over policies that have traditionally belonged to the realm of the 'national' rather than that of the 'international'. The superiority of EU legislation, EU laws on cultural issues, the common currency, European citizenship and the European defence policy are clear examples of the EU's impact on all national spheres, including the economic, political and social domains. The EU has become the 'ultimate step before global governance' (National Front 2004: 62),[21] which plainly contradicts the party's insistence on 'national solutions to national issues' (Gollnisch 2009a). Overall, the relationship between France and the EU is seen to have resulted in a 'negative balance' for France (de Danne 2010).[22]

ELECTORAL INCENTIVES AND THE NATIONAL FRONT'S DOMESTIC STRATEGY

How may we explain the National Front's rejectionist EU position? Placing the party's strategy in the context of French domestic politics, this section demonstrates that, due to a number of institutional constraints, the National Front has prioritised a policy of differentiation that would enable it to create its own niche in the system. The National Front engages in adversarial politics. Its political agenda concentrates on specific issues, such as immigration, globalisation and the EU. Its extreme policies on these issues enable the party to achieve policy divergence and at the same time undermine the legitimacy of the French political system. The National Front's rigid Eurosceptic position is integral to this political strategy. The party claims that it is the only political force in France whose main purpose is to protect the French people from European and global external forces.

The National Front is one of the most politically successful far right parties in Western Europe (DeClair 1999: 115). Despite its extremist ideology, the party has become a strong actor in the system, 'giving rise to a "tripolar" pattern of party competition' (Bornschier and Lachat 2009: 360). Its electoral gains have allowed it not only to become a major force in French domestic politics, but also to perceive itself as such, arguing that it is 'the 3rd or 4th force in the system' (de Danne 2010). Party officials accept that 'we are a small party only from the point of view that we are not represented in the National Assembly', but 'in reality we are not small; we are important in setting the debate, have influence on the society, and provide an intellectual challenge' (de Danne 2010).

However, unlike other far right parties in Europe, its success in the polls has not translated into either significant numbers of legislative seats or political office. Domestic institutional constraints produce strong biases against small parties. The French two-round electoral system results in the over-representation of large parties and the underrepresentations of small parties. It tends to incentivise pre-electoral coalitions; however, there is no evidence that participation in such coalitions contributes to gaining more seats among small parties (Blais and Loewen 2009: 352). Since pre-electoral coalition formation in France does not promise high electoral pay-offs and may come at the cost of ideological compromise, the National Front is effectively encouraged to compete as a single force in the political system. At the same time, mainstream French parties have, for the most part, adopted a strategy of non-co-operation with the National Front, which has contributed to further polarisation and has kept the party out of the National Assembly. The National Front has been discredited for its extremist ideas and its anti-system character. This can be seen in sharp contrast to the pre-electoral behaviour of the conservative Movement for France. In the 2007 legislative elections, for example, the Movement for France ran as part of the 'Presidential Majority' electoral block. It obtained only 1.2 per cent of the vote, which translated into two seats in the National Assembly. The National Front, on the other hand, ran independently in the same elections. It gained 4.3 per cent of the vote in the first round, but it ultimately won no seats in the National Assembly.

The French semi-presidential system also contributes to the marginalisation of small parties. Presidential elections by definition entail a 'winner takes all' outcome, which discourages third-party candidates. A candidate must win the majority of the votes in order to be elected. Candidates failing to be elected do not make any concrete political gains in terms of effective power within the political system. For example, the 2002 elections proved to be a significant victory for Jean-Marie Le Pen and a major shock to the French political system. Despite qualifying for the second round, however, the party leader did not gain any real power in terms of representation and office. This inability of the party to access power is realistically accepted by party officials, who also argue that they are not willing to co-operate with any other French political force either pre- or post- elections (de Danne 2010; de la Tocnaye 2010; de Saint-Just 2010; Salagnac 2010). The other French political forces are seen as responsible for French decadence and decay (Martin 2010), and as such coalitions are seen as compromise or even treason (de Danne 2010).

French institutional constraints, in combination with the National Front's unconventional ideology, have led to the party's effective exclusion from the political system. Competition between the National Front and other parties has developed into a zero-sum game, in which the National Front is the player experiencing constant losses despite electoral gains. This exclusion provides additional incentives for the party to engage in adversarial politics. The National Front holds diametrically opposed views compared to the rest of the party system on most political issues, especially those on which it considers itself to have a comparative advantage. This is consistent with Mayer's (1998: 17) evaluation of the National Front's political strategy, which suggests that the party seeks 'to polarise the political debate around their ideas, and replace the traditional left/right cleavage with a new one, which sets the National Front against the "gang of four", as Front National likes to refer to the established parties, evoking the image of collusion'. This strategy consists of, first, treating mainstream parties as a single block, in order to reduce 'the differences of values, policies and practice between them to mere gradations' (Flood 1997: 112); and, second, competing on a new political division that mainstream parties do not [yet] engage in. Smartly, the National Front has identified new issues since the 1990s. It has promoted forms of solidarity that go beyond social class, and it has engaged in nationalist politics. The National Front competes on the new

Table 4.2 The socio-demographic profile of National Front voters

		2002		2007		2012	
		All voters (n=1000)	FN voters (n=54)	All voters (n=2000)	FN voters (n=56)	All voters (n=2014)	FN voters (n=266)
Gender	Male	48.1	61.11	41.55	51.79	44.89	46.99
	Female	51.9	38.89	58.45	48.21	55.11	53.01
Age	Up to 35	34.5	22.22	21.9	25	19.86	23.31
	36-50	30.1	38.89	30	33.93	26.61	27.07
	51-65	19.8	24.07	28.75	26.79	28.3	31.58
	65 or more	15.6	14.81	19.35	14.29	24.83	17.67
Employment Status	Employed	54.6	61.11	50.35	46.43	46.33	48.5
	Student	8.3	1.85	7.35	7.14	3.28	2.63
	At home	6.8	5.56	3.95	7.14	4.47	4.51
	Retired	23.7	24.07	32.15	28.57	34.11	30.45
	Unemployed	4.5	5.56	4.4	10.71	7.05	9.02
	Other	2.1	1.85	1.7	0	4.52	4.89
Education	Low	25.8	18.52	43.3	67.86	23.73	24.06
	Medium	58.3	68.52	33.8	25	45.53	59.77
	High	15.2	12.96	22.3	5.36	29.99	15.79
Religiosity	Every week	5.5	3.7	6.4	3.57	6.11	3.01
	Every month or several times a year	21.7	27.78	23.8	14.29	14.65	13.91
	Once a year or less	28.8	22.22	60.55	78.57	59.68	68.8
	Never	10	14.81	8.6	3.57	18.72	13.91
Urban vs rural	Rural	23.7	24.07	24.9	39.29	35.1	46.24
	Urban	76.3	75.93	75.1	60.71	64.9	53.76
Left-right (0–10)	Mean	5.12	6.92	5.47	7.46	4.65	6.41
	Std. deviation	2.55	2.69	2.48	2.03	2.47	2.29

Source: The Comparative Study of Electoral Systems (CSES Module 2, 3 and 4).
Notes: Vote choice in presidential elections (1st round).

cleavage that differentiates between the winners and losers from globalisation (Kriesi et al. 2006), and within this division it seeks to push for particular policies that are exclusive to its own agenda, such as the effects of immigration, European integration and globalisation. It is only by selectively focusing on particular policies that the National Front can polarise the debate and present its ideas as the polar opposite of what the other parties are offering.

This strategy of creating its own distinctive niche in the system is also partly demonstrated in the type of voter the party attracts (see Table 4.2). The National Front's voters tend to form a coherent core and have remained largely faithful to the party since the 1980s (Mayer 2002b; Mayer 2013a, 2015; Stockemer and Amengay 2015). Support for the party tends to depend more on education and gender, rather than social class and religion. National Front voters tend to be predominantly male, have low to medium levels of education and are significantly underrepresented among highly educated groups of society. They tend to be slightly overrepresented among the unemployed, especially in 2007. In 2002, the party expanded its electoral base, gaining votes from rural areas and smaller French towns, mainly among farmers who had traditionally supported the centre-right Union for a Popular Movement. The positions of these voters largely resemble those of the core National Front supporters, as they equally reject immigration, have an authoritarian vision of society and tend to be in favour of the death penalty (Mayer 2007: 439).

National Front supporters have values that set them apart from the remaining French society (Mayer 2002a; 2002b; 2007). They are significantly more to the right compared to the French electorate. They do attract some left-wing voters, too, but these 'Leftist Lepenists' tend to be a minority. Indicatively, only 16 per cent of the workers who intended to vote for Jean-Marie Le Pen in the 2007 presidential elections claimed to belong 'mostly to the left' (Mayer 2007: 438). The party's electorate has an ethnocentric and authoritarian vision of society. It is somewhat anti-Semitic, and it is in favour of the re-establishment of the death penalty (Mayer 2002b). It overwhelmingly believes that there are too many immigrants in France, that immigrants from North Africa will never become French and that the French people no longer feel at home in France (Mayer 2002b: 505–06). There is a strong correlation between the importance one attaches to the issue of immigration and voting for the National Front (Mayer 2007).

This trend continued under new party leadership. Marine Le Pen has followed in her father's footsteps and has employed a similar strategy of policy differentiation. The European financial crisis has changed the context, however, and has resulted in economic issues and financial becoming relatively more salient in the party's agenda (Ivaldi 2015). Marine Le Pen's 2012 campaign focused on social protection and economic redistribution, which – in line with party ideology – was justified in terms of exclusion, the rights of the in-group and the doctrine of national preference, which Marine Le Pen labelled a national 'priority'. As the campaign progressed, the focus returned to more familiar issues, including immigration, Europe and globalisation (Shields 2013). Despite Marine Le Pen's attempt to diversify her electoral audience, in 2012 she attracted an electorate that is socially and ideologically similar to her father's. The key differences included a younger electorate and a more narrow gender gap, with a greater number of women voting for the party in 2012. Beyond these differences, Marine Le Pen seems to have attracted more support from the party's existing pools of voters, rather than expanding its pool of voters to new socio-demographic categories (Mayer 2013a, 2015; Stockemer and Amengay 2015).

THE EU ISSUE AS A DIFFERENTIATION TOOL

The French institutional and electoral context has produced strong biases against the National Front. Despite continuous electoral accomplishments, the party has not been able to achieve significant representation. This effective marginalisation from the party system has encouraged the National Front to prioritise an adversarial and issue-based logic of electoral competition. The National Front has a lot more to win, including media coverage, by being controversial than by being accommodating. The party thus adopts policies that allow it to dissociate itself from the other parties in the French political system. Its decision to make the EU an electoral issue fits within this domestic political strategy of policy differentiation. The party's rejectionist position on European integration represents a clear and different option to the electorate. Strong criticism of the EU becomes a strategic tool for the party, in an effort to demonstrate to the French electorate that it represents a different, powerful and independent actor in the party system.

This may be illustrated through an examination of the 2005 European Constitution referendum campaign. Although highly divided, the Socialists and the Greens supported the European Constitution, as did the Union for a Popular Movement. The 'no' campaign was diverse, ranging from the far left French Communist Party, the Workers' Struggle and the Revolutionary Communist League, on the one hand; to Philippe de Villiers right-wing Movement for France, and Nicolas Dupont-Aignan's France Arise, a break-away party from the Union for a Popular Movement, on the other. This cross-party campaign against the European Constitution was united by its focus on 'the negative socio-economic impact and cultural consequences of globalisation for France's economic and political future' (Startin 2008: 94). The radical left condemned the European Constitution because they saw the EU as a capitalist project that ran counter to their vision of the 'Socialist United States of Europe' (Workers' Struggle 2004; Revolutionary Communist League 2006: 18), and that perpetuated the ultra-liberal logic of the Maastricht Treaty (French Communist Party 2004). The right-wing opponents of the Constitution put forward a 'variable geometry,' or, 'à la carte' alternative Europe, relying on intergovernmental co-operation. It was only the National Front, however, that advocated the repatriation of all competences, the renegotiation of all European treaties and the organisation of a referendum on French EU membership. Furthermore, although the right-wing French Eurosceptics tend to share the National Front's views on nation-state sovereignty, they did not adopt its vision of Europe. During that campaign, the National Front was the only party against the totality of EU policies, maintaining that France should not be bound by international legislation, and advocating the absolute supremacy of the European nation-state over any other institution, which essentially amounted to withdrawal from the EU.

The National Front perceives both conservative and far left parties as potential electoral competitors, given that their target electorates and some of their policies often tend to overlap. In this context, the party has additional incentives to increase its differentiation and portray itself as a unique – albeit rather extremist – political alternative. By claiming that 'it was the first Eurosceptic party in France' (Salagnac 2010),[23] the National Front presents itself as the 'owner' of Euroscepticism in France. It claims to be different from the far left, both in terms of the focus and the justification of criticism. Unlike the far left, the National Front does not only criticise the EU with reference to the economy, but also for encouraging immigration (Schénardi 2009). In addition, it justifies its disapproval of the EU on the basis of 'economic patriotism' (de la Tocnaye 2010),[24] and its 'willingness to retain the nation's prominence' (de Saint-Just 2010).[25] The National Front also stresses its distance from French conservative parties: 'Philippe de Villers and Nicolas Dupont-Aignan have been elected to the National Assembly thanks to the Union for a Popular Movement' (de Danne 2010), which ties them to the mainstream. In particular, de Villiers is perceived as having 'sold out' to the Union for a Popular Movement (Schénardi 2009).[26] This rejectionist Euroscepticism has a two-fold effect. It allows the party to differentiate itself from its immediate competitors in terms of policy, while at the same time it preserves its anti-party and anti-establishment status.

This link between the party's effort for differentiation and the question of Europe became even more prominent in the later few years of the 2000s. Nicolas Sarkozy, leader of the centre-right Union for a Popular Movement, openly politicised immigration and national identity during his 2007 presidential campaign, effectively hollowing out a large part of the National Front's political agenda (Mayer 2007: 441). Indeed, a number of party officials argue that Sarkozy won precisely because he borrowed National Front ideas (Schénardi 2009; Gollnisch 2009a; de Danne 2010; de Saint-Just 2010). Sarkozy increased the salience of immigration and challenged the National Front's ownership of this issue, which proved to be an effective strategy, as some traditional right-wing voters returned to his party in 2007.[27] Jean-Marie Le Pen received 10.4 per cent of the vote in the first round of the 2007 presidential elections, with approximately 1,700,000 less votes, compared to the second round of the previous 2002 elections.

Effective exclusion from the party system has served to sharpen the party's claims (Schénardi 2009).[28] It has further encouraged the party to employ the EU issue as part of its exclusive policy toolkit, and engage in contentious politics by arguing that 'we are imprisoned within the EU. It is a prison'; 'we do not need a villain'; and 'the European Parliament is a masquerade' (Salagnac 2010).[29] Acknowledging that the party mobilises those voters who strongly identify themselves with the national community (Schénardi 2009; Gollnisch 2009a), it seeks to defend the 'New Paradigm' against the EU. The party's agenda is patriotic and social: 'We believe in the preservation of national identity and stand out for the social rights of the people' against the EU (de Danne 2010). Marine Le Pen continued this strategy by according the greatest importance to the EU issue in her 2012 electoral campaign, as compared to other presidential candidates. The question of Europe was the second-most mentioned issue after the economy and ahead of immigration (Dehousse and Tacea, 2015: 153–54). This strategy of differentiation has allowed the National Front to claim ownership of the EU issue, and present itself as providing a unique – yet extremist – niche in the French political system.

THE ROLE OF GLOBALISATION IN THE NATIONAL FRONT'S EUROSCEPTIC AGENDA

The National Front's rejectionist Euroscepticism is ultimately linked to its master frame, i.e., opposition to globalisation. The party views this phenomenon as a threat to the nation-state, with detrimental effects on Frenchness at all levels, including cultural, social and economic (Hanley 2001: 310). Instead of protecting the European peoples against the threats arising from globalisation, the EU is seen as an incubator for them. The party argues that the EU is the 'Trojan horse of the ultra-liberal forces of globalisation, with the European Treaties since Maastricht imposing free and undistorted competition, which [...] prohibits any type of patriotic interventionism' (National Front 2012a: 5).[30] Globalisation is perceived as commencing 'by the standardisation at the European level' (Lang 2001).[31] The National Front labels this phenomenon 'Euro-globalisation' [*Euro-mondialisme*], and it often argues that the entire EU project is an American fabrication (e.g. de Danne 2010). Jean-Marie Le Pen argued that 'not only does Europe fail to constitute a protection for French businesses but also contributes to the acceleration of the processes of deregulation, liberalisation of services, and the opening to global competition' (Le Pen 2006: 2).[32] European and national elites are portrayed as 'traitors', unreservedly surrendering to free-market economics and the forces of globalisation (National Front 2009: 1).

Rejection of the EU becomes a tangible scapegoat for the perceived negative consequences of globalisation, including insecurity, unemployment, competition for scarce resources with non-natives, rising inequalities, powerlessness, alienation and demographic change. All problems facing France are attributed to the EU for failing to mitigate the negative effects of globalisation. For example, the party criticises the EU for having 'sacrificed French agriculture to America', and it condemns the single market for 'responding to its own logic' (Salagnac 2010).[33] French farmers are seen as 'victims of globalisation that pay the consequences of a disastrous European agricultural policy' (Au Front 2008: 6).[34] The party views the French 'no' to the European Constitution as the expression of the people's frustration with the devastating effect of European integration and globalisation on French industry and agriculture. A speech of Jean-Claude Martinez in the EP captures this very well:

> The French people's will expressed by the 2005 referendum broke the wild wave of ultra-liberalism and unrestrained free-trade that for the past 20 years swept and destroyed our coal, steel, textile, leather, spare parts, home appliances and automobile industries. This wave sowed the desertification of our fishing ports, our Languedoc-Roussillon vineyards, our sheep, cattle and poultry breeding, our Caribbean bananas, our Reunion plantations, our farms and plunged the women, the men, the workers and labourers of our country into social insecurity (Martinez 2006a).[35]

A systematic analysis of the National Front's MEP speeches demonstrates the comparative salience of issues relevant to the phenomenon of globalisation. During the fifth Parliamentary Term (1999–2004), the National Front elected five MEPs, including Charles De Gaulle, Bruno Gollnisch, Carl Lang, Jean-Marie Le Pen and Jean-Claude Martinez. Marie-France Stirbois replaced Jean-Marie Le Pen in April 2003, following the suspension of the latter's EP mandate. During the sixth Parliamentary Term (2004–2009), the National Front elected seven MEPs. Whereas Marine Le Pen, Fernand Le Rachinel and Lydia Schénardi were elected for the first time, Bruno Gollnisch, Carl Lang, Jean-Marie Le Pen and Jean-Claude Martinez renewed their mandate.[36] Only three National Front MEPs were re-elected during the seventh Parliamentary term (2009–2014): Bruno Gollnisch, Jean-Marie Le Pen and Marine Le Pen. For the most part of this fifteen-year period, National Front MEPs have remained non-attached, i.e., they have not formally affiliated themselves with any other political group in the EP. Transnational collaboration has been confined to the party's participation in the short-lived Technical Group of Independent Members (1999–2001) and the Identity, Tradition and Sovereignty group (2007) (see Startin 2010). Following the 2014 EP elections, Marine Le Pen established the Europe of Nations and Freedom Group. MEP speeches during the eighth EP term (2014–2019) are not included in this analysis.

The content analysis of National Front's MEP speeches demonstrates that they have employed the majority of their speaking time in the EP to discuss issues that arise from the EP's agenda as opposed to domestic issues (see Table 4.3; also see appendix for information on the coding procedure). Within the domestic issues category, which occupied, on average, 8 per cent of the coded sentences, the most salient issues included references to the national government and institutions, at 30.15 per cent, followed by references to social policies, at 28.64 per cent, and references to the national economy and economic policies, at 17.58 per cent. Although questions of domestic immigration featured in MEPs' speeches, this policy did not occupy a prominent role in their agenda. During the seventh EP term, social policies –including health, employment and welfare –were the primary focus of MEPs, at 47.59 per cent ahead of references to the national government and institutions, at 30.34 per cent.

Similar to the Italian National Alliance (see chapter 6), the National Front MEPs employed the EP platform in order to discuss EU-related issues. On average, approximately 92 per cent of the party's MEPs' sentences referred to EU-related policies. This percentage varies from 88.44 per cent during the fifth EP term to 92.22 per cent and 95.29 per cent during the sixth and seventh EP terms, respectively. The most salient category here relates to EU rules and procedures, at 25.17 per cent on average over the fifteen-year period. The National Front's MEPs are staunch critics of the EU system of governance. They used a quarter of their speaking time to criticise various European treaties, arguing that EU-imposed harmonisation of law removed state sovereignty, and was geared towards the creation of a centralised and unitary superstate. They presented the EU as an incompetent organisation run by a group of oligarchs who failed to respect the results of EP elections and European referendums. They argued that the system was unnecessarily complicated and technocratic, entailing that member states lost their sovereignty even in areas in which they had negotiated opt-outs. They disagreed with the ways in which decisions were made at the EU level. They accused the EU of failing to tolerate dissenting voices and different points of view, and of creating instruments that restricted freedom of expression. In particular, they

Table 4.3   Salience of issues in National Front MEPs' European Parliament speeches

	Overall	*5th term*	*6th term*	*7th term*
General breakdown				
Domestic	8.03	11.56	7.78	4.71
EU	91.97	88.44	92.22	95.29
Domestic issues				
Crime	2.93	3.19	3.56	0.00
Economy and economic policies	17.58	11.03	23.37	15.86
Environment and energy	9.64	18.38	5.35	0.00
Foreign policy	3.02	2.45	4.36	0.00
Government and institutions	30.15	29.66	30.50	30.34
Immigration	8.03	5.88	10.30	6.21
Social policies	28.64	29.41	22.57	47.59
EU-related issues				
EU agriculture and fisheries	5.48	6.86	5.61	3.85
EU economy and economic policies	22.20	14.45	25.56	23.61
EU enlargement	3.28	4.39	3.20	2.31
EU environment and energy	3.27	2.85	3.78	2.73
EU foreign and security policy	7.77	11.69	6.11	6.97
EU justice	1.94	3.33	1.45	1.48
EU research and technology	0.65	0.42	0.78	0.64
EU rules and procedures	25.17	18.94	26.82	28.30
EU security and borders	9.24	8.62	10.07	8.29
EU social policies	16.01	20.70	13.62	15.84
EU trade and co-operation	3.91	6.95	1.22	5.94
European culture and history	1.08	0.80	1.79	0.03

Source: EP online archives.
Notes: N=1515 speeches/13172 sentences (fifth term: N=302 speeches/3529 sentences; sixth term: N=778 speeches/6376 sentences; seventh term: N=435 speeches/3267 sentences). See appendix regarding coding procedure.

were concerned with parliamentary immunity, arguing that the EP discriminates against specific MEPs. The MEPs' focus on EU rules and procedures increased over time ranging from 18.94 per cent during the fifth EP term, to 26.82 per cent and 28.3 per cent during the sixth and seventh EP terms, respectively. This suggests that the party's MEPs employed the EP platform in order to push for their rejectionist agenda, which increased in focus over time.

The second and third most salient categories include EU economy and economic policies, at 22.2 per cent, and EU social policies, at 16 per cent on average, across the period under investigation. Sentences coded in these two categories were predominantly framed in terms of criticising the EU and its policies for accelerating the devastating effects of globalisation on the economy and decreasing social standards. National Front MEPs argued against the four freedoms of the EU – i.e., the free movement of capital, goods, services and people – which they viewed as resulting in deindustrialisation, pressure on wages, unrestrained speculation and unemployment. They accused the EU of employing the Eurozone crisis as an instrument to justify the further deepening of integration in the form of a European superstate, which only served capitalism as opposed to Europeans' interests and well-being. They opposed any co-operation on fiscal matters, were critical of the EU budget and viewed the adoption of the Eurocurrency as detrimental to national economies. National Front MEPs criticised the EU for failing to adopt the policies necessary to protect European workers, industries and consumers from the adverse effects of globalisation. While they argued that globalisation might lead to inequalities and human rights violations, both within Europe and beyond, they staunchly criticised the EU's approach of prioritising human rights issues and the constitutional protection of minorities. Interestingly, while the party's MEPs criticised the EU for promoting uncontrollable migration, the EU security and borders category, which included references to border security, immigration and Schengen, is not as salient. This category was fourth in importance, with just 9.24 per cent of coded sentences on average throughout the fifteen years. This suggests that, contrary to the core expectation in the literature that far right parties prioritise cultural frames (e.g. Ellinas 2010), the National Front has also insisted on the negative economic and social consequences of France's EU membership, blaming the EU for failing to mitigate the adverse effects of economic globalisation.

The argument that the EU facilitates globalisation is prominent in party campaigns during both national and European elections. For example, during its 2009 EP election campaign, the party called the EU a 'scam' that destroyed identities, sovereignties and freedoms. It was called a 'Euro-global space open to all winds, to all flows of people, products and capital' (National Front 2009: 4).[37] Bruno Gollnisch gave an interview to the party's magazine, in which he argued that 'the World is sick. Europe is sick. France is sick' (Au Front 2008: 7),[38] indicating that Europe was on an intermediate level between the global and the national levels, accelerating the negative effects of globalisation. One of the party's pre-electoral slogans was 'Against the Europe of Banksters', suggesting that Europe was being run by profiteering and dishonest individuals (Au Front 2008: 5).[39] The negative effects of the Eurozone crisis exemplified that the party was 'right' to oppose globalisation and European integration (National Front 2009: 1; Le Pen 2016a). Similar frames have persisted in national elections, with Marine Le Pen launching her domestic 2012 and 2017 presidential campaigns with references to economic globalisation and European integration as the root causes of French decline. In both campaigns, Marine Le Pen promised to roll back the tide of globalisation and European integration by reasserting French sovereignty, and she accused her rivals of being 'servants' of the banking and finance industries (France24 2012; Vinocur 2017). Marine Le Pen has presented herself as a different voice, fighting in the name of the people in order to stop immigration and ensure full employment for the French people. She has argued that developments such as the Trump vote, Brexit and the 2015 Greek bailout referendum were essentially 'referendums against an unfettered globalisation imposed upon people, which has today clearly showed its limits' (Marine Le Pen 2016b). Following Brexit, she insisted that 'the European Union is objectively a total failure. It's a social failure, it's an economic failure, it's a failure in terms of power, it's a diplomatic failure' (Marine Le Pen 2016a). She promised to give the French people the 'four sovereignties that the EU has stolen' – including monetary, legislative, territorial and economic sovereignty – and she offered the prospect of a 'just, proud, sustainable and prosperous France' (Le Pen 2017).[40]

Extreme policy preferences on the EU, and framing the EU as a question of globalization serve to satisfy the perceived needs of the party's niche electorate: i.e., low-skilled, low-educated voters with anti-immigrant and authoritarian attitudes, who tend to see globalisation as a threat. This group of people is likely to consider themselves to be victims of globalisation. Economic liberalisation and the outsourcing of production affects professions that attract lower-level employees, and workers in traditionally protected sectors. At the same time, low-paying, low-skilled jobs are mostly threatened by the influx of immigration. These voters also tend to identify strongly with the national community, and they view globalisation and the EU as promoting uncontrollable immigration and creating a cultural melting pot. Policy vote among these societal groups becomes a means of defending their socio-economic status in opposition to what they see as 'devastating' European and global forces. The party's unconditional opposition to the EU project is the only such position in the French party system, and it has attracted the most anti-EU voters in France (Goodliffe 2015: 332). By adopting a 'losers' programme that consists of the fusion of cultural and economic protectionism, the party has created its own unique niche in the system: 'Our electorate is poor and a victim of globalisation and European integration. We carry the questions and anxieties of the French' (de Saint-Just 2010).[41] Voters 'choose us for the consequences of globalisation, namely unemployment, immigration, low purchasing power, lost social gains and insecurity' (Schénardi 2009).[42] The party's rejectionist Euroscepticism addresses this niche electoral clientele: 'Our position is really the position of our electorate' (Schénardi 2009).[43]

CONCLUSION

The aim of the chapter has been to examine the rejectionist type of party-based Euroscepticism, though the detailed investigation of the anti-system French National Front. Positioning the party's domestic strategy within the context of French electoral and institutional constraints, the chapter has shown that the National Front's rejectionist Euroscepticism may be explained by its attempt to undermine the legitimacy of the French political system and to polarise the domestic debate. Although the party accepts Europe as a cultural and geographical entity, it rejects the principle of integration at the EU level, is utterly against the EU's policy and institutional practice, and opposes the future building of a European federal state. The party argues that European co-operation may only take place outside the EU framework on a bilateral or trilateral basis. Projects are thought to work much better outside the EU, and nation-state co-operation should only occur on a case-by-case basis. The party's effective exclusion from the political system, despite constant and rising popular demand for its ideas, has resulted in a strategy of policy divergence and exaggeration of ideological differences. The National Front has a lot to win, including more attention and media coverage, by engaging in adversarial and confrontational politics, rather than by being accommodating. Its position concerning the EU has become a strategic tool for further differentiation from what it portrays as the domestic pro-EU consensus. This allows the party to create its own electoral niche, and signal to the electorate that it represents a different, powerful and independent actor in the party system.

The party has portrayed the EU as a form of regional globalisation that promotes ultra-liberal economic policies and encourages immigration. In doing so, it has insisted on the economic and social consequences of globalisation, arguing that the EU is a superstate serving the needs of financial institutions as opposed to fulfilling European citizens' interests and promoting their wellbeing. This framing has allowed the party to claim that it is the only political force in France whose main purpose is to protect the French people from European and external global forces. It is also in line with the perceived needs of the party's niche target electorate: i.e., the low-skilled, low-educated voters with anti-immigrant and authoritarian attitudes, who tend to feel that they have suffered from the devastating consequences of globalisation. Globalisation and European integration are seen as the root cause of French economic, social and cultural decline. To address this question, the party proposes a nationalist solution that includes repatriation of all competences from the EU back to the nation-state, including monetary, legislative, territorial and economic sovereignty.

Chapter 5

Conditional Euroscepticism

The Greek Popular Orthodox Rally

Εμείς υιοθετούμε την Αριστοτέλεια λογική της μεσότητας.

We apply Aristotle's logic of the median.

—Asterios Rontoulis, LAOS MP, 2009

The previous chapter has explored in detail the first variant of far right Euroscepticism identified in this book, i.e., the rejectionist position on European integration. This chapter proceeds by examining the conditional pattern of far right Euroscepticism. Parties that belong to this group are not against the principle of co-operation at a European multilateral level. They oppose, however, the EU's policy and institutional practice, and have doubts about the future building of a European polity. To shed light on this type of far right Euroscepticism, this chapter analyses the case of the anti-liberal Greek Popular Orthodox Rally (LAOS). LAOS views Europe as a continent sharing common cultural, historical and religious characteristics, and, for this reason, it supports European co-operation at a higher, multilateral level. Although the party presents strong criticisms against the EU's policy and institutional practice, it accepts that some policies may be managed at the European rather than the national level. European nation-states should co-operate in the context of a confederation that would recognise and protect member states' historic, cultural and ethnic particularities. LAOS supports European integration under certain conditions. These include the predominance of intergovernmental decision-making, the use of plebiscitary politics for every major EU decision or treaty change and the preservation of each member state's cultural uniqueness. The party is against the future building of a European polity, and it criticises major treaties for giving birth to a European superstate to the detriment of national sovereignty.

The main body of the chapter provides a detailed examination of LAOS's position on European integration and its significance within the context of Greek domestic politics. It is divided into five sections. It commences with an analysis of the party's core ideology, showing that, similar to other far right parties, it is characterised by nationalism, authoritarianism and strong leadership. In doing so, it shows that although the party is highly critical of liberal democracy, it does not seek to overthrow the regime. LAOS seeks radical change within the system through constitutional reform. This chapter continues with a detailed examination of the party's position on European integration through the analysis of where the party stands on four indicators, including the definition, principle, practice and future of European integration. It proceeds by placing the party's domestic strategy within the cultural, institutional and historical constraints provided by the Greek party system. In an effort to ensure its political survival, LAOS has distanced itself from the country's dictatorial past, has prioritised a strategy that would allow it to target voters from mixed social constituencies and has adopted an accommodative stance towards co-operation with other parties. The adoption of a conditional position on European integration may be situated within the party's electoral strategy. LAOS's Euroscepticism is an attempt to reflect Greek public opinion, and in doing so it presents itself as a trustworthy partner at both the domestic and EU levels. LAOS has avoided radical anti-EU statements and has selected its specific criticisms on the basis of what it perceives to be representative of Greek public opinion. The party has framed its Eurosceptic argumentation with reference to pressing domestic questions, such as security, which are both relevant to Greek voters and integral to its policy toolkit. This has allowed LAOS to articulate a nuanced anti-EU argument and occupy a unique – yet non-extremist – niche in the party system.

THE 'ANTI-LIBERAL' GREEK LAOS

Georgios Karatzaferis established LAOS on 14 September 2000, after being expelled from the centre-right New Democracy on 9 May 2000 (In.gr 2000) for openly criticising the then-leader, Costas Karamanlis, and other New Democracy MPs, such as Aris Spiliotopoulos.[1] The creation of LAOS was essentially the product of division between, on the one hand, Karamanlis's attempt to present New Democracy as a moderate and renewed force of the Greek centre-right (Lyrintzis 2005), and the ultra-nationalist branch of the party, on the other (Georgiadou 2008; 2009). LAOS is characterised by centralised structures and the strong personality of its leader (Dinas 2008: 605; Tsiras 2012: 110). A journalist by profession, Karatzaferis is a charismatic communicator with his own nationwide broadcasting channel, ART (formerly TeleAsty and Telecity), and the founder of the party's weekly newspaper, *A1*.

Since its establishment, LAOS has enjoyed a piecemeal but constant rise in support in all types of elections, including regional, national and European (see Table 5.1). LAOS made its electoral debut in the 2002 municipal and prefectural elections, when its leader came in third in the Athens-Piraeus prefecture election, with 13.6 per cent of the vote, gaining four seats in the prefectural administration. LAOS first ran in national parliamentary elections in 2004, when it received 2.19 per cent of the vote. This electoral result was below the 3 per cent threshold and did not allow the party to enter the Greek parliament. The 2004 EP elections marked the party's electoral breakthrough, however. With 4.12 per cent of the Greek vote, Karatzaferis became the party's first MEP. This position enabled him not only to develop a pan-European political network, but also to increase his political status, both domestically and abroad. LAOS achieved representation in the Greek Parliament following the 2007 general election, when it gained 3.8 per cent of the Greek vote, which translated into ten parliamentary seats. This was a great achievement for LAOS, as it was the first time that a far right party was represented nationally in Greece since 1977. Its relative electoral success continued in both the 2009 EP and national elections, when the party elected two and fifteen representatives, respectively.

The party's electoral fortunes changed, however, with the outbreak of the Greek sovereign debt crisis. First, the party was no longer seen as an anti-establishment force, as it voted in favour of Greece's first bailout programme in 2010, and agreed to formally support Lucas Papademos's co-operation government in a three-party coalition cabinet with PASOK

Table 5.1 LAOS election results (National and European)

Year	Election	Percentage	Votes	Seats
2004	Parliamentary	2.19	162,103	0
2004	European	4.12	252,429	1
2007	Parliamentary	3.80	271,809	10
2009	European	7.15	366,616	2
2009	Parliamentary	5.63	386,205	15
2012 May	Parliamentary	2.89	182,925	0
2012 June	Parliamentary	1.58	97,099	0
2014	European	2.69	154,029	0
2015 Jan	Parliamentary	1.03	63,669	0
2015 Sept	Parliamentary	-	-	-

Source: Greek Ministry of the Interior (www.ypes.gr)

and New Democracy in 2011 (Psarras 2011; Kathimerini 2012). Second, the Greek crisis resulted in high levels of electoral volatility and the fragmentation of the party system (Vasilopoulou and Halikiopoulou 2013). The extreme right Golden Dawn and the newly formed nationalist Independent Greeks also populated the right-wing political space, both putting forward an anti-immigrant and anti-bailout agenda. This resulted in LAOS losing parliamentary representation from 2012 onwards at the domestic level. Ultimately, the party leader decided that LAOS would not run in the September 2015 elections, which he characterised as 'prefabricated' (NewsBomb 2015). On 8 April 2016, without disbanding LAOS, Karatzaferis announced the formation of 'National Unity', a new coalition of right-wing parties, in collaboration with former New Democracy cabinet minister Panayiotis Baltakos (Terzis 2016). National Unity claims to provide a patriotic and popular right-wing alternative to what is seen as New Democracy's centrism, elitism and neoliberalism. That said, National Unity is in its infancy, with no clear policy positions, and its electoral success remains to be seen. Karatzaferis continues his political agenda as the official leader of LAOS, and the party's website continues to be regularly updated with the activities of the party leader and its members.

Similar to other far right parties in Europe, nationalism, traditionalism and a critique of modernity characterise LAOS's ideology. Karatzaferis has positioned the party within what he calls the 'European patriotic right'. In order to avoid marginalisation, he has actively sought to pacify the extremist and neo-fascist elements of the party, and he has consistently refused to be associated with the Greek 1967–1974 dictatorship. He has also been critical of other far right politicians in Europe, including Jean-Marie Le Pen, for having fascist mentality which I consider an enemy of society and democracy (Eleftherotypia 2006).[2] Despite insisting on the democratic credentials of the party, LAOS's ideology is based on the slogan 'fatherland, religion, family' (*Πατρίδα, Θρησκεία, Οικογένεια*),[3] which in the Greek context is associated with authoritarian regimes, including the Metaxas dictatorship (1936–1941) and the Colonels' regime (1967–1974) (Gazi 2013).

LAOS primarily competes along the nationalism versus internationalism dimension of political contestation, as demonstrated by the party's slogan, 'Greece is what unites us all' (LAOS 2003: 1).[4] Its MPs view the left-right division as obsolete, especially after the fall of the Berlin Wall in 1989. By establishing LAOS, Karatzaferis (2009) seeks to provide what he calls the 'middle ground' between neoliberalism and socialism. The party's political programme is based on the logic of patriotic interventionism; i.e., nationalism and patriotism inform all party polices, including the economy, the environment, security and foreign affairs (Aivaliotis 2009; Chrisanthakopoulos 2009; Polatides 2009; Rontoulis 2009).

The nation constitutes the party's founding principle, which is key to the logic of patriotic interventionism: '[LAOS] is a Greek-centred party that advocates the long-term interests of the Greek people and the nation. Greek civilisation, Greek spirit and Greek values inspire the formulation and implementation of its policies' (LAOS 2003: 7).[5] The party adopts an ethnic understanding of the Greek nation (Halikiopoulou et al. 2013), i.e., defined by ascriptive, rather than voluntaristic, criteria, such as language, religion and community of birth. For LAOS, Orthodoxy is integral to Hellenism and Greek national identity. Karatzaferis talks about a 'congenital relationship between the two',[6] and he views the Greek Orthodox Church as key to Greek nation-building, as it is 'thanks to the Church that Greece became a free nation after four centuries of serfdom' (LAOS 2004: 2; 2012).[7] The party enjoys support from the Greek Church, and it became particularly popular with the late Archbishop Christodoulos, who admitted sharing a common vision with Karatzaferis (Tsatsis 2006). LAOS seeks to appeal to the 'Greek patriot', i.e., those Greeks defined by their love for Orthodoxy and the fatherland, a point also maintained by Archbishop Christodoulos, who argued that LAOS's voters were good Christians (Ta Nea 2002).

The party is also defined by its authoritarianism. It supports a strong justice system (LAOS 2012: 12), is a champion of a strong Greek army (LAOS 2003: 13) and argues that the Greek Armed Forces deserve greater recognition (LAOS 2012: 10). The party maintains that immigration should be strictly controlled and that immigrants must be assimilated in order to be 'Greeks both in the soul and the spirit' (LAOS 2007: 44).[8] It is against illegal immigration, claiming that 'it plagues Greek society and is catastrophic in many areas' (LAOS 2003: 23).[9] LAOS views Greece as having a serious demographic problem, which should not be managed by increasing the number of immigrants, because 'Greece has a small number of inhabitants and the proportion of the population has already been altered [by high levels of immigration]' (LAOS 2007).[10]

LAOS is against the 'New World Order' and has sometimes insisted on the links between globalisation and international Zionism (Tsiras 2012: 120). While the party claims that it is democratic (LAOS 2012), it is openly critical of liberal democracy, but seeks change through constitutional reform. For example, the party advocates the peaceful and democratic overthrow of Greek political forces, and argues that PASOK and New Democracy are unable to serve the national interest and lack a vision for the nation's progress (LAOS 2003: 7). This may be accomplished through constitutional change, such as giving more power to the President of the Republic, and establishing an advisory body to the President (*Συμβούλιο Αρίστων*) consisting of, among others, the Chief of Armed Forces and the Archbishop of Athens and all Greece (LAOS 2012: 9). Consistent with its illiberal credentials, LAOS advocates a constitutional provision that would legally differentiate between nationality and citizenship and prescribe that foreigners may only become Greek citizens but not Greek nationals. In addition, the party questions the Greek system of government and representation, claiming that democracy should lie in the hands of the people. Politics should be the expression of the general will of the people, which explains the party's consistent attempt to promote the use of referendums for issues that it describes as 'of high national importance'. LAOS seeks the institutionalisation of the government's obligation to hold a referendum if requested by a minimum of 10 per cent of MPs and/or one million citizens (LAOS 2003: 9; 2007: 16; 2012: 9). It advocates a referendum on a number of issues, including the EU entry of Turkey and the Former Yugoslav Republic of Macedonia (FYROM) (LAOS 2007: 22), Greek immigration policy (LAOS 2007: 44), the euro (LAOS 2007: 45), Greek labour policy (LAOS 2007: 60) and FYROM's official name (LAOS 2007: 84).

LAOS's CONDITIONAL EUROSCEPTICISM

LAOS defines Europe as a cultural entity, standing on a 'tripod' composed by ancient Greek democracy, Roman legal tradition and Christianity (Rontoulis 2009). Greece's contribution to European civilisation is portrayed as paramount. 'The West belongs to Greece because it has been established on the virtues born by our civilisation, including democracy, humanism, research, lack of excess and harmony' (LAOS 2003: 8).[11] LAOS views Greece's relationship with the EU – the major political and economic organisation of the continent – as a necessary coexistence. Given that European civilisation and identity are built on Greek values, Greek identity also has a European component. If Greece did not participate in this framework, it would be as if it were denying its European identity (LAOS 2003: 8).

This cultural definition of Europe is closely related to a spatial/border definition. Because Christianity is one of the three defining features of European civilisation, EU borders must stop at the Urals and the Mediterranean, excluding non-Christian countries to the east and south, including Turkey. This definition of Europe provides a partial justification of LAOS's opposition to Turkey's EU accession. European co-operation should occur only with reference to a clear definition of Europe, both in spatial and cultural terms (Rontoulis 2009). If the EU accepted a non-Christian country such as Turkey, the European construction would collapse: 'Turkey does not belong to the EU for geographic, cultural, religious and political reasons' (LAOS 2007: 22).[12]

LAOS is in favour of the principle of European integration, and Greek co-operation at a European multilateral level. The party supports Greek EU membership, and criticises any political argumentation in favour of Greece's withdrawal from the EU. LAOS recognises that Greece's future is, to a large extent, linked to the EU. It is not 'dogmatically anti-European but at the same time it does not accept that "we have to surrender to the EU powers that erode our national sovereignty"' (LAOS 2007: 4).[13] It favours a type of multilateral European collaboration in which all decision-making would be held in an intergovernmental fashion among free and sovereign nations. It approves a system 'promoting the co-operation of European peoples in economic, social policy and cultural policies' (LAOS 2004: 2).[14]

LAOS supports a 'united Europe of Nations' (LAOS 2003: 8).[15] It argues that a European confederation would be the only viable framework for co-operation whereby member states could preserve their distinct roles (Polatides 2009), and 'where the historic, cultural and ethnic roots of European peoples would be recognised and protected' (LAOS 2007: 23).[16] It is only within this framework that Greece and other member states could preserve 'veto power on issues considered to be of national importance' (LAOS 2003: 12).[17] These might include policies traditionally thought to belong to the realm of the nation-state, including currency or foreign policy, but they could also vary from one country to another, depending on national specificities. Note that the word 'confederation' was used to contrast with the word 'federation' employed by some political elites as a synonym of 'supranationalism'. The EU should not become a federal superstate (Georgiadis 2009). Member states should have distinct roles, and decision-making should be intergovernmental based on the principle of unanimity (Polatides 2009).

LAOS has been ambivalent vis-à-vis Greece's EMU membership. On the one hand, LAOS is an active supporter of Greek economic convergence towards the economies of the most developed EU countries (LAOS 2007: 40). On the other hand, the euro is seen as having had negative consequences on Greek development policy, exports and tourism. Greece's EMU entry is portrayed as partly responsible for rising prices affecting Greek consumers (LAOS 2004: 2). The party supported a referendum on whether Greeks preferred the restoration of the drachma over remaining in the Eurozone (LAOS 2007: 45). However, during the Greek sovereign debt crisis, the party did not overtly advocate a Greek exit from the Eurozone; indeed Karatzaferis saw the resolution of the Greek crisis within – rather than outside – the Eurozone, advocating Greek co-operation with other EU countries that also suffered from liquidity problems (LAOS 2012; Naftemporiki 2012). As the crisis deepened, party rhetoric changed with the leader arguing that the euro was expensive for Southern European countries and that any monetary policy should be decided at the national level.[18]

Despite the fact that LAOS promotes a form of European collaboration, it criticises the EU's policy and institutional practice. These criticisms point towards three conditions under which LAOS would be willing to support the European project. These include intergovernmental decision-making, the use of plebiscites for EU-related issues and the preservation of the cultural uniqueness of each member state. First, decisions should only be taken through an intergovernmental framework of decision-making that would allow each member state to safeguard its national interest. LAOS supports co-operation in a number of policies, including immigration, energy, economy, development, defence, security and foreign policy (LAOS 2007). Key to this co-operation, however, is the preservation of national veto power, especially regarding national issues (Voridis 2009). LAOS is against any additional policy transfer to the EU without unanimity.

Second, LAOS seeks the wider use of plebiscitary politics for all major EU decisions and treaty changes (LAOS 2007). One of the party's key goals is to promote democracy. Citizen participation is likely to become a positive learning process that would ultimately lead to citizen support of European integration. The party is open about its Eurosceptic position and argues that 'in fact, it is through Euroscepticism that the EU will be re-established on the basis of popular consent' (Rontoulis 2009).[19] The introduction of pan-European referenda for the ratification of every major decision and treaty change at the EU level, including the European Constitution and the Lisbon Treaty, would lead to more transparency and accountability at the EU level, and would ultimately encourage LAOS's support of the EU.

Third, the cultural uniqueness of each member state should be maintained. This issue is of outmost importance to LAOS, and is inextricably linked to its definition of Europe. Whereas the party accepts the common cultural underpinnings of European civilisation, it maintains that the European peoples should be able to preserve their national differences, including religion, tradition and language (Karatzaferis 2005; Georgiou 2009). The EU should respect the history and traditions of each member state, and should not attempt to produce policies that cast a shadow over the cultural and national differences of its member states. The EU is encouraged to establish policies that seek to enrich a common European culture by promoting mutual respect of each member state's histories, traditions and civilisations.

LAOS opposes the policy and institutional practice of European integration, and sets conditions under which it would support integration. The party also opposes the deepening of European integration and the future construction of a European polity. LAOS has criticised the European Constitution because it introduced new supranational institutions, including a European President and a Foreign Minister (LAOS 2005). Given that the Lisbon Treaty is perceived to include 90 per cent of the text and stipulations of the European Constitution (Chrisanthakopoulos 2008), it has also been rejected as the 'greatest fraud against the peoples of Europe' (Karatzaferis 2008).[20]

By giving the EU full legal personality, the treaty is thought to give birth to a superstate, weakening national parliaments in favour of the 'Brussels Directorate' (Karatzaferis 2008: 3). Since the Treaty compromises the principle of unanimity, it is unclear whether Greece would be able to 'maintain [its] veto power regarding Skopje's EU accession' (Karatzaferis 2008: 2).[21] A further criticism relates to the fact that the European public has not been given the opportunity to ratify these projects through national referenda. According to the party leader, by not holding a referendum on the ratification of the Lisbon Treaty, the Greek government went against the will of the people (Karatzaferis 2008: 1).

Opposition to the future of European integration is also informed by a cultural justification. The European Constitution is thought to promote the weakening of national identities in favour of an 'American style cultural melting pot' (LAOS 2005: 6).[22] Given that the Constitution did not include a reference to Christianity, the EU is also seen as 'promoting the de-Christianisation of Europe' (Rontoulis 2009),[23] which runs against the party's basic values and beliefs. The EU disempowers the nation-state to the benefit of Brussels. The fading away of the nation-state is likely to lead to the development of multicultural consciousness whereby the Greek people would forget their nation, their motherland, their national heroes and Greek literature (Chrisanthakopoulos 2008). LAOS opposes the future creation of a European polity, arguing that member states should not be downgraded into the provinces of a European federation governed by stronger states (LAOS 2005: 5). The party's position on European integration has been neatly summarised as follows: 'We do not want a federation. We want a confederation of nation-states. We are neither against the EU nor do we believe in Greece's withdrawal from the EU. Greece has benefited from EU membership. Rather, we are against giving away our sovereignty on issues of national importance, e.g. Skopje and Turkey' (Georgiadis 2009).[24]

ELECTORAL INCENTIVES AND LAOS's DOMESTIC STRATEGY

Why has LAOS adopted a conditional Eurosceptic strategy? To answer this question, this section positions LAOS's strategic incentives within the context of Greek domestic politics. It shows that due to a combination of cultural, electoral and party competition constraints, LAOS has prioritised a strategy that would enable it to widen its electoral appeal and achieve political representation. LAOS has adjusted its strategy by distancing itself from Greece's dictatorial past, adopting an accommodating stance towards co-operation with other parties and putting forward policies that appear consistent with Greek public opinion.

Since the restoration of democracy in 1974 and until the outbreak of the Greek sovereign debt crisis in early 2010s, Greek party system dynamics were not conducive to the rise of the far right.[25] Until the crisis, the Greek party system was characterised by the dominance of two main competitors: i.e., the centre-left PASOK and the centre-right New Democracy. In the period from 1977 to 2009, PASOK and New Democracy jointly occupied between a 'minimum of 251 (in 2009) and a maximum of 287 (in 1981 and 1985) out of 300 parliamentary seats' – that is, 83 and 95 per cent, respectively (Vasilopoulou and Halikiopoulou 2013: 524). Pappas (2003) suggests that post-1981, Greece evolved into a classic two-party system characterised by the concentration of political forces. This is a manifestation of the zero sum dynamics of Greek party politics and a political culture characterised by the 'polarisation of political conflict and rhetoric' (Legg and Roberts 1997: 142; see also Mavrogordatos 1984; Seferiades 1986). Greek adversarial politics are also the result of the electoral system, a form of reinforced proportional representation with a 3 per cent threshold that gives bonus seats to the winner. This facilitates single-party governments while at the same time disfavouring pre-electoral alliances and penalising small parties. For example, in the period from 2004 to 2009, Greece scored a moderately high 7.2 on the index of disproportionality and had 2.5 effective number of parties at the legislative level (Gallagher et al. 2011: 391).[26]

As a result of these electoral dynamics, parties that fail to gain representation tend to cease to operate or become exceptionally weak.[27] Given the delegitimisation of right-wing extremism following the collapse of the Colonels' regime and New Democracy's ability to absorb voters with far right and pro-monarchist views (Georgiadou 2011; Vasilopoulou and Halikiopoulou 2015), the Greek far right was presented with additional constraints. For almost three decades after the fall of the military junta, it was confined to the margins of the party system, receiving much less than 1 per cent of the national vote, albeit with few exceptions associated with Greece's democratisation (Table 5.2). For example, the National Alignment's success during the 1977 national elections may be understood as related to the process of democratic transition, which entailed the legalisation of the Communist Party and public sector purges of junta collaborators (Clogg 1987: 184; Dimitras 1992: 260). The relative success of the Progressive Party and the National Political Union in the 1981 and 1984 EP elections has been attributed to the debate regarding the release of the junta leaders from prison (Clogg 1987: 185; Dimitras 1992: 266). In 1984, the National Political Union invited Jean-Marie Le Pen, the then-leader of the French National Front, to Athens, which provoked violent demonstrations and contributed to the party's weak electoral result in the 1985 national elections (Clogg 1987: 185). Moreover, as Davis argues, 'Perhaps the greatest impediment to the rise of neo-populist parties has been

Table 5.2   Far right electoral results in Greece post-1974

Year	Election	Name of Party	Percentage	Seats
1974	Parliamentary	National Democratic Union	1.1	0
1977	Parliamentary	National Alignment	6.8	5
1981	Parliamentary	Progressive Party	1.7	0
1981	European	Progressive Party	2	1
		Movement of Greek Reformers	0.9	0
1984	European	National Political Union	2.3	1
		Progressive Party	0.2	0
		United Nationalist Movement	0.1	0
1985	Parliamentary	National Political Union	0.5	0
1989 June	Parliamentary	National Political Union	0.3	0
1989	European	National Political Union	1.2	0
		United Nationalist Movement	0.2	0
		New Politicians	0.2	0
		European Economic Movement	0.1	0
		National Militants	0.1	0
1989 Nov.	Parliamentary	-	-	-
1990	Parliamentary	National Party	0.1	0
		Nationalist Alignment	0.03	0
1993	Parliamentary	National Party	0.14	0
1994	European	Golden Dawn	0.11	0
1996	Parliamentary	National Political Union	0.24	0
		Hellenism Party	0.18	0
		Golden Dawn	0.07	0
1999	European	Front Line	0.75	0
		Hellenism Party	0.26	0
		Hellenic Front	0.2	0
2000	Parliamentary	National Coalition	0.21	0
		Front Line	0.18	0
		Hellenism Party	0.09	0
2004	Parliamentary	Popular Orthodox Rally	2.17	0
		Hellenic Front	0.09	0
2004	European	Popular Orthodox Rally	4.12	1
		Hellenic Front	0.25	0
		Patriotic Alliance	0.17	0
2007	Parliamentary	Popular Orthodox Rally	3.8	10
2009	European	Popular Orthodox Rally	7.15	2
		Golden Dawn	0.46	0
		Greek Union	0.06	0
2009	Parliamentary	Popular Orthodox Rally	5.63	15
		Golden Dawn	0.29	0
2012 May	Parliamentary	Popular Orthodox Rally	2.9	0
		Golden Dawn	7	21
		Independent Greeks	10.6	33
2012 June	Parliamentary	Popular Orthodox Rally	1.6	0
		Golden Dawn	6.9	18
		Independent Greeks	7.5	20

(Cont. . . .)

Table 5.2   Far right electoral results in Greece post-1974 *(Cont. . . .)*

Year	Election	Name of Party	Percentage	Seats
2014	European	Popular Orthodox Rally	2.69	0
		Golden Dawn	9.4	3
		Independent Greeks	3.46	1
2015 Jan	Parliamentary	Popular Orthodox Rally	1.03	0
		Golden Dawn	6.3	17
		Independent Greeks	4.8	13
2015 Sept	Parliamentary	Popular Orthodox Rally	-	-
		Golden Dawn	7	18
		Independent Greeks	3.7	10

Source: Dimitras (1992) up to 1990 elections; the remaining updated by the author.

the tremendous growth of the Greek welfare state and the populist actions of the PASOK party during the 1980s' (Davis 1998: 168).

The Greek sovereign debt crisis altered these dynamics and provided opportunities for small parties to gain political representation (Vasilopoulou and Halikopoulou 2013; 2015). Until then, however, political survival was the major challenge faced by new parties of the right, including LAOS. The party's predominant strategy since its establishment in 2000 was to disassociate itself from the country's dictatorial past, in order to create a solid voting base and achieve stable parliamentary representation. With a view to attracting votes from across the political spectrum, LAOS downplayed its radical elements and portrayed itself not as an extreme party, but rather as a party of the middle ground that advocates mainstream ideas shared by the Greek electorate. This was intended to ultimately allow the party to win enough seats in the national parliament in order to hold a strong blackmail potential, whereby any Greek government would be obliged to co-operate with LAOS in order to pass legislation.

Party officials have confirmed this strategy, arguing that they represent the 'average Greek person', with their views being consistent with the majority of the Greek electorate (Georgiou 2009).[28] Party policies are not deemed to be extreme, because 'we apply Aristotle's logic of the median' (Rontoulis 2009).[29] In fact, 'we may not be mainstream, just because we have not governed. We have, however, mainstream ideas' (Polatides 2009).[30] The two-party system was seen as an impediment to the 'mainstreamisation' of LAOS, while the predominance of PASOK and New Democracy in power was characterised as 'insanity' (Georgiou 2009). Despite being critical towards its mainstream competitors, LAOS has adopted an accommodating stance towards co-operation. The party supported coalition governments and – much before the Greek sovereign debt crisis – it expressed an interest in co-operating, not only with centre-right New Democracy, but also with the centre-left PASOK (Georgiadis 2009; Polatides 2009; Rontoulis 2009).

LAOS has viewed its participation in a governmental coalition as a likely development only if the party was able to transcend the country's bipolar political culture. Karatzaferis has argued (2006): 'Greece is no longer a bipolar society. This has already been tried. Our political discourse is positively received all the way from the Communist left to the far right. Everyone listens to us because we are saying what is obvious. [...] We do not have restrictions. We accept what is good. All parties have patriots'.[31] The party's official newspaper has confirmed on a number of occasions the leader's understanding of the political uncertainty small Greek parties may face. For example, shortly after the 2009 EP elections, Karatzaferis argued that LAOS's victory should not be equated to Political Spring's short-term electoral success in the 1990s. He confirmed his vision of LAOS becoming an established force in the Greek party system, arguing that 'we are here to stay, and we will stay' (Karatzaferis quoted in A1 2009b: 5).[32]

Note that, although Greek political conflict is mostly structured along the left-right dimension, polarisation is not necessarily based on cleavages as understood in the Western European context, namely, historical divisions between clearly defined societal groups that are in opposition to one another (Lipset and Rokkan 1967; Lyrintzis 2005: 244). Greece experienced limited industrialisation, and civil society tends to be weak and fragmented (Featherstone 1990). The Greek political world has historically been based on clientelistic structures (Legg and Roberts 1997: 144; see also Mitsopoulos and Pelagidis 2011). Notwithstanding, Greek parties manipulated the content of the left-right divide in order to appeal to every Greek voter (Lyrintzis 2005: 244). In this respect, although New Democracy and PASOK place themselves in the centre-right and centre-left spaces of political contestation, respectively, they essentially adopt catch-all electoral strategies, seeking to make broad appeals and attract support from a variety of different classes (Legg and Roberts 1997: 144).

Similarly seeking to widen its appeal, LAOS has strong incentives to go beyond the left-right and adopt a catch-all electoral strategy. This is demonstrated in the party leader's attempt to recruit politicians from both the left and the right of the political spectrum, as well as non-experienced politicians, including civil servants and celebrities. 'We accept all those who agree with our patriotic analysis of Greek politics regardless of whether they previously belonged to other parties, e.g. New Democracy, PASOK, etc.' (Rontoulis 2009).[33] For instance, LAOS's elected representatives have included Chrysanthakopoulos, who was a PASOK MP following the 1996 and 2000 elections; Voridis, who was the President of the far right Greek Front; Polatides, who was a President of the Prefectural Committee of New Democracy's youth club; Anatolakis, who was a famous footballer; and Georgiou, who was a high-ranking civil servant.

Interestingly, the socio-demographic profile of LAOS's voters tends to be similar to other far right parties in the sense that the party primarily attracts male, middle-aged, religious voters who are residing in urban areas. Unlike other far right parties, however, LAOS's voters do not primarily have lower education levels; rather, they tend to have medium levels of education, which includes individuals who have completed secondary education, those with postsecondary non-tertiary education, and those with incomplete higher education (see Table 5.3). Ideologically, LAOS's voters tend to be primarily right-wing, scoring on average between 5.86 and 7.29 in 2007 and 2009, respectively, on a scale from 1 to 10, where large values indicate self-identification with the right. At the same time, if asked more specifically, LAOS's voters tend to vary in terms of their values, with 27 per cent claiming to be

Table 5.3   The socio-demographic profile of LAOS voters

		2007		2009	
		All voters (n=1000)	*LAOS voters (n=41)*	*All voters (n=1022)*	*LAOS voters (n=24)*
Gender	Male	42.8	65.85	49.41	62.5
	Female	57.2	34.15	50.59	37.5
Age	Up to 35	29.5	34.15	33.86	29.17
	36-50	31.9	43.9	26.91	41.67
	51-65	24.8	9.76	21.23	20.83
	65 or more	12.4	12.2	18	8.33
Employment Status	Employed	50.2	63.41	47.36	62.5
	Student	9.5	7.32	6.36	0
	At home	9.3	2.44	13.11	16.67
	Retired	20.2	17.07	21.72	12.5
	Unemployed	6.2	7.32	9.1	8.33
	Other	4.1	2.44	2.15	0
Education	Low	15.9	7.32	31.41	25
	Medium	49.2	60.98	36.69	50
	High	32.9	24.39	31.51	25
Religiosity	Every week	18.9	24.39	14.48	20.83
	Every month or several times a year	60.3	58.54	64.38	66.67
	Once a year or less	9.7	7.32	6.46	4.17
	Never	9.3	7.32	14.09	8.33
Urban vs rural	Rural	20	19.51	18.1	12.5
	Urban	79.1	80.49	80.14	87.5
Left-right (0-10)	Mean	4.95	5.86	5.33	7.29
	Std. deviation	2.76	2.49	2.46	1.88

Source: 2007: EES Voter study 2009 (Egmond et al. 2013); 2009 The Comparative Study of Electoral Systems (CSES Module 3)
Note: 2007: Vote choice in previous general election; 2009: vote choice in current general election

nationalists, 15 per cent as conservatives and 6 per cent as socialists. Surprisingly, a relatively high percentage of LAOS's voters perceived themselves as liberals and ecologists at 16 and 8 per cent, respectively (see Figure 5.1). This suggests that the party's strategy to widen its appeal was somewhat successful, and it confirmed its leader's contention that 'LAOS attracts voters from all political streams' (A1 2009b: 5).[34]

THE EU ISSUE AS AN ACCOMMODATION TOOL

During the period between LAOS's establishment and the Greek crisis, the domestic electoral context provided constraints to the rise and continued political existence of the far right. LAOS sought to be seen as offering an agenda with the potential to attract Greek voters irrespective of ideology, social background or economic status. The adoption of a conditional position on European integration may be situated within the party's electoral strategy. Greeks have been pro-EU membership since the late 1980s, but, from 2001 onwards, they became somewhat reluctant towards the European project. LAOS's conditional Euroscepticism is an attempt to align with Greek public

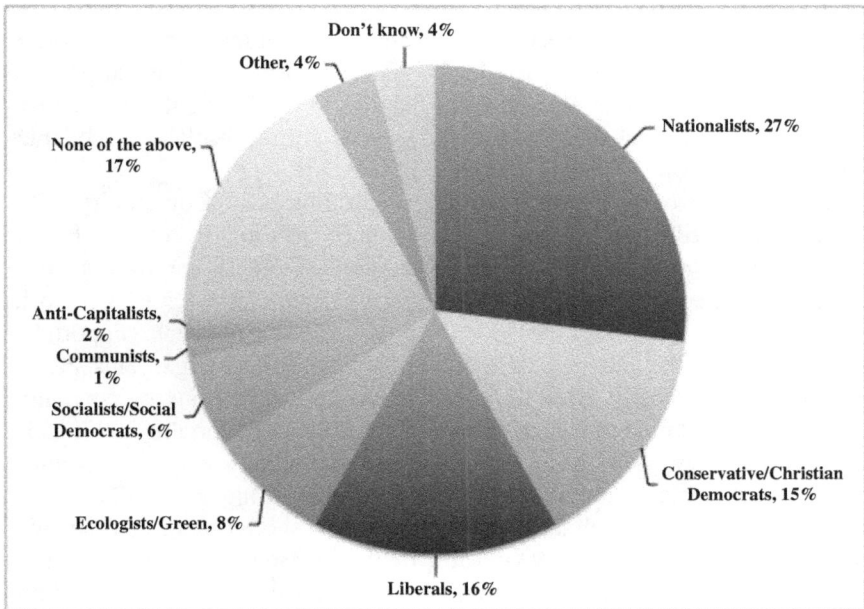

Figure 5.1   **Ideological self-placement of LAOS's voters.** *Source*: Public Issue (2009a) EP Elections public opinion survey, N=291.

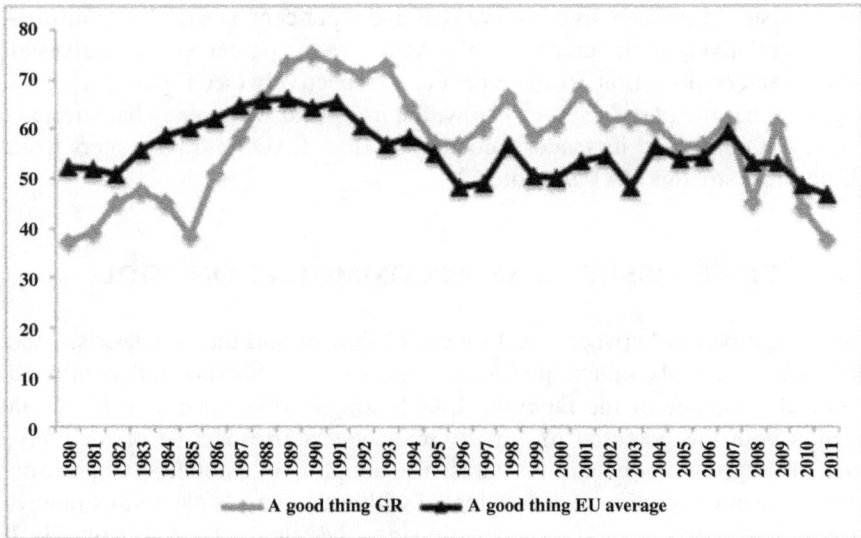

Figure 5.2　Greek and EU-wide support for membership of the European Union, 1980–2011. *Source*: Eurobarometer, European Commission. ('Generally speaking, do you think that Greek membership of the European Community (Common Market) is ...?').

opinion, and in doing so it serves as a means to present itself as a trustworthy partner at both domestic and EU levels. That is not to say that the party is centrist. As discussed above, the party belongs to the far right party family. Rather, its conditional EU position allows it to portray itself as a moderate force in Greek politics.

Greek public opinion was sceptical about European Community (EC) membership until the mid-1980s, when it underwent a major shift (see Figure 5.2; see also Verney 2011). Support started to rise from 1986 onwards, coinciding with Greece securing EC loans and the change of PASOK's rhetoric on membership (Featherstone 1994a: 155). Since 1988 Greek support for membership of the European Union was above EU average. This public Europhilia was mostly utilitarian and linked to expectations of economic development and modernisation (Economides 2005; Vernardakis 2007: 153). Greek voters viewed the European project as a solution to problems pertaining to Greek society, and as a means of providing a higher quality of life. They preferred 'EC-level action to overcome the shortcoming of their own conditions' (Featherstone 1994a: 156). Public opinion experienced fluctuation in the 1990s, however, but remained well above the EU average. From 2002 onwards, a small but steady decline may be observed, with positive attitudes towards membership dropping below the EU average in 2008, 2010 and 2011 at 45, 44 and 37 per cent, respectively.

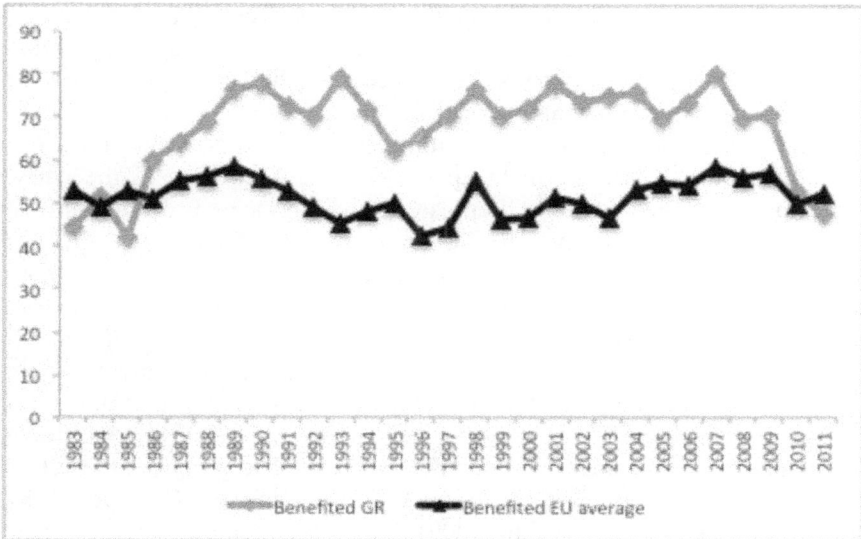

Figure 5.3 Greek and EU-wide perception of benefit from EU membership, 1983–2011.
Source: Eurobarometer, European Commission. ('Taking everything into account, would you say that Greece has on balance benefited or not from being a member of the European Union?').

This declining trend of Greek public support of European integration, which was present prior to the Greek sovereign debt crisis, may also be observed in people's emotional reactions towards Europe. In a public opinion poll held in 2009, only 23 per cent of respondents viewed the European project with hope. Indifference was at 27 per cent, whereas reservation and fear attained 28 and 14 per cent, respectively (Public issue 2009b). Despite this rising reluctance towards the EU, Greeks overwhelmingly believe that their country has benefited from EU membership (see Figure 5.3). Greek perception of benefit from EU membership is not only high in its own terms, but it has also been persistently above EU average. In the period from 1986 to 2010, agreement that Greece has benefited from EU membership was on average 19.48 points higher than the EU average, with this difference being at its highest at 28.6 and 26.4 per cent in 2003 and 2001, respectively (see also Clements et al. 2014). LAOS's conditional Euroscepticism in the 2000s tends to mirror this lukewarm and somewhat contradictory public opinion. The party leader acknowledges that 'at a political level, LAOS's agenda coincides with the real agenda of Greek society' (A1 2009b: 4).[35] Echoing the utilitarian character of Greek EU public opinion, LAOS portrays itself as the only party promoting Greek national interest to the EU level. For instance, the party leader argues that

'we go to Europe with specific goals and objectives!' (A1 2009a: 4).[36]
While the EU project is not entirely rejected, it becomes questioned and
distrusted. Membership is considered necessary, however, given that the
Greek public perceives benefit from it.

Conditional Euroscepticism has allowed LAOS to occupy a unique –
yet non-extremist – niche in the party system. According to the party,
Greek party policies on the EU represent two extreme ends of the political
spectrum. On the one hand, the Communist Party of Greece (KKE) has
adopted a rejectionist policy, arguing that Greece should not be a member
of the EU, which is seen as a product of capitalism and imperialism. On
the other hand, PASOK and New Democracy are unconditionally Euro-
phile, accepting EU treaties, laws and regulations without any criticism
(Rontoulis 2009). Instead of blindly rejecting co-operation or unreservedly accepting integration in every policy sphere, LAOS's conditional
Euroscepticism is framed as a centrist position. The party sees itself as
reconciling the two opposing poles of Euro-rejection and Euro-philia, by
standing in the middle (Voridis 2009). Its Euroscepticism is not a sterile
rejection of the EU; rather, it is portrayed as constructive criticism of the
EU project (Chrisanthakopoulos 2009). The term 'Eurosensitive' is often
preferred because of its positive connotation (Aivaliotis 2009). The party
is 'sensitive' towards EU treaties and decisions that involve relinquishing
state sovereignty. By showing that it is neither an unconditional EU supporter nor a fervent Eurosceptic, LAOS cultivates an image of compromise and reduced hostility. It seeks to convey the message that it does not
hold extreme views and that it can be trusted as a moderate political actor
(Georgiou 2014).

THE ROLE OF GREEK SECURITY IN
LAOS's EUROSCEPTIC AGENDA

LAOS's conditional Euroscepticism is ultimately framed with reference to
Greek security concerns and the question of Turkey. Given that – at least
until the crisis – the EU issue was not particularly salient among the Greek
electorate (Vernardakis 2007), the party did not expect citizens to cast
their vote primarily on the basis of EU politics (Georgiadis 2009). This
explains why LAOS has linked its EU criticism to domestic security issues
that are both relevant to voters and integral to its policy toolkit, such as the
name of FYROM, the perceived constant threat from Turkey, Greek borders, the situation in Northern Cyprus and Greece's relations with Albania
and Kosovo (LAOS 2009).

Table 5.4 Support for further EU enlargement in Greece

	Turkey			FYROM		
Year	In favour (%)	Not in favour (%)	Don't know (%)	In favour (%)	Not in favour (%)	Don't know (%)
04/2000	39	53	8	-	-	-
11/2000	26	66	8	47	40	13
10/2001	26	65	9	54	33	13
03/2002	-	-	-	43	39	18
10/2002	23	72	5	41	45	14
05/2005	26	70	4	45	47	8
10/2005	20	79	1	46	52	1
09/2006	24	75	1	52	47	1
03/2008	22	78	0	24	76	0
11/2010	21	76	3	24	72	4

Source: Eurobarometer, European Commission ('For each of the following countries and territories, would you be in favour or against it becoming part of the European Union in the future?')

LAOS's choice to focus on Greek security issues in its European discourse is linked to its master narrative that centres on the nation. The party portrays Greece's neighbours as posing a threat to Greek territory, religion and cultural heritage. This is consistent with Greek nationalist political culture, which is based on ethno-cultural bonds, i.e., defined by ascriptive criteria such as blood, language, religion and the need to maintain the nation as a homogenous unit (Vasilopoulou and Halikiopoulou 2015: 81). Greeks distinguish themselves from their Turkish neighbours on the basis of ethnicity and religion. They also differentiate themselves from neighbouring slavic populations because the latter could not 'raise a claim on classical Greek culture' (Triandafyllidou et al. 1997: 194). Greece's relationship with its neighbours tends to be framed as an identity question. It constitutes a major citizen concern that cuts across party lines and ideologies, and may be easily stirred up by politicians and/or religious leaders (see Featherstone 1994b).

Territory, the country, and the homeland are very important in the hearts and minds of Greeks. In a survey carried out in October 2007 on the occasion of the national holiday celebrating the heroic 'no' of 28 October 1940, 82 per cent of respondents answered that they would give their life for their borders and homeland (Public Issue 2007). Greeks are also overwhelmingly against Turkey's and FYROM's EU membership, with opposition rising over time (see Table 5.4). In 2008, 84 per cent of Greeks believed that the Greek government should veto FYROM's EU and NATO accession if there were no agreement on the country's name (Public Issue 2008). Greek support for European integration is partly due to citizen insecurity regarding Greco-Turkish relations and the perception that Turkey poses a threat to Greece (Vernardakis 2007: 153–54). For example, 50 per cent of respondents felt that

Greece should rely on the EU in order to resolve its security issues (Public Issue 2008).

In a context where the question of Greek security remains largely uncontested, LAOS sees its role as the essential guardian of Greek national interests at the European level. For LAOS, security issues strongly affect all problems pertaining to Greek society. This is especially true because the Greek government spends a great share of its budget on defence. If security was no longer a problem, the defence budget could be allocated to different projects, including education, welfare, road construction and the building of schools (Rontoulis 2009). The party argues that Greece should formulate a long-term foreign and security policy independent from both international organisations and domestic party politics. This 'national' policy should be solely guided by 'the interest of the country and the Greek nation' (LAOS 2007: 21).[37] Greece should thus maintain its veto power in the EU to avoid being overridden by the preferences of other member states when it comes to deciding on issues related to Greek security (Georgiadis 2009).

The question of Greek security also enables LAOS to criticise other Greek parties for being selfish and failing to protect the national interest at the European level. The party portrays itself as the only 'voice' fighting for Greece in Europe:

> Our voice in the European Parliament will shake other Europeans [...] a voice against injustice and defeat, a voice addressed not only to Europeans but also to Greeks who with their compliance have risked writing the bleakest page of Greek history yet. Generations of Greeks have kept Greece upright with sacrifice. They have given her dignity, recognition, respect and prestige. These properties are unfortunately sacrificed on the altar of selfish goals. We should neither settle nor become compliant. Both here and in Europe! Greece first! With this slogan we will give our battle in Europe (LAOS 2004: 5).[38]

Towards the end of the 2000s, these criticisms transformed into outright condemnation of Greek political parties for acting against Greek national interests at the European level, and more specifically, in the EP.

> The vote of a large majority of our national partisan representatives in the European Parliament is evidence of surrender and national degradation. [...] Greek MEP votes have become arrows against our homeland. We do not blame them for their foolishness. But we do call on them to explain under whose orders and with the promise of what in return they carried out their blasphemy against Macedonia (LAOS 2008: 6).[39]

An analysis of the party's EP speeches demonstrates that its MEPs have employed the time allocated to them in Plenary to promote issues related to Greek foreign and security policy. Karazaferis was elected as the party's first

Table 5.5 Salience of issues in LAOS's MEPs' European Parliament speeches

	Overall	*6th term*	*7th term*
General breakdown			
Domestic	19.29	23.34	16.86
EU	80.71	76.66	83.14
Domestic issues			
Economy and economic policies	32.82	19.47	43.91
Environment and energy	5.78	8.89	3.19
History and culture	6	10.58	2.20
Government and institutions	2.73	1.68	3.59
Security and borders	47	52.16	42.71
Social policies	5.67	7.21	4.39
EU-related issues			
EU economy and economic policies	26.90	13.76	34.17
EU enlargement	6.91	9.66	5.38
EU environment and energy	10.87	7.32	12.83
EU foreign and security policy	17.41	26.87	12.19
EU research and technology	1.56	1.68	1.50
EU rules and procedures	9.49	7.98	10.32
EU security and borders	9.78	15.74	6.48
EU social policies	14.21	10.83	16.07
European culture and History	2.87	6.15	1.05

Source: EP online archives.
Note: N=713 speeches/4753 sentences (sixth term: N=123 speeches/1782 sentences; seventh term: N=590 speeches/2971 sentences). See appendix regarding coding procedure.

MEP following the 2004 EP elections. In September 2007, he was elected as an MP in the Greek Parliament, and he handed over his EP seat to Georgios Georgiou, a former Greek ambassador. The party elected two MEPs following the 2009 EP elections, including Nikolaos Salavrakos, who was LAOS's legal consultant, and Niki Tzavela, a former New Democracy MP and MEP who rejoined New Democracy in February 2014. The party's MEPs were affiliated with the Independence/Democracy group during the EP's sixth parliamentary period (2004–2009), and the Europe of Freedom and Democracy Group during the EP's seventh parliamentary period (2009–2014).

The content analysis of LAOS's MEP speeches reveals an interesting pattern (see Table 5.5; see appendix for information on coding procedure). A number of themes recur, which may be grouped into two broad categories, including references specific to the EU, and references to domestic Greek politics. LAOS MEPs dedicated approximately a fifth of their reserved speaking time in the EP to domestic issues rather than issues deriving from the EP's agenda. This breaks down to 23.34 and 16.86 per cent during the EP's sixth and seventh terms, respectively. This is surprising, given that the EP controls the agenda and MEPs are often invited to give 'explanation of vote' speeches to clarify why they voted for or against an EU report. This finding suggests the party's MEPs employed the EP platform, not only to present and promote their views on aspects of European integration, including EU policies and treaties, but also to discuss and raise awareness of a variety of domestic issues.

The most frequent EU-related issues include EU economy and economic policies at 26.9 per cent, followed by EU foreign and security policy in second place at 17.41 per cent, EU social policies in third place at 14.21 per cent and EU environment and energy in fourth place at 10.87. When it comes to domestic issues, the most salient issue in MEPs speeches related to Greece's security and borders at 47 per cent, followed by the economy and economic policies at 32.82 per cent. Interestingly, whereas 52.16 per cent of the sentences were dedicated to Greek security and 19.47 per cent to the economy during the sixth EP term, this percentage changed to 42.71 and 43.91, respectively, during the seventh EP term, indicating that the economy gained prominence over time. When LAOS MEPs discussed Greek security, they primarily referred to Cyprus and Turkey, followed by the Balkans (Albania and FYROM), Greek borders, immigration and terrorism. Greek security concerns also featured within a number of EU-related categories, including EU foreign and security policy, EU enlargement and EU security and borders. For example, EU foreign policy was often discussed with reference to Greece's neighbours. In addition, LAOS MEPs consistently argued that Turkey should not be a member of the EU. They expressed concern regarding immigration and the EU's borders to Turkey. Beyond criticising the EU for its enlargement policy, they also targeted Turkey for not being eligible for EU membership, as it is culturally different, occupies the northern part of Cyprus and fails to respect international borders (Georgiou 2014).

This analysis indicates that while the Eurozone and Greek crises somewhat altered the focus in favour of the economy, the party's MEPs claimed ownership of the issue of security with reference to both EU and domestic issues. They also sought to push domestic issues, such as Turkey and Greek borders, onto the EP agenda, framing them not only as Greek, but also as EU issues. Interestingly, party MEPs did not employ the EU as a scapegoat for the absence of resolution of Greek national issues. They appeared to have accepted a potential resolution of Greek security issues within the EU framework. Note that, unlike Karatzaferis, Georgiou and Salavrakos, who maintained a common approach by broadly referring to similar issues, Tzavela was not as much concerned with security. She talked a lot more about issues related to the environment and energy. She spent much of her time discussing the issue of gas supply in Europe, a topic of special interest to her after she wrote a report on industrial, energy and other aspects of shale gas and oil. Unlike other LAOS MEPs, Tzavela also voted in favour of many EP reports and spoke positively of the EU's procedures, practices, and decisions, especially towards the end of her tenure, when she was in the process of rejoining New Democracy.

By linking its conditional Eurosceptic position to Greek security concerns, LAOS has been able to portray its policies as the expression of public opinion (Polatides 2009; Georgiou 2014), making them relevant to the average Greek person independent of party identification. In a speech during the 2009 EP electoral campaign, the party leader argued: 'They ask me, why do you insist on Turkey not becoming an EU member? Because I listen to the Greek heart, soul and consciousness, which has been reported in a survey as being 78 per cent against Turkish EU accession' (Karatzaferis, quoted in A1 2009a: 5).[40] The insistence on these issues is intended to mobilise voters in its favour, especially given that the mainstream governing parties in Greece have increasingly adopted a much more conciliatory agenda on these issues (Ker-Lindsay 2007). It allows the party to portray itself as the 'only party that gives a battle in the EU' (Aivaliotis 2009),[41] and that 'convincingly expresses the policies that satisfy the common sentiment' (Papadopoulos 2009: 18).[42] The party further pursued this agenda through the publication of a seventeen-page party document entitled 'The documentation of shame', which outlined how Greek MEPs voted in the EP on issues predominantly related to Greek security concerns. The purpose of this pamphlet was to inform Greek citizens on 'which MEPs have openly and without shame or inhibitions supported Turkish or Skopje's interests' (LAOS 2008: 2).[43]

The 2009 EP election manifesto was equally devoted to issues relating to Greek security concerns. Nineteen out of the twenty-four pages of the 2009 EP election manifesto criticise Greek political parties for not promoting Greek security interests at the European level (LAOS 2009). The front cover depicts a Greek man dressed in a traditional uniform, reminiscent of the Greek War of Independence from Turkey. Sitting on a locked ballot box, he looks depressed and disheartened, and his attire is wrinkled and soiled. The slogan on the front page reads, 'Fellow compatriot, some people humiliated you in Europe! Learn the truth and forget the fairy tales!' (LAOS 2009). This was used as a strong communication tactic to convey that Greeks had been internationally humiliated without being able to react. The underlying message was to criticise the two main Greek parties for having supported Turkey's EU accession, insinuating that LAOS was the only Greek party that took these matters seriously.[44]

CONCLUSION

This chapter has analysed the second pattern of far right Euroscepticism, i.e., conditional Euroscepticism, through the detailed analysis of the anti-liberal

Greek LAOS. Placing the party's strategy in the context of domestic electoral constraints, it has demonstrated that the party's choice to adopt a conditional position on European integration is consistent with its attempt to reflect Greek public opinion and promote itself as the guardian of Greek national interest. The chapter has shown that LAOS accepts the principle of European integration at a higher multilateral level. It is, however, against the institutional and policy practice of EU co-operation given that intergovernmentalism is not the established decision-making procedure. The party is also against the future building of a European polity. LAOS supports European integration under the condition that member states keep their veto power on issues of national importance, European citizens have more stake in the decision-making process through plebiscitary politics and the EU does not pose a threat to member states' cultural particularities.

In its quest for political survival, LAOS has adopted a flexible communication strategy by rejecting verbal extremism and under-emphasising ideological distinctiveness. The party's conditional Eurosceptic position has been employed to construct an image of respectability, and disassociate itself from extremism and the country's dictatorial past. Its position on the EU has been an excellent accommodation tool. It has allowed the party to differentiate itself from every other party in the Greek party system on this dimension, while at the same time strategically integrating itself in the middle ground of Greek politics. It has enabled the party to present itself not only as a moderate force in the system, but also as the only party that can truly understand Greek public opinion and listen to what Greek citizens have to say. By associating its Euroscepticism to questions related to Greek security, the party has capitalised upon an issue that resonates well with the Greek electorate. Framing its Euroscepticism with reference to Greek security concerns has allowed the party not only to portray an image of being the sole guardian of Greek national interests at the European level, but also to criticise Greek parties for essentially failing to prioritise such issues.

The chapter has illustrated the ways in which Euroscepticism may be employed as part of a party's agenda in the domestic party system. LAOS's conditional Euroscepticism can be thought of as a marketing decision serving to differentiate LAOS from both the margins and the mainstream, and to demonstrate that it occupies the middle ground in Greek politics. Adopting a conditional EU position and linking it with the issue of Greek security concerns, LAOS has portrayed itself as occupying a unique niche in the Greek party system.

Chapter 6

Compromising Euroscepticism
The Italian National Alliance

Sarebbe eccessivo dire che è la destra che ha contribuito a scrivere la Costituzione europea. Diciamo che il governo italiano, un governo di centrodestra, è stato impegnato in questo obiettivo.

It would be excessive to say that the Right contributed to the writing of the European Constitution. Let us say that the centre-right Italian Government was committed to this goal.

—Gianfranco Fini, leader of the National Alliance, 2003[1]

This chapter explores the final variant of far right Euroscepticism, namely, the compromising position on European integration. Compromising Eurosceptic far right parties tend to accept that Europe is bound by a common culture, they support the principle of co-operation at a European multilateral level, they broadly support the institutional and policy practice of European integration, but they express qualified opposition to the future building of a European polity. To further explore this Eurosceptic variant, this chapter examines the normalised Italian National Alliance. The National Alliance viewed Europe as a cultural and – in particular – a Christian entity. It supported the principle of European co-operation at a higher multilateral level and within the context of the EU project. The party accepted, by and large, the EU's policy practice and recognised the importance of European institutions. According to the National Alliance, the European nation-states were instrumental in the construction of the European project. Thus, the EU was seen as beneficial only to the extent that it promoted and safeguarded each member state's national interest. The party expressed modest support for the European project, and its criticisms remained technical for their most part.

It was argued, however, that the EU suffered from a democratic deficit and that, to the party's disillusionment, it was solely an economic rather than a political project. The party's compromising Euroscepticism can be thought of as a relative commitment to the European project coupled with feelings of disenchantment regarding specific aspects of the EU's trajectory.

Placing the National Alliance's Euroscepticism in the context of changing developments in domestic Italian politics, this chapter argues that the crisis of the Italian party system in the early 1990s, which paved the way towards the establishment of the Second Italian Republic, opened political opportunities for the party to rebrand itself and reshape its identity away from its anti-democratic tradition. While similar to other far right parties in Europe, its ideology was characterised by the centrality of the nation and a strong belief in traditionalism, and the party adopted a strategy of institutional entrenchment, which combined de-radicalisation and normalisation. The National Alliance avoided controversial statements, and sought to become part of the system through coalition formation with larger parties of the right; and government participation. This allowed the party to progress from an anti-system party in the First Italian Republic into a rehabilitated party in the Second Republic. The chapter conducts a detailed analysis of the party's Euroscepticism, and demonstrates that, in its quest for political entrenchment, the National Alliance changed its EU policy from a relatively hard and critical position to one of compromising Euroscepticism. The question of Europe was integral to its leader's strategy of becoming the head of the Italian centre-right, and it became a political tool in his effort to appear as a statesman on an equal footing with other centre-right leaders abroad. The party framed its position on European integration with reference to questions of Italy's international status and foreign policy, trying to promote a strong Italian presence in the world. Its policy on the EU was essentially a litmus test, proving that the National Alliance was no longer an anti-system party, and provided the party and its leader with long-sought national and international legitimacy.

THE 'NORMALISED' ITALIAN NATIONAL ALLIANCE

The National Alliance was the offspring of the neo-fascist Italian Social Movement (MSI). The MSI had been founded in 1946 by a group of Mussolini's Italian Social Republic supporters. The party had been essentially anti-system. It opposed liberal democracy and its institutions, because they 'had put a seal on Fascism's destruction' (Newell 2000: 469). During the decades after World War II, the MSI had oscillated between a strategy of insertion (*inserimento*) and one of re-radicalisation as a result of the diverging factions within the party. The first was anti-bourgeois, anti-capitalist, non-conformist and revolutionary, while the second was authoritarian, clerical and corporatist (Ignazi 1994). Essentially there was a division between a radical, violent, hard-line MSI faction and a moderate faction inclined to co-operate with other conservative forces in order to enter normal Italian politics (Ignazi 2003: 36–37). These differences aside, both factions' ideological and cultural references had been characterised by fascist nostalgia. As a result, under the postwar democratic regime, the party's legitimacy was heavily questioned. Despite being viewed as outside the Italian political spectrum, however, the MSI was one of the most electorally successful far right parties in Europe. From the 1950s onwards, its electoral results had spanned from approximately 5 to 9 per cent of the Italian vote in national and European elections, indicating that its strategy of insertion had been to an extent successful (see Table 6.1).

The postwar Italian regime, commonly referred to as the First Republic (from 1948 to 1993), was characterised by ideological polarisation between an anti-communist bloc led by the centrist Christian Democracy in office (Bull 2004: 550) and the strongest communist party of the Western world in opposition (Roux and Verzichelli 2010: 12). Such a division was not conducive to an alteration of power, and it had resulted in political compromise and a policy of consociation in the legislature (Fabbrini 2006: 146). The MSI had been the only party in postwar Italy overtly claiming a right-wing position. For fear of being associated with fascism, no other party wished to collaborate with the 'right'. Therefore, despite the fact that the party was electorally successful in relative terms, it was essentially marginalised in the postwar political system.

During the period from 1993 to 1996, however, Italian politics witnessed significant changes, which provided electoral opportunities for the MSI and were conducive to the rebranding of the party into the National Alliance (Ignazi 1994: 65; Bianchi 2007: 84; Morini 2007: 150). Scandals related to political corruption led to the fall from power of old parties and the emergence of new parties. In addition, the change of the electoral law in 1993, from proportional to a partially compensatory mixed-member system, introduced a somewhat majoritarian logic in the Italian party system (Renwick et al. 2009). This resulted in the gradual stabilisation of a new bipolar system, which no longer relied on consensual politics (Fella 2006). The political landscape of the Second Republic was divided into two camps broadly associated with the left and the right, ending the ostracism of the right, and, by extension, that of the MSI, which was also not involved in the clean hands [*mani pulite*] judicial investigation into political corruption (Ignazi 2005: 334). The presence of Silvio Berlusconi's newly established Forza

Table 6.1   Italian social movement and National Alliance election results (National and European)

Year	Election	Percentage	Votes	Seats
1946	Chamber of Deputies	-	-	-
1946	Senate	-	-	-
1948	Chamber of Deputies	2	526,882	6
1948	Senate	0.7	164,092	1
1953	Chamber of Deputies	5.8	1,582,154	29
1953	Senate	6.1	1,473,645	9
1958	Chamber of Deputies	4.8	1,407,718	24
1958	Senate	4.4	1,150,051	8
1963	Chamber of Deputies	5.1	1,570,282	27
1963	Senate	5.3	1,458,917	14
1968	Chamber of Deputies	4.5	1,414,036	24
1968	Senate	4.6	1,304,847	11
1972	Chamber of Deputies	8.7	2,894,722	56
1972	Senate	9.2	2,766,986	26
1976	Chamber of Deputies	6.1	2,238,339	32
1976	Senate	6.6	2,086,430	15
1979	Chamber of Deputies	5.3	1,930,639	30
1979	Senate	5.7	1,780,950	13
1979	European	5.5	1,909,055	4
1983	Chamber of Deputies	6.8	2,511,487	42
1983	Senate	7.4	2,283,524	18
1984	European	6.5	2,274,556	5
1987	Chamber of Deputies	5.9	2,281,126	35
1987	Senate	6.5	2,121,026	16
1989	European	5.5	1,918,650	4
1992	Chamber of Deputies	5.4	2,107,037	34
1992	Senate	6.5	2,171,215	16
1994	Chamber of Deputies	13.5	5,202,698	23
1994	Senate	6.3	2,077,934	8
1994	European	12.5	4,108,670	11
1996	Chamber of Deputies	15.7	5,870,491	28
1996*	Senate	37.3	12,185,020	116
1999	European	10.3	3,202,895	9
2001	Chamber of Deputies	12	4,463,205	24
2001*	Senate	42.5	14,406,519	176
2004	European	11.5	3,736,606	9
2006	Chamber of Deputies	12.3	4,707,126	71
2006	Senate	12.4	4,235,208	41
2008*	Chamber of Deputies	37.4	13,629,464	272
2008*	Senate	38.2	12,511,258	141

Source: http://elezionistorico.interno.it/index.php; http://www.parlgov.org/; http://www.electionresources.org/

Note: Before 1994, the party was called Italian Social Movement. From the 1990s onwards, the National Alliance runs as part of pre-electoral coalitions with other parties of the right. The party officially disbanded in 2009.

*Results reported here refer to the entire pre-electoral coalition. It was not possible to find the National Alliance's separate results.

Italia also contributed to the MSI's legitimation. Having no links with the old regime, Berlusconi offered political backup to the MSI during the 1993 local elections endorsing the party secretary, Gianfranco Fini, for the Rome mayoralty. The MSI's resounding success during these elections increased the party's coalition potential. Berlusconi recognised that 'if the left was to be beaten' (Fella 2006: 12), the MSI had to be considered as a legitimate electoral partner. Such a belief led him to coalesce with the MSI – launched as National Alliance – for the 1994 elections, when the party scored an unprecedented 13.5 per cent of the Italian vote in the Chamber of Deputies elections and 6.3 in the Senate elections (see Table 6.1). This resulted in the National Alliance participating in the first Berlusconi Cabinet from May to December 1994.

The impressive electoral result was not necessarily due to the MSI providing a radically new message to the electorate. Fini openly stated his belief that Mussolini was Italy's greatest statesman even as late as 1994, provoking strong international criticism (Locatelli and Martini 1994: 143). At the 1995 Fiuggi Congress, the party officially changed its name into the National Alliance. But this was no more than a change in the name, rather than a change in political personnel, organisation and ideology (Ignazi 2003, 2005; Tarchi 2003). The Theses of the Congress 'failed to acquire the status of a historic, path-breaking "manifesto" of the new party' (Ignazi 2005: 337). An overwhelming majority of the 1995 Congress participants continued to positively evaluate fascism (Baldini and Vignati 1996; Ignazi 2003: 46). The new party also presented elements of continuity with regards to its organisational structure (Morini 2007: 160; Ignazi et al. 2010: 200).

From the mid-1990s, its leader was in a constant quest for a 'winning ideological formula' (Fella and Ruzza 2006). The party's ideology constantly changed, conditional upon its electoral fortunes and whether it would participate in government or remain in opposition. During the period of the rise and fall of the first Berlusconi government (1994), MSI-National Alliance sought to consolidate its newly found legitimacy in the new centre-right ground. In doing so, the party first and foremost declared its fidelity to the tenets of liberal democracy. At the same time, it maintained traditional themes of law and order, and ideas generally associated with the conservative right. While in opposition (1995–1999), the party's economic policies departed from statism and protectionism. The National Alliance imitated Berlusconi's Forza Italia through its support of neoliberal policies and limited state intervention (National Alliance 1998). The party, however, maintained its focus on traditional values and themes, such as the centrality of the family, the right to life, national sovereignty and law and order (Tarchi 2003). During the 1999 European elections, however, the party failed to draw voters away from Forza Italia, and thus its primary emphasis shifted back to more traditional positions, presenting itself as the 'socially advanced wing of the centre-right' (National Alliance 2001; Tarchi 2003: 163).

The party showed a dramatic, if incremental, drive, during the 2000s to distance itself from the past, with a view to becoming a considerable force of the Italian centre-right. The National Alliance participated in the House of Freedom's coalition governments led by Berlusconi (Berlusconi II cabinet 2001–2005; Berlusconi III cabinet 2005–2006). The party proceeded with an official collaboration with Forza Italia to launch a federation of parties under the banner 'People of Freedom' in November 2007. The two parties ran jointly in the 2008 national elections. The National Alliance was not officially disbanded until early 2009. Fini stepped down from party leadership in 2008 after being elected to the post of President of the Chamber of Deputies, and was succeeded by Ignazio La Russa. Following the party's dissolution, a significant number of National Alliance politicians remained within the People of Freedom.

These changes, however, did not imply that the role of the nation would cease to be instrumental in National Alliance's ideology. History, tradition, customs, collective memory and common religious sentiment were seen as the 'founding elements of the Nation' (National Alliance 2000: 2). The party (2000: 2–3) argued that a 'people without national conscience not only forgets its past but also lacks cohesiveness in the present and is deprived of a future'.[2] The party's nationalism in the 2000s was not one that focused on race and ethnicity. Rather, it was 'based on a belief in the nation-as-empire' (Spruce 2007: 101). The National Alliance (2002: 11) maintained that a 'healthy national sentiment [. . .] should not be confused with nationalism,'[3] i.e., nationalism should not necessarily be associated with violence and aggression (Fini 2003: 17; Campi 2006: 95). In a somewhat primordial understanding of nationalism, the party viewed Italy not as a state created during the nineteen-century Risorgimento, but as a nation, or 'fatherland' (*patria*), dating back to the era of Ancient Rome and Ancient Greece (National Alliance 2002: 11). In fact, the party claimed ownership of the term '*patria*' (Spruce 2007: 106), and presented a strong sense of pride in Italy's long past:

> Italy is the place that has best emulated Greek philosophy, mediated by Christianity, the Roman political and legal tradition, the medieval social expression and the best insights of humanism into an organic whole not prejudiced by language nor religion (National Alliance 2001: 2).[4]

This imperial vision of Italy could also be seen through the party's portrayal of the country's civilising mission in the world: 'The Italian genius has helped diffuse European ideas around the world, shaping the politics and culture of other territories' (National Alliance 2001: 2–3).[5] The party's imperial understanding of the Italian nation is related to the concept of diversity, which explains its insistence on the principle of subsidiarity. The wealth of the nation is conditional upon respecting internal specificities. This, however, did not imply support for federalism, as the latter was thought to disintegrate the nation-state. In line with fascism's focus on a strong state, National Alliance (2000: 3) argued that the state should always intervene in emergency situations.

The imperial – rather than ethnic – vision of the nation explains why, although the party was tough on immigration, it avoided ethno-populist frames, such as that immigrants steal jobs from Italians (Fella and Ruzza 2006: 195). The 2002 Bossi-Fini Law on clandestine immigration illustrates this point. It reduced regular entrance into the country and made the granting of resident permits conditional upon the immigrant having a contract of employment. The party's primary focus was on rules governing immigrants rather than their perceived threat to the nation (Fella 2006: 16). The law helped cement National Alliance's tough stance on immigration, but it also dissociated it from the hard-line inflammatory rhetoric of the Northern League. Having said that, some National Alliance politicians associated immigration with criminality and lack of citizen safety (La Russa 2005). The party maintained traditional authoritarian positions on issues relating to security and law and order, and it attached importance to traditional family and Catholic values (Fella 2006: 13; Ruzza and Fella 2009: 155, 164). Security remained a prime electoral theme during the party's 2008 electoral campaign (National Alliance 2008b), when the party hardened its positions with Fini, declaring that if elected he would make the Bossi-Fini Law even stricter (Fini 2007a).

In its quest to carve out a political identity distinct from the populism of its centre-right competitors, the National Alliance avoided anti-elitist and populist appeals after 1998 (Ruzza and Fella 2009: 166). This would mark a clear break from the party's past and would also provide an alternative to the Northern League and Forza Italia. Although Fini was a charismatic leader who was able to modulate his party's image in order to enhance his party's legitimacy (Lee 2000: 372; Hainsworth 2008; Griffin 2011: 203), its calm and measured presence in Italian politics was antithetical to that of Berlusconi and Bossi. To further develop the party's electoral appeal, 'Fini sought to distinguish the AN from the populism and neo-liberalism of the LN and FI [...] presenting the party as the social conscience of the right' (Fella 2006: 15). Ignazi has argued that the party was on the fringe of the contemporary radical right (Ignazi 2003: 52), especially after merging with Forza Italia towards the end of the 2000s. However, 'elements of anti-political and exclusionist discourse remain important [...] despite the apparent adoption of a quite conventional conservative and state welfare interventionist programme' (Ruzza and Fella 2009: 142). The party's policies lacked coherence, the MSI symbol continued to feature in party literature, the party's visual propaganda covertly celebrated elements of fascism (Cheles 2010), and the party 'struggled to define exactly what it stands for and what holds it together' (Fella 2006: 22).

THE NATIONAL ALLIANCE'S COMPROMISING EUROSECPTICISM

The party's transformation from the neo-fascist MSI into the post-fascist National Alliance in the mid-1990s entailed a shift in its EU position. From a strong Eurosceptic position in the 1980s and early 1990s (Conti 2009: 206), the party moved towards a more conciliatory view of European integration, entailing modest support for the project. Earlier expert surveys have indicated that, during the 1980s, the party was very close to the rejectionist Eurosceptic end of the spectrum. On a seven-point scale where 1 indicates strong opposition to European integration and 7 strong support, Ray's expert survey positioned the party at 1.63 in the 1984 and 1988 expert surveys. During the following decade, the party modestly moved to 1.88 and 2.55 in the 1992 and 1996 expert surveys, respectively (Ray 1999: 300). The MSI had recognised the importance of co-operation, but it 'never enthusiastically supported integration because of its fear of loss of national autonomy and independent decision-making' (Kritzinger et al. 2004: 958). The dramatic change in its position occurred from the mid-1990s onwards, when the party started expressing a moderate stance towards integration in line with what it perceived as de Gaulle's notion of 'Europe of fatherlands' (Fella and Ruzza 2006: 190). The 1995 Fiuggi document stated: 'The idea "Europe of Father-lands", integral to the 1960s Gaullism, can guarantee through intelligent adjustment the historic unity of the nation-states characterising the civilisation of the continent' (National Alliance 1995: 61).[6] The EU was envisaged as a confederation of equal member states, respecting cultural particularities and identities against a 'federal, centralizing superstate' (Tarchi 2003: 166). From the mid-1990s onwards, the National Alliance's EU position may be categorised within the compromising pattern of Euroscepticim.

Similar to other far right parties in Europe, the National Alliance viewed Europe as 'a spiritual and cultural reference, product of the history and characteristics of its peoples, from ancient Greece to Rome and Christianity' (National Alliance 2002: 6).[7] Europe is not only a geographical area, but also 'something deeper, a type of civilisation layered over centuries of history' (National Alliance 2004: 5),[8] a 'European fatherland' (National Alliance 2000: 4).[9] Europeans are distinguished from other cultures in terms of their history, moral standards and way of life. 'When we speak of values such as personal

dignity, the rule of law, solidarity, the family, respect for life, we inadver-
tently refer to principles that the Judaeo-Christian roots have given to Europe'
(National Alliance 2004: 6).[10] Religion was thought to serve as a uniting element of Europe and its peoples, and as such featured prominently in the party's
political discourse. For example, the National Alliance lobbied for a reference
to Christianity in the preamble of the European Constitution, and regretted that
Europe's Christian roots ultimately were not mentioned (Angelilli 2007). The
party maintained that a 'reference to Europe's Judaeo-Christian roots becomes
the necessary recognition of the continent's secular unity' (National Alliance
2004: 6).[11] Cristiana Muscardini, one of the party's MEPs, argued:

> It is our hope that, with regard to the preamble, the Intergovernmental Confer-
> ence will come to an agreement on the acknowledgement of the roots from
> which the Union has sprung to life. The ancient history of Greece and Rome, the
> Judaeo-Christian traditions and the secular, liberal values which came gradually
> to be established cannot be disregarded because it is from them that the future of
> Europe is drawing cultural and moral strength (Muscardini 2003).[12]

Whereas the party perceived national and European identities as distinct,
these were not necessarily posited as antithetical or competing. Instead, they
were understood through a framework of concentric circles. National identity
constitutes the first circle, closest to the individual, while European identity is
the second wider circle of identification. It is only by finding the similarities
and differences of European peoples that it would be possible to acquire the
consciousness of European citizenship (National Alliance 2002: 6). European
citizenship, however, still implies 'the need to safeguard our own identities
and our own traditions too' (Muscardini 2007a).[13]

The National Alliance was in favour of the principle of European co-
operation at a higher multilateral level. The party believed that it is in the
European States' best interest to pool their resources in order to better manage
issues of international and transnational character. The party supported Italy's
membership of the EU; its proposed framework for co-operation was intergovernmental based on the primacy of the nation-state. The party favoured
a 'confederation in which nation-states delegate part of their sovereignty to
central institutions for the management of specific sectors while maintaining
their autonomy' (Muscardini 2009).[14] 'Europe cannot be formed against the
Member States and against national interests' (Tatarella 2008).[15] National
specificities constitute Europe's wealth, and the EU should not 'negate the
nation-state but rather constitute a Confederation of nation-states; in this
sense the states and their interests would contribute to rather than obstruct
the formulation of European interests and priorities' (National Alliance
2002: 6).[16] Key party politicians accepted that Italy benefited more from the

European community and much less from the EU (e.g. Muscardini 2009). The party nevertheless opposed a 'single Europe' that adopted the same policies for all member states without considering national and regional specificities.

The nation-state was seen as both central to the creation of a united Europe, but also, empowered by it. 'It is through the states and the national governments [...] that the Confederation of States could acquire a "political personality" [...] and the States would find their centrality' (National Alliance 2002: 6).[17] This vision of Europe resembles the Gaullist belief of integration based on the strength and integrity of the nation-state. 'Our documents and political positions have been inspired by the Gaullist model' (National Alliance 2006b: 16).[18] The party leader specified that 'we are in favour of delegating some powers of the State; but we are against abandoning national sovereignty. "The Europe of nations" should prevail where every member state can maintain its identity in a non-centralised structure' (interview of Fini, in Fini and Staglieno 1999: 29).[19] This was contrasted to the creation of Europe as a superstate: 'The Right has always supported a Europe of nations rich by its identities and cultures that should be respected and cannot be reversed by a superstate' (National Alliance 2004: 6).[20] The party was clearly against the creation of a European federal structure: 'We oppose a type of European integration that would represent the creation of a single model. We are in favour of a Europe that respects the diversities and cultures that enrich it' (Muscardini 2009).[21] The nation-state must be central to EU decision-making, and the 'pluralism of national sovereignties' must be preserved (National Alliance 2004: 8). The party leader argued that the 'best way to participate in the European club should not involve giving up one's national prerogatives, history, culture and identity. Being good Europeans presupposes being good Italians' (Fini, in Campi 2006: 108).[22] The strength of European integration stemmed from the notion of unity in diversity: 'European political unity must be established while at the same time safeguarding national identities and diversities' (Angelilli 2001).[23] European co-operation should not be an unconditional surrender of power to European institutions; rather, 'integration should take place when necessary [and] decentralisation where possible' (National Alliance 2002: 6).[24]

It is worth noting that the National Alliance portrayed itself as the only party in Italy, seeking not only to preserve, but also to promote, Italian national interests to the EU level. 'Italy [...] should develop and assert its characteristics in a united Europe' (National Alliance 2004: 12).[25] Fini criticised other Italian parties for their unconditional Europeanism that did not allow them to upload Italian interests to the EU: 'Europeanists in words, we have never taken European institutions seriously, we did not make every effort to insert our officials in the bureaucratic structure of the Communities' (Fini, in Campi 2006: 108).[26] Italy had assumed a deterministic 'agree and get along' position towards the EU in order to create an EU 'at all costs but without any values' (National Alliance 2002: 5). The party pointed to the fact that 'it is only in recent years, and thanks to the Right, that we can speak of the "rediscovery of the national interest" (National Alliance 2004: 12).[27] Using the EU as a tool for domestic criticism, the National Alliance criticised the Italian left for supporting the creation of a European superstate against the culture and traditions of the European peoples (National Alliance 2004: 8).

The party supported the practice of European integration. It espoused EU co-operation on a number of policies, including the economy, energy, the environment, immigration and borders, security and justice. Policies of particular interest to the party related to technology and foreign policy. It saw a benefit from European integration to the extent that the EU did not attempt to establish uniform policies for all member states irrespective of geography, climate and financial considerations. 'We are against regulations in some sectors that extend from the North Cape to the island of Lampedusa' (Muscardini 2009).[28] The practice of European integration was thus filtered through a systematic cost-benefit analysis conferred upon Italian national interests (Conti 2003: 26).

However, this support for EU policy practice did not translate into uncon-ditional support for EU institutions. The National Alliance criticised the EU for being distant from citizens' interests and needs, thus suffering from a democratic deficit. The EU was portrayed as a technocratic government, lack-ing citizen participation and popular legitimacy. The EU's decision-making procedures were thought to be opaque and distant from European peoples. 'EU decisions, far from being taken in the Parliament, arise from Council meetings and are implemented by the Commission. The Council decides in secrecy and the Commission implements them in a politically "non-responsi-ble" manner. These paradoxes clearly contradict the democratic spirit inher-ent in Europe' (National Alliance 2002: 6).[29]

The party criticised the European Commission for being a hyper-bureau-cracy incapable of designing and implementing a common policy (National Alliance 2004: 7). The technocratic EU was seen as averse to the process of democratic participation. The people, instead of being active decision-makers, had become passive consumers of European legislation (National Alliance 2002: 5). European bureaucrats had created an overregulated, soulless Europe 'incapable of asserting the roots of its own identity' (National Alliance 2006a: 12).[30] The main challenge for the party was to create a Europe where institu-tional structures would enjoy direct citizen accountability (National Alliance 2004: 8). EU regulations were portrayed as excessive, too hard and complex to understand: 'Establishing the curvature of bananas or the diameter of peas or the length of contraceptives, and believing that this means you are regulating the market is a sign that you are a thousand miles away from the daily life of the citizens' (Muscardini 2007b).[31]

The EU was seen as struggling between two antithetical conceptions. The first referred to a technocratic European superstate alien to democratic participation and legitimacy. The second related to a political union of sovereign nation-states, collaborating in areas of mutual interest. The party's vision of co-operation related to the second conception, i.e., a political union defined as a confederation of European nation-states where all members would contribute without compromising their sovereignty (National Alliance 2000: 4). The maintenance of diversity was an important principle of the party, which argued that the 'future of Europe cannot be marked by centralised uniformity but by unity in diversity' (National Alliance 2002: 5).[32] European co-operation would only succeed if it developed 'with the peoples' in a project of concentric circles of sovereignty primarily governed by the principle of subsidiarity (Muscardini 2009). The future of European integration would be successful only by respecting and preserving member state specificities, which is precisely what was seen as uniting and enriching the EU. Indeed, the EU should find a balance between national interests, on the one hand, and European common interests, on the other. For example, although the party supported the European Constitution, it argued that it should not be 'exploited for party-political purposes against governments that have been duly elected by their own citizens. The European Union must not run the risk of becoming a place where political groups join in the battle to attack freely made national decisions on ideological grounds' (Muscardini 2005).[33]

The party's view of the EU during the 2000s was rather pessimistic. It deplored the existence of a technocratic and elitist EU, which was the product of social democratic policies (National Alliance 2002: 5). EU enlargement was seen as an additional impediment to the EU becoming a strong political power. The EU was criticised for prematurely enlarging in 2004 to the countries of Central and Eastern Europe (National Alliance 2006a: 12–13). The EU should 'deepen in order to enlarge, resulting in reinforced co-operation in areas of strategic importance' (National Alliance 2002: 5).[34] Fini expressed his disillusionment towards future co-operation within the EU, arguing that the 'future of Europe, at this point, is nothing more than a vast marketplace ruled by a purely economic logic' (Fini, in Campi 2006: 106).[35] The party envisaged the EU as a European club consisting of few selected countries with a common vision and limited bureaucracy. Because the prevailing EU model was perceived to be technocratic and lacking legitimacy, the EU was portrayed as a socialist construct, disoriented and fragmented with protectionist and introverted tendencies. As such, the future building of a European polity appeared inconsistent with the party's vision of co-operation.

ELECTORAL INCENTIVES AND THE NATIONAL ALLIANCE'S DOMESTIC STRATEGY

How may we understand the development of National Alliance's Euroscepticism? The party's move towards a compromising stance on European integration may be seen in the context of changing developments in domestic Italian politics. The crisis of the Italian party system in the early 1990s, which paved the way for the establishment of the Second Italian Republic, opened political opportunities for the National Alliance to differentiate itself not only from its fascist past, but also from the parties of the First Republic, which were accused of corruption. Under these new political conditions, the National Alliance prioritised a strategy of institutional entrenchment, which combined de-radicalisation, i.e., avoiding controversial statements, extremist policies and anti-democratic references; and normalisation through coalition formation with larger political groups of the right and ultimately access to political power. This strategy would enable the party to gain legitimacy and consolidate its position within the centre-right of Italian politics.

Since the collapse of the old regime at the beginning of the 1990s, the National Alliance went through two key phases. The first commenced roughly in 1993, when the party enjoyed unprecedented electoral success in local elections, and lasted until the end of the decade. During these years, the party sought to move away from right-wing extremism in order to partake in 'normal' Italian politics as a respectable and legitimate partner of the right. This entailed renaming the party and rebranding it from neo-fascist into post-fascist/conservative. The former MSI attempted to reshape its identity, ideology and values away from its anti-liberal and anti-democratic tradition. Its strategy consisted of avoiding open confrontation with other political parties, discouraging party members from committing violent acts and changing the traditional mass party organisational structure – reminiscent of fascism – by introducing local branches (Ignazi 2005). This largely resembled its strategy of *inserimento* during the 1950s and 1960s, pursued by former leaders in order to become politically accepted within the anti-communist bloc (Bianchi 2007: 75; Ruzza and Fella 2009: 15). The party's attempt to construct an image of respectability in the 1990s contributed to its rehabilitation and ultimate participation in a short-lived cabinet led by Berlusconi in 1994, which translated into five ministries and the prestigious post of Deputy Prime Minister. During the remaining years of the 1990s, the party remained in opposition. Its full integration into the political system occurred from 2001 onwards, when the party participated in the second and third Berlusconi cabinets (2001–2005; 2005–2006). The National Alliance held a few ministries, and Fini was appointed to the posts of Deputy Prime Minister (2001–2006) and Minster of Foreign Affairs (2004–2006). This second phase marked a

decisive break from the past. During the 2000s, the party enjoyed governmental status in one of the longest running cabinets in the history of Italian
politics. Access to political power further stimulated a desire for consolidation and institutional entrenchment, and a drive for a leading position within
the governmental coalition.

Fini's role in guiding the party's ideological evolution during these two
phases was crucial, as he was able to respond to opportunities provided by
changing political circumstances (Campi 2006: VI; Fella and Ruzza 2006:
183). Ideological transition did not occur without internal opposition (Ruzza
and Fella 2009: 144, 153). It was, rather, facilitated by the centralised
organisation of the party whereby the President enjoyed ample powers and
incrementally made 'any real control over him by collective bodies a highly
remote possibility' (Ignazi et al. 2010: 207). Fini was playing a game both at
party and individual levels. On the one hand, he wished to retain leadership
of the party, which led him to occasionally adopt hard-line positions. On the
other hand, Fini competed as a potential heir to Berlusconi and aspired to
become President of the Republic, which explained his expressed moderation
and lack of clarity in his policy positions (Ruzza and Fella 2009: 158). As a
result of this two-level political agenda, the party appeared to put forward two
different types of right-wing political culture (Campi 2006: 62–63).

The National Alliance's electoral coalition with Forza Italia and the Northern League did not consistently enjoy amicable relations. As early as the 1998
Verona Congress, the National Alliance evoked neoliberal policies, overtly
borrowing from Forza Italia (National Alliance 1998). In the 1999 European elections, the party stood on a joint list with the Christian Democratic
Segni Pact party against Berlusconi, which scored a lower-than-anticipated
electoral result. This led National Alliance to shift its focus away from the
economy to its traditional themes of security and law and order, and to rejoin
the Forza Italia-Northern League 'House of Freedoms' coalition for the 2001
elections. Following the coalition's electoral victory in 2001, the opportunity appeared for Fini to 'position himself as a possible future leader of the
post-Berlusconi centre-right' (Fella 2006: 15). A rift between Tremonti, the
Italian Treasury Minister, and Fini over the economic policy of the coalition
became a dispute between Forza Italia and the Northern League, on the one
side and the National Alliance, on the other (Fella 2006: 18). The political
priorities of the coalition appeared to be dominated by the 'personal interests
of Berlusconi and the political priorities of the Northern League' (Ruzza
and Fella 2009: 154), which provoked a feeling of resentment within the
National Alliance. Choosing to run alone in the 1996 elections, the Northern
League had proven to be indispensible to Forza Italia (Pasquino 2008: 346),
which gave the impression that it was more important to Berlusconi than the
National Alliance.

Table 6.2   The socio-demographic profile of the National Alliance's voters

		1996		2001		2006	
		All voters (n=3708)	AN voters (n=437)	All voters (n=1553)	AN voters (n=143)	All voters (n=1439)	AN voters (n=95)
Gender	Male	48.3	59.27	53.31	62.24	49.27	56.84
	Female	51.7	40.73	46.49	37.76	50.73	43.16
Age	Up to 35	37.78	37.53	15.39	19.58	33.36	40
	36-50	37.46	36.84	26.4	25.87	27.17	32.63
	51-65	21.04	20.14	35.22	37.06	22.45	17.89
	65 or more	3.72	5.49	22.99	17.48	17.03	9.47
Employment Status	Employed	53.21	56.98	5.09	9.79	49.62	52.63
	Student	13.4	10.3	3.8	4.2	11.47	15.79
	At home	16.05	12.59	19.25	18.18	13.48	9.47
	Retired	8.82	9.84	7.15	3.5	22.24	17.89
	Unemployed	8.52	10.3	4.7	3.5	2.78	2.11
	Other	0	0	52.99	52.45	0.42	2.11
Education	Low	27.08	24.26	33.81	27.97	46.14	34.74
	Medium	31.34	32.72	34	38.46	45.59	58.95
	High	23.46	25.4	18.61	19.58	8.27	6.32
Religiosity	Every week	24.38	21.74	41.15	46.85	19.32	16.84
	Every month or several times a year	36.11	40.05	31.62	32.87	49.69	54.74
	Once a year or less	20.12	22.88	8.11	8.39	8.55	11.58
	Never	19.39	15.33	11.46	3.5	17.79	16.84
Urban vs rural	Rural			33.61	23.78	34.54	36.84
	Urban			59.5	67.13	65.46	63.16
					135		
Left-right (0-10)	Mean	5.21	7.09	5.14	8.24	5.13	8.04
	Std. deviation	2.51	2.2	2.61	1.71	2.67	1.71

Source: 1996: EES Voter Study 1999 (Eijk et al. 1999); 2001: EES Voter Study 2004 (Schmitt et al. 2009); 2006: The Comparative Study of Electoral Systems (CSES Module 2)
Note: 1996: Vote choice in previous general election; 2001: vote choice in previous general election; 2006: vote study in current general election

Berlusconi's decreased popularity towards the end of the 2001–2006 cabinets and a sceptical climate within the coalition (De Sio 2007: 98) brought about a discussion regarding leadership change and a possible move towards a European-style centre-right that would not ally with extremist parties (De Sio 2007: 107). This provided the perfect opportunity for Fini to portray himself as the future leader of the Italian centre-right. His choice was backed up by a series of positive public evaluations of Fini as a politician (Ruzza and Fella 2009: 147) and as a potential future leader of the coalition (Campi 2006: 29). Fini's charismatic personality contrasted the populist appeals made by both Berlusconi and Bossi, and gave the National Alliance an image of respectability. In addition, the rift with Tremonti had revealed that the National Alliance was not a hard neoliberal party, and the various disputes with Bossi had served as a reminder that the party had a comparatively less harsh stance on immigration. The discussion over the post-Berlusconi leadership of the centre-right, however, did not last very long. Despite losing the 2006 elections, Berlusconi was thought to have won the electoral campaign, which contributed to his re-empowerment within the coalition (De Sio 2007). Berlusconi's strong personality obstructed Fini's leadership aspirations. However, despite various disputes, the National Alliance collaborated with Forza Italia to launch the People of Freedom in 2007 and ran jointly in the 2008 elections. This clearly indicated that policy differences and past disagreements were not considered strong enough to deter right-wing electoral and governmental alliances.

The attempt to appear as a uniting force within the Italian right is, to some extent, also demonstrated in the socio-demographic makeup of the party's voters (see Table 6.2). Similar to other far right parties in Europe, the party consistently attracted more male than female voters in the domestic electoral contests of 1996, 2001 and 2006. It also received more support from individuals residing in urban areas. In terms of age and employment, however, party voters were similar to the electorate, with the party attracting slightly younger voters in the 2001 and 2006 elections. Unlike other supporters of other far right parties, National Alliance supporters were not distinguished by their low education status. They were, however, significantly different from the electorate in terms of their strong identification with the right.

From an anti-system party in the First Italian Republic, the National Alliance progressed into a rehabilitated mainstream party in the Second Republic. However, its position within the centre-right was based on shaky agreements. Forza Italia and the Northern League appeared to be on better terms with each other rather than with the National Alliance, repeatedly questioning the importance of the latter in the centre-right Italian political landscape. The National Alliance was likely to increase its significance in the party system only through assuming leadership of the centre-right. Failing to do so, the

National Alliance and its leader were likely to be continuously overshadowed by Berlusconi. The party viewed its role as creating a new right-wing alliance that would be pivotal to the future development of the country: 'We want to create a Grand Alliance for Italy which would act in the present but also would look to the future in order to restore hope for those who think that Italy has no prospects and has been relegated to the margins of history' (National Alliance 2008a: 1).[36] This project was based on traditional right-wing ideas, and was intended to 're-affirm the Italian model that derives from our history, our culture and our identity' (National Alliance 2008a: 2).[37] The party's insistence on creating this alliance to rule the 'Nuova Italia' (National Alliance 2008a: 3) implied a wish for radical change in Italian politics. As the collapse of the First Republic led to the party's rehabilitation and insertion in Italian politics, the creation of a Grand Alliance under the aegis of the National Alliance was expected to result in the party's full entrenchment in the Italian political establishment. Interestingly, this idea of a 'Grand Alliance' that would bring Italian right-wing forces together based on cultural references was very similar to the MSI's project of the 'Grande Destra', i.e., the Great Right that would combat communism (Ignazi 1994: 7).

THE EU ISSUE AS A TOOL FOR POLITICAL ENTRENCHMENT

Political transition from the First to the Second Italian Republic provided opportunities to the National Alliance to shed its fascist past and rebrand itself as a moderate force of the new Italian centre-right political space. During the Second Republic, the party became Berlusconi's electoral and governmental partner, further consolidating its position within the party system. Fini's appointment to the prestigious posts of Deputy Prime Minister and Foreign Minister signified the system's acceptance of the party as a legitimate force in the Second Republic. However, the National Alliance remained subordinate to Berlusconi's Forza Italia, which involved a constant risk of 'being chased back into the ghetto to which it had been confined for almost half a century prior to the early 1990s' (Newell and Bull 2002: 635). In its quest for political entrenchment, the National Alliance changed its EU policy from a relatively hard and critical position to one of compromising Euroscepticism. This stance provided the party and its leader with long-sought national and international legitimacy. Fini employed the EU issue as a political tool that would ultimately enable him to appear as a statesman on an equal footing with other centre-right leaders abroad.

Fini's role as a representative of the Italian government in the Convention for the Future of Europe (2002–2006), which debated and drafted the European Constitution, provided the perfect opportunity for the party to establish its international standing. Berlusconi, who was under investigation for charges including tax evasion and bribery, was discredited abroad (Newell and Bull 2002: 629). The international press led by *The Economist* criticised Berlusconi arguing that he 'stands for sleaze, if not outright criminality' (*Economist* 2001b) and is 'not fit to lead the government of any country, least of all one of the world's richest democracies' (*Economist* 2001a). Fini argued that the Italian centre-right government should nonetheless appoint its own representative in the Convention to counterbalance the appointment of left-leaning Giuliano Amato as Vice Chairman of the Convention. He thus put himself forward for the nomination of Italy's representation in the European Convention: 'I said to Berlusconi: I am available to do this' (Fini 2003: 43).[38]

Fini assumed the role of the representative of the Head of State of Italy in a Convention that was unique in its kind and had the potential for a historical role (Fini 2003: 42–44). His participation also had domestic political relevance, driven by a 'desire to occupy myself with Community politics, which increasingly determine the choices of national politics' (Fini 2003: 44).[39] Fini presented himself not only as the representative of the National Alliance, but also, and perhaps most importantly, as the main representative of Italy's executive branch, thus assigning himself decision-making powers. He marketed himself as a 'leading actor of the Convention's success' (Fini 2003: 46).[40]

The Convention was a high-profile political arena where Fini was able to introduce himself to other European leaders and political elites. To liaise with them, Fini portrayed himself, his party and the Italian government as like-minded as far as the future of the EU's architecture was concerned. This was a great challenge. Not only was the National Alliance divided on the EU issue (Quaglia 2005: 285), but Forza Italia, the strongest party in the Italian governmental coalition, was also only functionally supportive of the EU (Conti 2009). During his participation in the Convention, Fini insisted on avoiding the use of the word 'federal'. He proposed amendments with a view to safeguarding national sovereignty and limiting the EU institutions' powers on the member states. Fini was also against the right of movement within the EU for citizens of other countries, including refugees and migrants who already faced restrictions under the Bossi-Fini Law. He supported the inclusion of a reference to Europe's Christian roots in the Constitution's preamble, confirming his vision of Europe as a Christian club. Fini also advocated the creation of a common defence policy, which was somewhat inconsistent with his attempt to safeguard national sovereignty, given that such a common policy would accelerate integration (Di Quirico 2003: 31–33).

Notwithstanding the inherent contradiction between Fini's personal enthusiastic contribution to the European Convention, on the one hand (Angelilli 2007), and his argument against a federal Europe, on the other, representing Italy in the European Convention gave Fini status, prestige and credibility, both domestically and abroad. Fini appeared as a statesman on the same foot-ing as his European counterparts. This was essential if he was to realise his personal desire to lead the Italian centre-right. In the Convention, Fini was able to project an image of managerial competence. He was a professional politician with experience in international relations, unlike other politicians from the ruling coalition, and Berlusconi himself who had repeatedly made errors on the international arena (Di Quirico 2003: 23). At the same time, Fini's position on the maintenance of national sovereignty, his opposition to federalism, his Christian-centric stance and his insistence on a strong defence policy were appreciated internally within the Berlusconi cabinet.

In line with literature that suggests that Fini is a weathervane, moving where political winds blow him (Marsiglia 2005), Fini responded to opportu-nities offered by external circumstances (Fella 2006; Fella and Ruzza 2006). In the 1990s, Fini utilised the opportunities provided by the breakup of the political system in order to reformulate his party and distance it from its discredited fascist past. In the 2000s, his role in the European Convention allowed him to portray his party as 'belonging to one of the greatest families of European political tradition which has largely contributed to the European cause and will continue to do so' (National Alliance 2004: 6).[41] While main-taining its traditionalist right-wing character, the party insisted on its political relevance. It was 'central but not centrist' (National Alliance 2002: 13–14).[42] Although participation in the European Convention did not satisfy Fini's quest for leadership, it contributed to his appointment as Foreign Minister in 2004 and President of the Lower House in 2008. Fini (2008) maintained that the 'two years I spent working on the European Constitution and my mandate as Foreign Minister have demonstrated that the National Alliance has simi-lar values to those of the European People's Party'.[43] In its 2006 campaign, which took place following the European Convention and Fini's appointment as Italian Foreign Minister, the party portrayed itself as the central force in the coalition with the 'right and obligation to aspire to permanently become the central force of the coalition through [...] its political and cultural project [...] from the point of view of a large national and popular party with European inspiration and credentials' (National Alliance 2006a: 2).[44]

Fini's leadership aspirations were also manifested in the run-up to the 2008 national elections, when he 'did not exclude the possibility of running for Prime Minister' (Fini 2007a).[45] He argued that an alternative system to that of the left was possible 'with or without Berlusconi' and that he had the ability to 'reconstruct the centre-right. Even if I have to do this on my own' (Fini 2007b).[46] In a book inspired by the twentieth anniversary of the fall of the Berlin Wall, Fini (2009) summarised his worldview. This book was addressed to those born in 1989 who had neither experienced Commu-nism nor lived during the First Italian Republic, and were thus presumably unaware of National Alliance's fascist past. Fini discussed the process of European integration within the context of rising levels of immigration in Europe. He presented the EU as lacking legitimacy with an ever-increasing gap between a bureaucratic Europe, on the one hand, and the European peoples, on the other. He insisted that the discussion on the Continent's identity and religious credentials should be resumed. The general tone was one of educating young Italians about the challenges lying ahead, reaffirming his view that 'away from Europe, Italy would increasingly become an outsider with regards to the processes of modernisation and globalisation' (Fini 2009: 136).[47]

ITALY'S INTERNATIONAL STATUS IN THE NATIONAL ALLIANCE'S EUROSCEPTIC AGENDA

The National Alliance's compromising Euroscepticism was framed with reference to the party's imperial vision of the Italian nation, and its attempt to enhance Italy's international status through co-operation within the EU framework. Rather than questioning the very existence of the EU, the National Alliance accepted that EU member states should club together in order to address the various social and geopolitical challenges facing the Western world. The party believed that the EU should become a global leader in international affairs, diplomacy and international trade. Europe was seen as a founding pillar of the West that should not be antagonistic to the United States (National Alliance 2004: 9). A strong EU should produce security in the world by conducting crisis management operations (National Alliance 2000: 4; 2002: 5). The National Alliance perceived the EU as a vehicle for the promotion of the Italian image abroad (National Alliance 1995: 61). Participation in such a leading international bloc would enhance Italy's global role and enable the country to become a driving force in international relations. Italy would lead the way in a dynamic Europe, by assuming international responsibilities and inserting itself within the Franco-German axis (National Alliance 2009: 9).

This global vision of the EU was linked to a belief in Europe's and Italy's civilising mission abroad. The party argued that 'Italy and Europe should play a dynamic role in international relations since there are important areas in the world where systematic violation of human rights takes place' (National Alliance 2000: 4).[48] For example, Christiana Muscardini (2007d), one of the party's leading politicians, argued that 'we want a political Europe able to inspire the desire for democracy in places in the world where millions of women and men still suffer a lack of freedom and the rule of law'.[49] Without a common foreign and security policy, Europe 'will remain weakened' (Muscardini 2007c) and 'will not be able to play a role in the world that is analogous to its economic and commercial weight and could be forced to accept choices made by others' (National Alliance 1999: 1).[50] Europe should become a strong player in international politics, making a concerted effort to tackle international crises, which thus far are managed by individual states, the United States or the United Nations. 'We have to anticipate future scenarios and cannot, as we were in the case of Kosovo, be unprepared and divided in the face of such a sensitive scenario' (Muscardini 2008).[51] This vision of Europe was portrayed as that of 'Euro-realism', whereby 'a Union of sovereign states is capable of acting effectively through the expression of a common will' (Muscardini 2007f).[52]

A systematic analysis of the party's MEPs' speeches in EP Plenaries also shows that they dedicated much of their time with a view to promoting the EU's global role and Italy's international status. The National Alliance was a member of the Eurosceptic Union for Europe of the Nations EP group with its MEPs occupying leading positions within the group. The party had consistently elected MEPs since the first EP election in 1979. The National Alliance ran jointly with the Sergi Pact during the 1999 EP elections. The analysis of MEP speeches during the fifth EP term (1999–2004) includes the speeches of Roberta Angelilli, Sergio Berlato, Cristiana Muscardini, Antonio Mussa and Adriana Poli Bortone. The analysis of the sixth EP term (2004–2009) comprises the speeches of Roberta Angelilli, Domenico Antonio Basile, Sergio Berlato, Alessandro Foglietta, Romano Maria La Russa, Cristiana Muscardini, Antonio Mussa, Umberto Pirilli, Adriana Poli Bortone and Salvatore Tatarella.

The first observation from the content analysis of their speeches relates to the very low prominence of domestic-related issues (see Table 6.3; see appendix for information on coding procedure). Contrary to LAOS MEPs, National Alliance MEPs dedicated only about 3 to 4 per cent of their time in EP Plenaries on issues of specific domestic interest. Table 6.3 provides a thematic breakdown of these domestic issues, but it is important to note that this percentage is very low, and that these references are mostly related to specific events that were current at the time of the speech, such as the waste crisis in Campania region, the Thyssen Krupp workers tragedy and the earthquake in Abruzzo. Similar to the French National Front, the National Alliance employed the EP platform to address a number of issues pertaining to the EU. No single policy issue predominated their EP agenda. The party's MEPs addressed a number of different topics, including EU social policy at 21.48 per cent of their time on average, EU rules and procedures at 14.14 per cent, EU foreign and security policy at 13.35 per cent, EU economy and economic policies at 11.71 per cent, and EU security and borders at 8.62 per cent. The salience of EU justice changed across the two EP terms, with MEPs dedicating 14.03 per cent of their time on EU justice during the fifth term, but only 3.53 during the sixth term. The salience of EU environment and energy increased to 7.63 per cent during the sixth term as opposed to 0.51 per cent during the fifth term.

Unlike the French National Front, however, National Alliance's MEPs approached EU policies and themes through the perspective of constructive criticism. Their negative evaluations referred to technical issues, and were mostly accompanied by practical recommendations for improvement. Although the party's MEPs were clearly against the construction of a federal EU, they worked proactively to improve the harmonisation of the EU's legal framework, which was seen as crucial to policy implementation. The theme of culture and tradition also appeared in the party's MEPs' speeches who supported EU projects, such as Socrates and other youth programmes. These were seen as a viable way of improving the integration and employability of young Europeans, but also as vehicles for the creation of European identity and citizenship. For example, Angellili (1999) argued that 'at this delicate stage for the European Union, while we begin to enlarge eastwards, while all the economic and financial changes linked to the creation of the single currency are already underway, we must not forget the value of culture, the specificity and diversity of European culture, its enhancement and its diffusion. Culture, which also means history, languages and traditions, must remain a fundamental and indispensable bond for European citizens'.[53] Indeed, the party's MEPs viewed European common cultural heritage – defined as the common heritage of national traditions rooted in Christianity – as the necessary means of fostering European integration beyond economic co-operation.

The EU social policy category enjoyed the most salience in National Alliance's MEP speeches, with 23.51 per cent during the EP's fifth term and 20.08 per cent during the EP's fifth term. This category includes references to health, infrastructure, workplace security, media policy and civil and consumer protection. True to the party's identity, MEPs approached the majority of social policies through a conservative nationalist perspective. For example, the party sought to preserve the traditional nuclear family consisting of two married heterosexual parents and their children, and maintained that the nation-state should remain sovereign in these policies. For example, La Russa (2006) argued that 'the family has always meant a father and a mother, a man and a woman, and I do not believe that the European Union, by promoting campaigns against hypothetical discrimination, can give itself the right to ride roughshod over national governments just to endorse the wishes of certain not exactly worthy lobbying groups. The European Union cannot act on matters of values, culture and the family as if it were dealing with the single market, asking the Member States to legalise homosexual unions for the sake of uniformity and a misplaced duty to protect people's rights; instead, it would be running the risk of undermining the system of values that lies at the heart of our age-old society' (see also Poli Bortone 1999).[54]

Table 6.3 Salience of issues in the National Alliances MEPs' European Parliament speeches

	Overall	5th term	6th term
General breakdown			
Domestic	3.31	2.50	3.86
EU	96.69	97.50	96.14
Domestic issues			
Economy and economic policies	6.87	22.50	0.00
Environment and energy	4.58	5.00	4.40
Immigration and minorities	23.66	2.50	32.97
Government and institutions	6.11	20.00	0.00
Social policies	36.64	5.00	50.55
Terrorism and justice	22.14	45.00	12.09
EU-related issues			
EU agriculture and fisheries	4.26	4.16	4.32
EU economy and economic policies	11.71	10.19	12.75
EU enlargement	7.13	6.73	7.41
EU environment and energy	4.73	0.51	7.63
EU foreign and security policy	13.35	14.16	12.80
EU justice	7.81	14.03	3.53
EU rules and procedures	14.14	13.26	14.74
EU security and borders	8.62	8.90	8.43
EU social policy	21.48	23.51	20.08
EU trade	4.70	0.06	7.90
European culture and history	2.06	4.48	0.40

Source: EP online archives.
Note: N=492 speeches/3958 sentences (fifth term: N=196 speeches/1601 sentences; sixth term: N=296 speeches/2357 sentences). See appendix regarding coding procedure.

The content analysis of speeches reveals that the National Alliance's MEPs also focused on questions of international relations with a view to promoting the EU's global status. Adding up the categories of EU foreign and security policy, EU enlargement and EU trade, which all relate – in different ways – to issues of international co-operation amounts to an overall salience of 25.18 per cent of the totality of EU-related themes. Unlike gender and family issues, MEPs sought a common strategy with regard to foreign and security policy, trade and external action. They were conscious of the challenges of globalisation and suggested that these may not be addressed by nation-states alone. The future of Europe was seen as inextricably linked to a common European foreign policy (Angelilli 2007).

They sought the EU's empowerment through trade and co-operation with other non-EU countries. For example, they tried to foster closer relations and political co-operation in the Mediterranean region, which they viewed as a 'gateway not just to the Middle East but also to the Atlantic, a cultural as well as economic area, consolidating the South-South dialogue but also the North-South and East-South dialogues' (Muscardini 2001).[55] By supporting

partnership agreements between the EU and southern Mediterranean countries, they sought to foster peace, democracy, stability and socio-economic
progress in the region, but also to place Italy at the centre of this political
strategy due to its geographic location (e.g. see Poli Bortone 2005). The
MEPs perceived the EU as a third geopolitical pole in addition to the U.S. and
China. As such, they urged the EU to take initiatives in the world, including
providing economic help to war-ridden countries; taking action against the
violation of human rights; cancelling third world countries' debt; dealing with
China in relation to the country's respect of human rights and compliance to
WTO rules; fostering peace in the Middle East; and fighting terrorism. It is
noteworthy that in discussing these issues, party MEPs seemed to assume
that the interests of different European nation-states converged in matters
of foreign affairs. In any case, this strategic framing of EU issues enabled
the party to portray its vision of Italy as a central player in EU politics – as
opposed to the Italian left, which was criticised for unconditionally supporting the EU without promoting the Italian national interest abroad (National
Alliance 2004: 11–12).

CONCLUSION

The main objective of this chapter has been to examine in detail the third
type of far right Euroscepticism and explain the way in which it is associated
with a party's domestic agenda. To shed light on this Eurosceptic variant, the
chapter has analysed the ideas, positions and political trajectory of the normalised Italian National Alliance. In doing so, it has also closely examined
the role of its party leader, Gianfranco Fini, in shaping the party's strategic
objectives and EU policy. It has placed the party's compromising Euroscepticism within the context of its transformation and re-branding from the
neo-fascist MSI to the post-fascist National Alliance. The chapter has shown
that the National Alliance had a cultural understanding of Europe primarily
defined by Christianity, but also by ancient Greek and Roman history. The
party supported the principle of co-operation at a European multilateral level.
Its vision of Europe resembled de Gaulle's notion of a 'Europe of fatherlands', whereby maintaining national interest was of vital importance for the
construction of the European project. The party criticised the EU for suffering from a democratic deficit, and for EU decisions being distant from the
European citizens. Its 'compromising' Euroscepticism was tailored as a type
of positive 'Euro-realism', which nonetheless carried a level of pessimism
regarding the EU's trajectory.

The question of Europe became a tool in the National Alliance's quest for
institutional entrenchment in the domestic party system. The party avoided

controversial policies in order to distance itself from its anti-systemic past and improve its collaboration potential with other domestic political forces of the right. Compromising Euroscepticism enabled the party to portray an image of respectability vis-à-vis the other parties in the system. Its EU position also allowed its leader to participate in the European Convention for the Future of Europe, which boosted his reputation both domestically and abroad, ultimately appearing as a statesman on an equal footing with other centre-right leaders. The party was in favour of a strong Europe in international affairs with Italy leading the way in a dynamic continent, assuming international responsibilities and inserting itself within the Franco-German axis. This framing of EU in terms of a vehicle for promoting Italy's international status advanced the party's vision of being a strong right-wing force fighting for Italian national interests abroad.

The analysis of the normalised Italian National Alliance has demonstrated that parties may move categories in the typology of far right Euroscepticism, based on a re-evaluation of their domestic political priorities. The discussion of this case has revealed the various dynamics behind a far right party's decision to change and soften its stance on European integration over time. Ultimately, it has given further weight to the book's argument that a party's position on European integration may be strategically employed at the domestic level for party political purposes. The extent to which a party's strategy may or may not be successful in electoral terms remains, however, outside the scope of this book.

Chapter 7

Conclusion

On the occasion of the 60th anniversary of the signature of the Treaties of Rome in 2017, the leaders of EU member states and of the European Council, the European Parliament and the European Commission met in Rome to reflect on the state of the EU. The ceremonial gathering in Rome resulted in the signing of the Rome Declaration, a short document, that reaffirmed their common interests, values and principles. The document commenced with the pronouncement of European unity:

> We, the Leaders of 27 Member States and of EU institutions, take pride in the achievements of the European Union: the construction of European unity is a bold, far-sighted endeavour. Sixty years ago, recovering from the tragedy of two world wars, we decided to bond together and rebuild our continent from its ashes. We have built a unique Union with common institutions and strong values, a community of peace, freedom, democracy, human rights and the rule of law, a major economic power with unparalleled levels of social protection and welfare.
>
> European unity started as the dream of a few, it became the hope of the many. Then Europe became one again. Today, we are united and stronger: hundreds of millions of people across Europe benefit from living in an enlarged Union that has overcome the old divides (European Union 2017: 1).

The 2017 Rome Declaration confirmed the EU's focus on European citizens, democracy and the rule of law, equal rights and mutually supportive co-operation, and the promotion of stability in the world. The signatories presented the 'Rome agenda', pledging to work towards safety, security, prosperity and sustainability, as well as a social Europe and a stronger Europe on the global scene. After a few paragraphs on these EU commitments, the document concluded:

We as Leaders, working together within the European Council and among our institutions, will ensure that today's agenda is implemented, so as to become tomorrow's reality. We have united for the better. Europe is our common future (European Union 2017: 2).

The declaration carefully avoided an explicit reference to the controversial expression 'multi-speed' Europe. Such co-operation has been considered risky. If multi-speed Europe was applied in a way that breached fundamental EU principles, such as the four freedoms of movement, capital, goods and services, it could potentially lead to the disintegration of the EU. The document insisted on an 'undivided and indivisible Union', but nonetheless accepted that EU states 'will act together, at different paces and intensity where necessary, while moving in the same direction' (European Union 2017: 1). The anniversary of the Treaties of Rome was also accompanied by the launching of the European Commission's White Paper on the Future of Europe a few days earlier on 1 March 2017. Sponsored by Commission President, Jean-Claude Junker, the paper presented five scenarios on how the EU could evolve by 2025, depending on how it chose to respond to contemporary challenges, including terrorism and security, the potential impact of new technologies on society and jobs and the rise of nationalism. The scenarios include 'carrying on', 'nothing but the single market', 'those who want more do more', 'doing less more efficiently' and 'doing much more together'. This White Paper marked the beginning of a process for the EU27 to decide on the future of their Union, and is a testament to the European Commission's realisation that the future of the EU is not guaranteed unless EU member states and institutions agree on a common direction. Interestingly, Junker's choice of five scenarios as opposed to one single strategy is an implicit acknowledgement of EU divisions and the difficulty of ensuring consensus among member states. This illustrates that, far from being a marginal phenomenon, Euroscepticism has become fundamental to the process of European integration.

Both documents were of great symbolic importance. They were written against a backdrop of political and economic insecurity and rising public Euroscepticism. They were issued following the EU's mismanagement of the Eurozone and refugee crises; the real prospect of Brexit as a result of the UK's 23 June 2016 referendum; and a changing international environment with Donald Trump becoming the President of the United States. The Eurozone crisis that erupted towards the end of the 2000s revealed disagreements between EU member states and consolidated the rise of public Euroscepticism (Vasilopoulou 2013). The Greek sovereign debt crisis introduced a – previously unthinkable – debate regarding a member state's place in the EU and the Eurozone and its potential exit. The crisis divided EU member states between those countries that are inside and those that are outside the Eurozone, and between creditor and debtor countries (Glencross 2013; Tsoukalis 2014). The necessity of fiscal transfers as a means of preventing the demise of the Eurozone (Hix 2015) revealed that income redistribution in the EU takes place not only within member states, but also across member states. The crisis resulted in rising public Euroscepticism manifested in the 2014 EP elections when Eurosceptic parties from both the right and the left of the political spectrum claimed victory across Europe. For example, parties with a strong anti-EU agenda were the main winners in Denmark and Britain, which are non-Eurozone members (Halikiopoulou and Vasilopoulou 2014). Euroscepticism was electorally manifested in Germany, a leading Eurozone creditor with no significant history of anti-EU sentiment (Arzheimer 2015). Eurosceptic parties were also on the rise in Greece, a traditionally pro-EU country, but one of the highest Eurozone debtors (Verney 2011, Vasilopoulou et al. 2014).

The migration crisis in 2015 became a source of major disappointment. For some Europeans, it revealed that the EU is poorly equipped to promptly resolve a crisis. For others, it demonstrated that the EU employed the migration crisis in order to gain more powers and encroach on member states' sovereignty. It further exposed substantive disagreements and a lack of co-operation between EU leaders. Member states' reaction towards the EU quota plan for relocating migrants over two years exemplified lack of solidarity with ministers from many EU states arguing that this was an issue of exclusive national sovereignty. Romania, the Czech Republic, Slovakia and Hungary voted against mandatory quotas. This policy prompted a referendum in Hungary on 2 October 2016, asking citizens: 'Do you want the European Union to be able to mandate the obligatory resettlement of non-Hungarian citizens into Hungary even without the approval of the National Assembly?' The Prime Minister publically criticised EU quotas and prompted voters to reject the policy. Although the overwhelming majority of Hungarians rejected EU refugee quotas at 98 per cent, low turnout below the 50 per cent threshold invalidated the referendum.

Both economic and migration crises raised concerns in some member states about the viability of the entire project, and revived discussions over Britain's relationship with the EU. On 23 June 2016, the UK held an in/out referendum, which resulted in popular support for the UK's withdrawal from the EU. Theresa May, the UK Prime Minister, was conspicuous by her absence from the EU leaders' meeting in Rome and did not sign the Rome Declaration. In fact, she was back at home in the UK, preparing a letter that would trigger Article 50, formally beginning the process of withdrawing from the EU. That letter was sent to the President of the European Council a few days later, on 29 March 2017. Brexit raised uncertainty among European circles, with Junker describing it as a failure and a tragedy (*The Guardian* 2017). It received, however, support from the President of the United States, Donald Trump, who praised the UK as being 'smart' for pursuing such a strategy, and has criticised the EU for being a flawed concept (BBC 2017). These developments have further weakened the legitimacy of European integration, signalling once and for all the end of the 'permissive consensus' era (Lindberg and Scheingold 1970). In the context of socio-economic insecurity and rising immigration, widespread opposition has replaced the vision of a strong Europe. The EU project is 'under serious stress' (Cramme and Hobolt 2015: 2).

A PARTY TYPE EXPLANATION OF FAR RIGHT EUROSCEPTICISM

Against the background of growing Euroscepticism, this book tackles one aspect of this phenomenon, i.e., far right party opposition to European integration. Challenging the notion that parties belonging to the same party family adopt similar positions on European integration, this study reveals wide variation in far right party EU attitudes and argumentation. It shows that far right parties display three patterns of opposition to European integration. These are the rejectionist, conditional and compromising patterns, which have been constructed based on the identification of four facets of European integration, including the definition of Europe, the principle, the policy practice and the future building of a European polity.

Why do far right parties oppose the EU to differing extents? To answer this question, this book puts forward a novel theoretical framework that links party type to Euroscepticism. In doing so, it provides a bridge between the literatures on party behaviour, far right parties and the study of Euroscepticism. The book's central argument is that far right parties' EU position responds to a broad set of ideological and strategic incentives, which include their relationship with democracy, their attitude towards the polity, their target electorate/social basis and their behaviour towards competitors. These four indicators allow the categorisation of far right parties into the anti-system, anti-liberal and normalised types. Far right parties are EU issue owners, politicising the question of Europe for electoral purposes. However, they do so in different ways. Anti-system far right parties tend to be rejectionist Eurosceptics, anti-liberal far right parties tend to accept co-operation under conditions and normalised far right parties tend to adopt a compromising position on the EU. This framework suggests that we need to go beyond the ideology versus strategy dichotomy in order to understand the ways in which political parties frame and debate the question of Europe. A party's ideological background may be a broad predictor of its general position on the EU and integration. It is, for example, able to predict that far right and far left parties tend to oppose European integration whereas mainstream Social and Christian Democrat parties tend to support it. When examining within party family differences, however, we need to view ideology and strategy as mutually enforcing, as a party's different relationship with democracy may be associated with a different approach to electoral politics and party competition.

Anti-system Far Right Parties and Rejectionist Euroscepticism

Anti-system parties reject both procedural and liberal democracy, and seek to undermine the legitimacy of the system. Their core principles are antithetical to the values of the regime, and opposition to the system tends to be an opposition of principle. They do not only seek to change the government; they believe in a fundamental change of the system itself. These parties' propaganda and actions stress their difference from all other party competitors, which they consider as part of the very system that they criticise. This anti-systemic character also becomes translated into a rejectionist position regarding the EU. These parties do not accept the principle of co-operation, and they suggest that the EU regime should be abolished. This adversarial strategy towards the EU increases policy divergence and distinguishes anti-system parties from their systemic competitors. It also becomes a strategic electoral tool, allowing these parties to demonstrate to the electorate that they represent a different, powerful and independent actor in the party system. This position serves to polarise the debate and attract a particular segment of the society, which sympathises with this type of non-conformist views. These parties articulate their anti-EU argumentation in a manner unique to their own worldview and dissimilar from all other parties, which allows them to portray themselves as the only real solution to societal problems.

Anti-liberal Far Right-wing Parties and Conditional Euroscepticism

Anti-liberal parties do not reject procedural democracy. They are, however, openly critical of liberal democracy. They tend to oppose the constitutional protection of minority rights and often target minority groups, including religious, ethnic and linguistic minorities in their domestic systems. In contrast to anti-system parties, anti-liberal far right parties seek radical change within the system rather than the change of the system itself. They tend to de-emphasise their radicalism, by arguing that their policies are close to the median voter, or the 'ordinary man'. Although they are keen to retain their core constituencies, they endeavour to also appeal to new voters and attract support from a wider variety of societal groups. Consistent with this electoral agenda, they adopt a conditional Eurosceptic position, i.e., they support the principle of European co-operation with a strong emphasis on intergovern-mental structures and the preservation of national sovereignty. The conditions under which they would accept co-operation relate to what they view as the concerns of the median voter. This allows them to attract anti-EU voters while at the same time cultivating an image of reduced hostility and modera-tion that could open up access to other potential constituencies that agree with the party's ideas but disagree with extremism. This has the dual advantage of differentiating anti-liberal far right parties from other anti-systemic competi-tors domestically, and appearing to occupy a middle – yet niche – ground in the domestic political arena.

Normalised Far Right Parties and Compromising Euroscepticism

In contrast to the above two types, normalised far right parties actively seek to become part of the system. While retaining their nationalism and authoritarianism, these parties are ambivalent – rather than openly critical – towards aspects of liberal democracy. By avoiding controversial statements and policies, they seek to appear to be legitimate government contenders. A compromising position on the EU, i.e., support for the principle and the practice of integration, but opposition to the future building of a European polity, enables them to project an image of support analogous to other main-stream conservative parties in Europe. These parties' Eurosceptic discourse is very nuanced. Their criticisms focus on aspects of European integration rather than the European polity as a whole. Their EU argumentation tends to be of a somewhat constructive character. A rejectionist, or conditional, Eurosceptic position could limit the likelihood of acquiring office, holding portfolios and becoming central in government coalitions. A qualified com-mitment towards the European project, on the other hand, may contribute towards the improvement of the party's reputation both at the national and EU levels. It may also increase the party's probability of occupying a leading role within the domestic centre-right, and thus becomes a tool for institu-tional entrenchment.

The Role of the National Context

One of the main findings of this research project is that the national context affects the way in which a party may choose to debate and/or politicise the question of Europe. This is especially true for far right parties. Given that nationalism is core to their ideology, their EU issue framing is largely conditional upon the specificities of domestic politics and history. Parties do not tend to discuss the EU in isolation. Instead they have a propensity to associate the EU with other issues of domestic relevance and frame it with reference to their own unique worldview. Naturally domestic issues vary from one national context to another, and may be employed in association with the EU issue in order to enhance aspects of party domestic agenda.

The book has shown that far right parties' anti-EU issue framing varies as a function of the interests they traditionally defend at the national level and the specificities of the domestic political context. The French National Front makes a clear connection between the EU and the wider issue of globalisation. It argues that the EU promotes globalisation at a regional level instead of protecting the European states from its dire consequences. It is often argued that the entire project is an American fabrication. The discussion of globalisation is quite prominent in the French context. The National Front's confrontational anti-EU and anti-globalisation agenda allows it to differentiate itself from the mainstream and facilitates its attempt to portray itself as the only party in France providing a 'unique' nationalist solution to new issues and problems, i.e., a return to the nation-state. The Greek LAOS links its Euroscepticism to domestic issues pertaining to Greek foreign and security policy. One of the party's main arguments is that a potential loss of Greek veto power at the EU level may result in Greece's inability to decide on key domestic issues, such as Cyprus and Turkey. These issues resonate well within Greek public opinion and are likely to produce high electoral returns. This choice to frame the question of Europe with reference to Greek security concerns enables the party to portray itself as the 'guardian' of Greek national interests. It also provides it with the opportunity to criticise other competitors for not 'uploading' Greek national interests onto the EU level. The Italian National Alliance associated the EU project with a greater role for Italy on the international arena. The party's EU argumentation was related to its foreign policy aspirations. The EU was seen as a vehicle for the promotion of the Italian image abroad. Italy should assume international responsibilities and become part of the Franco-German axis.

These findings are important for two reasons. First, they suggest that unless the EU issue is connected with an issue of domestic relevance, it bears less significance in and by itself. Second, they reveal that far right parties do not frame the question of Europe primarily in cultural terms. The content analysis of MEP speeches has demonstrated that economy, security, and foreign policy are very prominent frames. This entails that far right parties are increasingly creating a full and multidimensional policy agenda on how to address societal problems that goes beyond culture and immigration.

The Theme of Time

The categories proposed in this book are not fixed. Party behaviour is dynamic rather than static. Parties may transform agendas and shift their positions over time as a function of changing domestic conditions and electoral considerations. This suggests that parties may move from one model to another, and this may have an impact on how they position themselves on the question of Europe. The analysis of the Italian National Alliance reveals the dynamic nature of party positions within a framework of domestic constraints. It illustrates the ways in which shifting electoral interests may impact on EU positions. The National Alliance changed its position on the EU as part of its transition from a neo-fascist, anti-system party to a more moderate political contender. This transition took place within the context of Italian party system change following the collapse of Christian democracy in the early 1990s. From a relatively hard Eurosceptic position in the 1980s and early 1990s, (Conti 2009: 206), the National Alliance moved towards a conciliatory view of European integration in the 2000s. Its precursor, the MSI, recognised the importance of co-operation at the European level, but 'never enthusiastically supported integration because of its fear of loss of national autonomy and independent decision-making' (Kritzinger et al. 2004: 958). From the mid-1990s onwards, however, the party's EU position changed dramatically in line with its strategy of institutional entrenchment, which combined de-radicalisation and normalisation. The party expressed a moderate – yet sceptical – stance towards integration in line with de Gaulle's notion of 'Europe of fatherlands' (Fella and Ruzza 2006: 190). The National Alliance put forward a vision of a 'confederal' Europe of equal member states against a federal superstate.

It is noteworthy that, since Marine Le Pen became the leader of the French National Front in 2011, she has been attempting to modernise the party and improve its political acceptability. However, it is too early to evaluate whether this is a long-term strategy and the extent to which it is supported within the party. As of the time of writing, it has not fundamentally impacted the party's EU position. But if the process of modernisation and de-demonisation continues and is substantive rather than superficial, it is very likely to result in a change of the National Front's position to the EU from rejectionist to conditional Euroscepticism.

EXTENSIONS OF THE THEORY AND DIRECTIONS FOR FUTURE RESEARCH

This book has created a theory linking far right party type to Euroscepticism. It has shown that the development of a party's Euroscepticism should be placed within the context of its constant re-evaluation of where it stands within the party system, and its assessment of how the EU issue may be employed in order to achieve domestic political gains. In line with the most similar systems design, the book has conducted a controlled comparison of three similar far right parties that operate in similar political systems, but exhibit variation in the dependent variable, i.e., Euroscepticism. The three far right parties share the core characteristics of nationalism, authoritarianism and strong leadership, and they function in countries that are governed by a bipolar logic of competition. By choosing this research design, there is a trade-off between the internal and external validity of the argument (Gerring 2012). The analysis has established a causal link between party model and EU position in countries where the logic of party competition is bipolar. By doing so, it opens avenues for future research to examine and test whether this relationship also holds in a different universe of countries. Party models should be related to different party positions on the EU in countries that do not necessarily follow a bipolar logic of competition. For example, we may observe the anti-system National Democratic Party in Germany, which adopts a rejectionist position on the EU; and the anti-liberal Austrian Freedom Party, which puts forward a conditional position on the EU. Future research should thus test this theory's inferential robustness in the wider population of far right cases across Europe.

In constructing the theory linking party type to Euroscepticism, the chapters on individual parties have extensively discussed institutional and electoral incentives provided by each political system. In doing so, they have shown that it depends on individual parties to interpret these incentives and translate them into centripetal or centrifugal positions. There are instances in which more than one far right party operates in the same EU member state, thus facing similar institutional constraints, but adopting a different Eurosceptic position. Italy is an interesting example where three parties operate, but express different attitudes towards European integration. Based on the typology of Euroscepticism put forward in the second chapter of this book, the Italian Tricolour Flame is a case of rejectionist Euroscepticism, the Northern League belongs to the conditional Eurosceptic pattern and, as has been shown extensively in the book, the National Alliance has adopted a compromising Eurosceptic position. In Greece, LAOS has adopted a conditional position on European integration, whereas the Golden Dawn is a rejectionist Eurosceptic party despite the fact that they operate in the same political system. This suggests, therefore, that the effect of institutional incentives on party Euroscepticism is not deterministic. As shown in this book, LAOS is an anti-liberal party seeking to radically change the system from within. In contrast to LAOS, the Golden Dawn is an anti-system party, pursuing the complete delegitimisation of the system, and focusing on the 'need to revive and awaken the nation from its current degenerate condition' (Vasilopoulou and Halikiopoulou 2015: 10). Future research should establish the link between party type and Euroscepticism in a within-country case comparison research design.

This book has created a new framework for explaining Euroscepticism, taking into consideration the ways in which ideology and strategy become mutually reinforcing in determining a party's EU position. This analytical framework may also be extended to other non-mainstream party families, for example, the far left party family (see Table 7.1). This is true – with a caveat. The definition of Europe would need to be refined in order to adapt to different party family visions and representations of Europe. For instance, far left parties tend to define Europe in terms of geography and a space of Western capitalism (e.g. Halikiopoulou et al. 2012). The Greek, French and Cypriot Communist parties all adhere to a class-based analysis of society and economy (e.g. see March 2008; 2011). They are anti-capitalist and fight for workers' rights. Whereas the French and Greek Communist Parties are both electorally marginal, the Cypriot Progressive Party of Working People (AKEL) is an established and strong force in Cypriot politics. These three parties have adopted different positions on the EU. The Greek Communist Party supports Greece's withdrawal from the EU. It equates the EU with capitalism and argues that it exploits the working class. The French Communist Party does not support French EU withdrawal. It accepts the principle that European states should co-operate. But it associates the EU with a neo-liberal, free market economic model alien to the French socialist tradition. It would support the EU under the 'condition' that the latter would adopt a more socialist outlook. AKEL has come to terms with the fact that Cyprus' future is inextricably linked to European integration and, as a result, has supported the country's EU entry. The party views participation in the EU as an opportunity to push for a social Europe against neoliberalism.

The Greek Communist Party's rejectionist approach to European integration may be seen as integral to its anti-systemic character. The party is hostile to liberal democracy, denouncing social democrats and other political forces as bourgeois. It puts emphasis on extra-parliamentary struggle and advocates a different system of governance. In sharp contrast to the Greek party, the French Communist Party has discarded its anti-system credentials. Especially following its participation in Mitterand's government at the

Table 7.1   Wider applicability of the framework of Euroscepticism

EU Position	Far left party family
Rejectionist	Greek Communist Party
Conditional	French Communist Party
Compromising	Progressive Party of Working People

beginning of the 1980s, it adheres to the principles of the French system. It appears less prone to adopt a hard rejectionist position on Europe, and seeks to change the system from within. The EU attitude of the Cypriot AKEL may be seen as related to its role in the party system. It is one of the largest parties in the Assembly, and its General Secretary, Dimitris Christofias, was elected as the President of the Republic of Cyprus from 2008 to 2013.

Future research may be directed towards a systematic analysis of the EU positions within other party families. A number of questions remain: Why do some far left parties reject the EU as an accomplice to global capitalism, whereas others have decided to participate in the EU project and try to change the system from within? Preliminary answers to this question have been provided by Charalambous (2013), who has identified partisan, domestic and international factors influencing Communist parties' EU attitudes. However more systematic analysis is needed in order to place communist parties within specific patterns and identify exact causal mechanisms explaining this variation. In addition, future research should examine possible extensions of this framework to mainstream parties. For example, why are the British Conservatives very reluctant towards the EU project whereas the similarly conservative Greek New Democracy has a strong pro-EU attitude?

The book's model for conceptualising Euroscepticism is based on four indicators: the definition, principle, practice and future of European integration. Future research should test the relevance of this model to other relatively new issue dimensions, such as the environment and climate change. Conceptually, a party's position on key environmental issues may be measured as a function of party stance on the principle of international co-operation; the legal practice of various treaties and conventions regulating the interaction of humans and their natural environment; and the future governing of environmental practice. The book's framework may also shed light on far right party varied positions on the environment (e.g. see Gemenis et al. 2012).

The findings have also demonstrated that far right parties frame their Euroscepticism with reference to the domestic political environment. Future research is needed to systematically examine which national issues political parties tend to associate with the European issue. Are some issues emphasised in relation to the EU more in some contexts or by specific types of parties rather than others? Has this emphasis changed over time? What has been the effect of the Eurozone and the migration crises on this association? Two of the parties examined in this book, the Greek Popular Orthodox Rally and the Italian National Alliance, have linked the question of Europe to their national security and foreign policies, respectively. It would be illuminating to assess whether this connection is more prominent among parties of the right, or whether it also exists among the parties of the left. It could be argued that Europe belongs by definition to the realm of foreign policy and that this focus is consistent with far right party ideology. However, given increased political and economic interpenetration of the national and EU spheres, and the debate on whether more integration is needed in order to manage the crisis, the EU may no longer be seen as exclusively an issue of foreign policy. Related to this, how does the issue of globalisation feature in the anti-EU rhetoric of other parties? Is this a criticism that may be found only within anti-system parties, or it is becoming more widespread as a result of the Eurozone crisis?

Further research should also examine whether party rank-and-file members constrain party positions on European integration. Is there a difference of positions across the different organisational levels of political parties? Research has thus far shown that party elites tend to adopt less rigid positions compared to party members (Bochel and Denver 1983; Panebianco 1988). We still do not know whether the EU positions of the party in central office and the party in public office converge with or diverge from the positions of the party on the ground (for a short analysis of Conservative party members, see Webb and Bale 2014). Research has shown that the leader of the Italian National Alliance did not fully consult the party prior to making decisions (Fella 2006; Ruzza and Fella 2009). It would thus be informative to know whether Fini's participation in the Convention for the Future of Europe was an act endorsed by party members, or whether, by contrast, Fini went beyond the wishes of party members in order to increase his party's and his own personal status abroad. Questions of far right leaders' responsiveness towards their members remain largely under-researched.

CONCLUSION

Given that nationalism and authoritarianism are central to far right parties' belief systems, their negative attitudes towards the EU seem consistent with their ideologies. Cultural diversity and supranational decision-making promoted by the EU run counter to the far right's mission of defending the nation. The EU also promotes European citizenship and access to rights, pluralistic decision-making structures, cultural tolerance and social inclusiveness. The EU is a unique system run by complicated institutional arrangements, often seen as distant from the people. This book shows that – contrary to theoretical expectations – these parties do not oppose the EU project to the same extent. The way in which they frame, discuss and politicise the EU issue exhibits a great degree of variation. These positions are dependent upon party type, i.e., what this book terms the anti-system, anti-liberal or normalised categories, and have been governed by different domestic considerations.

More broadly, this project provides insights into the ways in which the dynamics of party competition and different party strategies across EU member states may influence the EU issue dimension, and how Euroscepticism may also shape domestic party politics. It brings party competition back into the analysis of Euroscepticism, and illustrates that it is increasingly problematic 'to talk in universal terms about a single contest over European integration' (Taggart 2006: 20). Within a wider context of global transformations, it is impossible to understand the process of European integration without unpacking specific party strategies within different European political systems. It is equally impossible to understand domestic politics without analysing Euroscepticism. This book can be seen as an important step towards the systematic integration of the comparative study of European domestic politics with the study of the EU.

Appendix

Coding MEP Speeches

Conventional content analysis of MEP speeches has been employed in order to examine how each far right party has chosen to frame the EU issue in the European Parliament. The coding consists of a total of 2,720 speeches of the MEPs of the French National Front, the Greek LAOS and the Italian National Alliance (Table A.1). These are available on the European Parliament's online archives at http://www.europarl.europa.eu/. The aim is to observe salient issues of Euroscepticism, as they are developed in the speeches of the three parties' elected representatives. This enables the assessment of the level of congruence between the attitudes of two faces of party organisation, that is whether the party in the central office, which produces the party literature, and the party in the public office, which delivers the speeches, are united on the EU issue, both in terms of their overall position and in their precise argumentation.

Content analysis is a technique for compressing large amounts of text into categories in a systematic manner. It is an 'empirically grounded method, exploratory in process, and predictive or inferential in intent' (Krippendorff

Table A.1 Number of speeches per party per EP term

EP term	France National Front	Greece Popular Orthodox Rally	Italy National Alliance	
5th 1999–2004	302	-	196	
6th 2004–2009	778	123	296	
7th 2009–2014	435	590	-	
Total	1,515	713	492	Total 2,720

2004: xvii), used to make valid and replicable inferences from texts. It provides a numerical description of an otherwise long text, indicating the presence or absence of specific issues in a text. The inferences drawn from the analysis are context-dependent. Its purpose is to 'identify and count the occurrence of specific characteristics of dimensions of texts, and through this, to be able to say something about the messages, images, representations of such texts and their wider significance' (Anders 1998). Because this type of analysis is 'useful for examining trends and patterns in documents' (Stemler 2001), it has been adopted for the purpose of processing MEP speeches.

The two main approaches to content analysis include emergent versus a priori coding (Stemler 2001), or inductive versus deductive coding (Elo and Kyngs 2008). Emergent or inductive content analysis involves identifying themes during the coding procedure. It is used when the main aim of the study is to describe a phenomenon, particularly in cases where literature is scarce. A priori or deductive content analysis tends to be based on a predetermined codebook or coding dictionary. Such an empirical approach is preferred when an existing theory or prior research exists about a specific phenomenon (Hsieh and Shannon 2005; Elo and Kyngs 2008). For the purposes of this analysis, a priori coding was preferred. Coders were provided with a codebook, which identified common themes that might arise as a result of the EP's agenda, including EU economy and economic policies, EU enlargement, EU environment and energy, EU foreign and security policy, etc. Within these themes, coders were free to create relevant subthemes in order to identify the precise topics to which the MEPs referred. To allow for party specificities, coders were also free to create additional overall themes, if this was necessary. This coding strategy captures the comparative salience of themes, as well as potential party-specific differences.

All calculations were based on the frequency of sentences. A 'core sentence' was defined as a sentence with a 'subject-verb relationship'. Phrases that did not include a verb were not considered as core sentences, and they were therefore not coded (for a similar technique, see Vasilopoulou et al. 2014). Each core sentence was coded once. This method produced a set of proportions per theme. The data were organised and coded manually using NVivo, which is a text-analysis software.

Notes

CHAPTER 1

1. Other potential explanations may include a country's historical relationship to fascism and a party's prior electoral success. Extensive discussion of how these variables have interacted with far right party strategies is included in subsequent chapters.

2. Based on the typology and identification of different patterns of Euroscepticism, the National Alliance is the only Western European party that belongs to the 'compromising' type. Other 'compromising' Eurosceptics include the Latvian TB-LNNK. Operating in Eastern Europe, however, makes TB-LNNK less comparable to the French National Front and the Greek LAOS. The Italian Northern League is not included in the place of the National Alliance because this party belongs to the 'conditional' Eurosceptic pattern. In addition, this party has a strong regionalist component, which would also increase variation in the controlled comparison.

CHAPTER 2

1. Capitals in the original. The TEU has been selected as the major Treaty establishing the European Union. Member state commitments are also deduced from the Lisbon Treaty, establishing the functioning of the European Union, which was signed in 2007 and entered into force in 2009.

2. Note that this definition of European identity directly applies to the far right's worldview and may not necessarily be shared by other parties or by the European public. For a detailed discussion of European identity from the citizens' perspective, see Bruter, M. (2005).

3. To clarify, the patterns suggested here are devised in order to provide useful information regarding party positions and discourse. They have indeed an ordinal character, namely, ranging from more to less opposition against the EU. However, measuring the exact distance between them is outside the scope of this chapter.

4. The analysis does not include the United Kingdom Independence Party. Although UKIP has been increasingly employing radical right themes, such as opposition to immigration wrapped in a populist rhetoric (Ford and Goodwin 2015), its establishment as a single-issue anti-EU party (Usherwood 2008) would not make it comparable for the purposes of this study. The Italian National Alliance is included, however, because of its fascist roots.

5. I acknowledge that each party's EU position may be nuanced and that there may be private disagreements within the party over the question of Europe. Given that manifestos represent official party programmes, however, they constitute the most reliable documents to assess a party's public stance.

6. Original: 'Sortir la France de l'Union européenne'.

7. Original: 'La France doit-elle reprendre son indépendance vis-à-vis de l'Europe de Bruxelles?'

8. Original: 'Liberons la France'.

9. Original: 'Leur Europe n'est pas la notre'.

10. The party has not substantively changed policies over time; its 2013 manifesto is a slightly updated version of its 2006 manifesto.

11. Original: 'Αποδέσμευση από διεθνείς οργανισμούς που δεν εξυπηρετούν τα εθνικά μας συμφέροντα. Ναι στην Ευρώπη των Εθνών, όχι στην Ευρώπη του κεφαλαίου και των τοκογλύφων'.

12. Original: 'μπορούμε μαζί να κάνουμε την Ελλάδα μεγάλη, κυρίαρχη και ανεξάρτητη'.

13. Original: 'Πρέπει να προωθήσουμε την ένωση όλων των Ευρωπαϊκών Λαών. Να ξεπεράσουμε παλιές έχθρες και αντιπαλότητες και αναδείξουμε τα στοιχεία εκείνα που μας ενώνουν, ώστε να δημιουργήσουμε μια πανίσχυρη Ένωση, από τον Ατλαντικό ως τα Ουράλια και πιο πέρα, που θα σέβεται όμως τις ιδιαιτερότητες του κάθε Έθνους και θα κατανοεί παράλληλα την κοινή μας καταγωγή'.

14. Original: 'The EU is a - Unia Europejska jest taką poza- i ponadnarodową strukturą quasi-państwową. Posiada interesy często rozbieżne z interesami poszczególnych narodów'.

15. Original: 'Unia Europejska dąży do wygaszenia narodowych kultur'.

16. Original: 'Unia Europejska znosi niepodległość poszczególnych państw'.

17. Original in English.

18. Original: 'Európa hármas talapzatra épült: a görög gondolkodásra, a római jogra és a keresztény erkölcsre'.

19. Original: 'Közösen megvalósítjuk a Nemzetek Európáját, amely a nemzetek sokszínűségére, egyenlőségére és kölcsönös érdekazonosságára épül'.

20. Original: 'Es gründet in der christlich-abendländischen Wertegemeinschaft'.

21. Original in English.

22. Original: 'Die FPÖ bekennt sich zu einem Europader freien und unabhängigen Vaterländer im Rahmen eines Staatenbundes souveräner Nationalstaaten'.

23. Original: 'Die FPÖ fordert die Aufrechterhaltung der Souveränität Österreichs in einem Europa der Vaterländer'.

24. Original: 'Das Zusammenwachsen Europas wird nur dann von Erfolg gekrönt sein, wenn es ohne Übereilung, auf Basis gleichberechtigter Zusammenarbeit der

Staaten und von deren Bevölkerungen getragen, erfolgt. Dies kann nur im Rahmen eines Staatenverbundes geschehen, der der historisch gewachsenen Vielfalt unseres Kontinents Rechnung trägt'.

25. Original: 'De EU vertoont steeds meer totalitaire trekken'.

26. Original: 'Het Vlaams Belang is voorstander van een confederaal Europa dat de eigenheid en het zelfbeschikkingsrecht van de naties respecteert. Geen Europese superstaat, maar een intergouvernementeel of confederaal samenwerkingsverband van soevereine naties'.

27. Original: 'Verenigd Europa ja, superstaat EU neen Wij zijn tegen een EU-superstaat die steeds dieper ingrijpt in de interne aangelegenheden van de verschillende lidstaten; de natiestaten zijn en blijven de peilers van verdere Europese samenwerking'.

28. Original: 'Een federaal Europa is onmogelijk en ongewenst omdat Europa een mozaïek is van volkeren, allemaal met een eeuwenoude geschiedenis, met een eigen taal en cultuur, rechtstraditie en met eigen specifieke collectieve doelstellingen. Er bestaat geen Europese identiteit in dezelfde zin als er een Amerikaanse identiteit is. Niemand beschouwt zich in de eerste plaats Europeaan en pas daarna Italiaan of Zweed'.

29. Original: 'Naast de ordelijke opdeling van België wil het Vlaams Belang een ordelijke ontmanteling van de EU en van de Eurozone [...]Het Vlaams Belang wil opnieuw een vrijwillige Europese (intergouvernementele) samenwerking zoals die bestond voor het Verdrag van Maastricht'.

30. Original: 'la realizzazione di un'Europa che sia una libera associazione dei popoli europei'.

31. Original: 'L'Europa dei Popoli non è quindi un Super Stato neo-centralista guidato da tecnocrati politicamente irresponsabili del loro operato'.

32. Original: 'si deve cercare di costruire un'Europa fondata sul rispetto delle realtà nazionali e territoriali, cedendo all'Unione Europea solo una limitata parte di sovranità,delimitando chiaramente le proprie competenze; vanno delimitati con precisione gli ambiti di intervento dell'Unione Europea, evitando norme ambigue ed indefinite'.

33. Original: 'Integrare significa ricercare tutto ciò che è comune e valorizzare tutto ciò che è specifico'.

34. Original: 'Ecco perché vogliamo un'Unione europea retta su un modello confederale, in cui i vari Stati membri mantengano inalterate le proprie sovranità, e dove le Regioni e i territori vedano riconosciuti le proprie specificità e differenze'.

35. Original: 'Più Europa dei Popoli, meno euro-burocrazia [...] Elezione popolare diretta del Presidente della Commissione europea, e ampliamento della potestà legislativa del Parlamento europeo'.

36. Original: 'Dansk Folkeparti ønsker et venskabeligt og dynamisk samarbejde med alle demokratiske og frihedselskende nationer i verden, men vi vil ikke acceptere, at Danmark afgiver suverænitet. Heraf følger, at Dansk Folkeparti er modstander af Den Europæiske Union'.

37. Original: 'Det betyder, at intet må sættes højere end den danske Grundlov'.

38. Original: 'Vi er modstandere af udviklingen i EU, som går i retning af Europas Forenede Stater. Dansk Folkeparti ønsker et tæt og venskabeligt samarbejde i Europa,

men samarbejdet skal begrænses til områder som handelspolitik, miljøpolitik og teknisk samarbejde. Vi er modstandere af indførelsen af en europæisk politisk union'.

39. Original: 'Dansk Folkeparti mener, at EU´s funktioner skal indskrænkes til at omfatte: * opgaver, som store befolkningsflertal i medlemslandene ønsker at løse gennem EU, ** opgaver, hvis grænseoverskridende karakter nødvendiggør fælles løsninger, *** opgaver, for hvilke der er afgørende stordriftsfordele i fælles løsninger'.

40. Original: 'Ο ΛΑ.Ο.Σ. δεν αρνείται την ευρωπαϊκή ταυτότητα της Ελλάδος'.

41. Original: 'Η ενσωμάτωση επομένως της χώρας μας στη Ε.Ε. μπορεί να γίνει μόνο στα πλαίσια μιας Συνομοσπονδίας και υπό τον όρο ότι θα προστατεύεται η ιδιαιτερότητά μας'.

42. Original: 'Εμείς δεχόμαστε μια Ευρώπη των Εθνών'.

43. Original: 'Στοχεύει μάλιστα στην αλλοτρίωση της εθνικής ταυτότητας και την κατάργηση της διαφορετικότητας των λαών'.

44. For Fatherland and Freedom/LNNK dissolved in 2011 and merged into the National Alliance.

45. Original: 'non annullando gli Stati nazionali bensì costituendo una Confederazione di Statinazione; in questo senso gli Stati e gli interessi nazionali contribuiscono e non sono di ostacolo alla formazione dell'interesse e delle priorità europei'.

46. Original: 'Ma la Destra ha anche sempre affermano il valore di un'Europa delle nazioni, ricchezza plurima di identità e culture, che vanno alimentate e rispettate e non possono essere annullate in un super Stato informe'.

47. Original: 'di nuovi paesi in un'Europa che si amplia geograficamente e politicamente, a cominciare dai icini prossimi dove massima è la proiezione italiana (Europa sud-orientale e balcanica)'.

48. Original: 'Eiropas Savienības darba kārtības jautājumu apspriešana ir svarīga, taču tā nevar aizvietot patstāvīgu ārpolitiku un ilgtermiņa mērķus'.

49. Original: 'Mēs stiprināsim ES valstu nacionālo suverenitāti'.

50. Original: 'Mēs atbalstām tādu Eiropu, kur atbildība un pienākumi tiek solidāri dalīti starp ES un dalībvalstīm, nevis federālas Eiropas "supervaras" radīšanu. ES kompetencē jābūt tiem jautājumiem, kuros tā var rīkoties efektīvāk nekā individuāla dalībvalsts'.

51. Original: 'Eiropas Parlamenta tribīne nedrīkst tikt izmantota Latvijas un citu dalībvalstu suverenitātes graušanai'.

CHAPTER 4

1. Original: 'Front d'opposition nationale pour l'Europe des patries'.

2. Following the election, Joëlle Bergeron became an independent and joined the Europe of Freedom and Direct Democracy (EFDD).

3. Original: 'On a le devoir d'aller aider les pays pauvres. Mais les Français d'abord'.

4. Original: 'Nous voulons aider l'Afrique. Mais nous voulons les aider chez eux. Non pas chez l'Europe'.

5. Original: 'accélèrent la décomposition du tissu social et des solidarités naturelles'.

6. Original: 'notre tradition européenne, parmi lesquels quatre essentiellement: la philosophie grecque, le droit romain, la spiritualité judéo-chrétienne et les lumières'.

7. Original: 'a inventé la liberté et l'égalité des Nations, se gouvernant librement, sans ingérence extérieure, modèle unique et sans équivalent ailleurs'.

8. Original: 'Seules des nations libres, puissantes et souveraines, rendront à la civilisation européenne son éclat dans le monde'.

9. Original: 'les Russes sont une grande nation européenne'.

10. Original: 'Mais la Russie, contrairement à la Turquie, appartient culturellement, spirituellement, géographiquement à l'espace européen'.

11. Original: 'une Europe « européenne », donc sans la Turquie, mais liée à la Russie'.

12. Original (in both manifestos): 'traités liant la France à l'Union européenne de Bruxelles (Rome, l'Acte Unique, Schengen, Maastricht, Amsterdam)'.

13. Original: 'La France doit-elle reprendre son indépendance vis-à-vis de l'Europe de Bruxelles?'.

14. Original: 'L'euro crée les disparités et mène a la catastrophe. C'est la concurrence déloyale parmi les pays'.

15. Original: 'Loin de conforter l'économie européen et française, il en accélère la mondialisation, c'est-àdire la fragilité structurelle'.

16. Original: 'Les Etas membres de l'UE peuvent faire face à la crise eux-mêmes'.

17. Original : 'Il faut [...] retrouver notre monnaie nationale pour garantir le pouvoir d'achat de nos compatriotes'.

18. Original: 'l'agriculture européenne est morte'.

19. Original: 'Le seul accès possible à la citoyenneté d'un pays est d'avoir la nationalité de ce pays'.

20. Original: 'une Europe des patries fondée sur la souveraineté de ses Etats, sur la préférence communautaire et sur des frontières la protégeant notamment de l'immigration et des délocalisations'.

21. Original: 'ultime étape avant le gouvernement mondial'.

22. Interviews with party officials have revealed a degree of internal variation in terms of intensity of opposition to the EU. Although, by and large, all interviewees disagreed with the EU project, blunt opposition to European integration came mostly (but not exclusively) from those politicians who have in some capacity worked in the EP. The EP seems to have thus produced a negative socialisation effect to the party's politicians (Kerr 1973; Hooghe 2001).

23. Original: 'nous ont été les premiers eurosceptiques en France'.

24. Original: 'on a la même position sur l'UE avec l'extrême gauche. Mais la justification est différente. A savoir, le patriotisme économique'.

25. Original: 'la volonté de garder la proéminence de la nation'.

26. Original: 'De Villiers est vendu à l'UMP'.

27. Another reason for this is that they saw Sarkozy as a more credible candidate compared to Jean-Marie Le Pen (Mayer 2007: 441).

28. Original: "On ne nous donne pas la parole. Ça a aiguisé notre revendication'.

29. Original: 'Nous sommes emprisonnés à l'intérieur de l'UE. C'est une prison', 'Nous n'avons pas besoin d'un méchant'; and 'Le PE, c'est une mascarade'.

30. Original: 'L'Union européenne ensuite, cheval de Troie de la mondialisation ultralibérale : les Traités européens imposent depuis le Traité de Maastricht le dogme de la concurrence libre et non faussée, interdisent [...] toute forme de patriotisme économique'.

31. Original: 'Nous sommes voilà simplement devant une étape supplémentaire de la globalisation à marche forcée, qui commence par l'uniformisation au niveau européen'.

32. Original: 'L'Europe, non seulement n'est pas une protection pour les entreprises françaises, mais elle contribue à accélérer la déréglementation, la libéralisation des services et l'ouverture à la concurrence mondiale'.

33. Original: 'L'UE a sacrifié l'agriculture française à l'Amérique [...] le marché répond à sa propre logique'.

34. Original : 'Victimes de la mondialisation, les agriculteurs français payent les conséquences d'une politique agricole européenne désastreuse'.

35. Original: 'La vague sauvage de l'ultralibéralisme et du libre-échange débridé qui, depuis 20 ans, déferlait et cassait nos charbonnages, nos aciéries, nos industries du textile, du cuir, de la machine-outil, de l'électroménager ou de l'automobile et semait la désertification dans nos ports de pêche, nos vignobles du Languedoc-Roussillon, nos élevages ovins, bovins, aviaires, nos bananeraies des Antilles, nos plantations de la Réunion, nos fermes, plongeant les femmes, les hommes, les ouvrières et les travailleurs de nos pays dans l'insécurité sociale, s'est cassée elle-même sur la volonté du peuple français exprimée par le référendum du 29 mai 2005'.

36. Ahead of the 2009 EP elections, Carl Lang and Jean-Claude Martinez left the party to run against the official National Front list.

37. Original: 'un espace euro-mondialiste ouvert à tous les vents, à tous les flux de personnes, de marchandises et de capitaux'.

38. Original: 'Le Monde est malade, L'Europe est malade. La France est malade'.

39. Original: 'Contre l'Europe des Banksters'.

40. Original: 'J'irai rendre aux Français les quatre souverainetés que l'Union européenne leur a volées. Je veux offrir aux Français une France juste, une France fière, une France durable, une France prospère'.

41. Original: 'Notre électorat est pauvre que souffre; victime de la mondialisation et de l'Europe. Nous somme porteurs des angoisses et interrogations des français'.

42. Original: 'Ils nous votent pour les conséquences de la globalisation, c'est-à-dire chômage, immigration, bas pouvoir d'achat, acquis sociaux perdus et insécurité'.

43. Original: 'notre position est vraiment la position de notre électorat'.

CHAPTER 5

1. Note that Costas Karamanlis was the Greek Prime Minister from 2004 to 2007 and from 2007 to 2009. Not to be confused with his uncle, Kostantinos Karamanlis,

who was the Greek Prime Minister from 1955 to 1958, from 1958 to 1961, from 1961 to 1963 and from 1974 to 1980, under various political alignments.

2. Original: 'Ο Λεπέν εκφράζει μια ιδιάζουσα φασιστική νοοτροπία, την οποία εγώ θεωρώ εχθρό της κοινωνίας και της δημοκρατίας'.

3. See https://www.youtube.com/watch?v=nuI-jazug70, accessed 8 December 2016.

4. Original: ''Ολους εμάς ενώνει η Ελλάς'.

5. Original: 'Είναι ένα κόμμα ελληνοκεντρικό, που προτάσσει τα μακροπρόθεσμα συμφέροντα του ελληνικού λαού, και του έθνους, διαπνέεται από τον ελληνικό πολιτισμό, το ελληνικό πνεύμα και τις ελληνικές αξίες στην χάραξη και εφαρμογή της πολιτικής του'.

6. See https://www.youtube.com/watch?list=PL321vpJQ29Q0zkNpWZx8Zmgh LRB9ueoIH&v=S0H11lk7xf0, accessed on 8 December 2016.

7. Original: 'την εκκλησία, που χάρις σ'αυτήν γίναμε έθνος ελεύθερο μετά από τέσσερις αιώνες δουλείας και σκλαβιάς'.

8. Original: 'να είναι Έλληνες στη ψυχή και στο πνεύμα'.

9. Original: 'Αποτελούν τη σοβαρότερη πληγή που ταλανίζει αυτήν τη στιγμή την ελληνική κοινωνία με πολλαπλές καταστροφικές συνέπειες σε διάφορους τομείς'.

10. Original: 'λόγω του μικρού αριθμού των κατοίκων της, έχει ήδη αλλοιωθεί σημαντικά η αναλογία του πληθυσμού της'.

11. Original: 'Η Δύση άλλωστε ανήκει στην Ελλάδα, αφού θεμελιώθηκε πάνω στις αρετές που γέννησε ο δικός μας πολιτισμός, όπως η Δημοκρατία, ο ανθρωπισμός, η έρευνα, το μέτρο και η αρμονία'.

12. Original: 'η Τουρκία δεν έχει θέση στην Ευρωπαϊκή Ένωση για γεωγραφικούς, πολιτισμικούς, θρησκευτικούς και πολιτικούς λόγους'.

13. Original: 'Δεν είναι ένα δογματικά αντί-ευρωπαϊκό κόμμα, χωρίς ωστόσο να αποδέχεται ότι «θα πρέπει να εκχωρήσουμε στην Ευρωπαϊκή Ένωση ακόμα και εξουσίες που ακυρώνουν την εθνική μας κυριαρχία»'.

14. Original: 'Δεχόμαστε δηλαδή ένα σύστημα που θα προάγει την συνεργασία των Ευρωπαϊκών Λαών στον τομέα της οικονομίας, της κοινωνικής πολιτικής και του πολιτισμού'.

15. Original: 'Ο ΛΑ.Ο.Σ. είναι υπέρ την ενωμένης Ευρώπης των ΕΘΝΩΝ'.

16. Original: 'όπου θα αναγνωρίζονται και θα προστατεύονται οι ιστορικές τόσο οι πολιτισμικές και οι εθνικές ρίζες όσο και τα ιδιαίτερα εθνικά χαρακτηριστικά των Ευρωπαϊκών λαών'.

17. Original: 'το δικαίωμα του βέτο για τα ζωτικά της θέματα'.

18. Party leader interview on RealFM, 28 March 2014, https://www.youtube.com/watch?v=RFj9Hu9HKs8, accessed on 11 December 2016.

19. Quote from the interview in Greek: 'εμείς υποστηρίζουμε ότι μέσω του Ευρωσκεπτικισμού πηγάζουν ποτελέσματα που θα κάνουν οικεία την ΕΕ στους πολίτες. Ενθεμελίωση της ΕΕ με βάση τους πολίτες'.

20. Original: 'Η μεγαλύτερη απάτη σε βάρος των λαών της Ευρώπης'.

21. Original: 'Και ποιος εγγυάται, κύριε Υφυπουργέ, ότι αν αύριο το πρωί με τη Συνθήκη επικυρωμένη θα έχετε ξανά το δικαίωμα του βέτο απέναντι στα Σκόπια'.

22. Original: 'όχι η κατάργησή τους μέσα σε ένα Αμερικανικού τύπου χωνευτήρι των λαών'.

23. Quote from the interview in Greek: 'Η ΕΕ θέλει τον αποχριστιανισμό της Ευρώπης'.

24. Original: 'Εμείς δεν θέλουμε ομοσπονδία. Θέλουμε συνομοσπονδία εθνών κρατών. Δεν είμαστε κατά της ΕΕ. Ούτε πιστεύουμε στην αποχώρηση της Ελλάδας. Η Ελλάδα έχει ωφεληθεί από την ΕΕ. Δεν θέλουμε την κατάργηση της ανεξαρτησίας για θέματα εθνικά πχ. Σκόπια και Τουρκία'.

25. It is outside the scope of the chapter to discuss the initial rise of LAOS (Gemenis and Dinas 2010; Tsiras 2012). Taking this relative success for granted and the constraints provided by the Greek party system, it seeks to explain how the issue of European integration sits within the party's wider strategy.

26. 'Disproportionality' refers to vote-seat disproportionality as measured using the least squares index (Gallagher and Mitchell 2004: Appendix B). The scale runs from 0 to 100, 0 being full proportionality and 100 full disproportionality. Effective number of parties at the legislative level refers to the level of fragmentation of seats (Laakso and Taagapera 1979).

27. Examples during the 1990s of splinter parties that did not last long in the Greek political landscape include Political Spring and the Democratic Social Movement (splinter parties from ND and PASOK, respectively).

28. Original: 'Το ΛΑΟΣ αντιπροσωπεύει το μέσο Έλληνα'.

29. Original: 'Εμείς υιοθετούμε την Αριστοτέλεια λογική της μεσότητας'.

30. Original: 'Μπορεί να μην είμαστε mainstream, λόγω του ότι δεν έχουμε κυβερνήσει. Έχουμε όμως mainstream ιδέες'.

31. Original: 'Δεν υπάρχει λοιπόν διπολισμός. Τους δοκίμασαν. Ο δικός μας ο λόγος έχει ευήκοα ώτα από την κομμουνιστική Αριστερά και αριστερότερα αυτής, μέχρι την άκρα Δεξιά. Μας ακούνε όλοι γιατί λέμε τα αυτονόητα. [...] Εμείς δεν έχουμε αγκυλώσεις, ό,τι καλό το παίρνουμε. Πατριώτες υπάρχουν σε όλα τα κόμματα'.

32. Original: 'Ήρθαμε για να μείνουμε και θα μείνουμε!'.

33. Original: 'Όποιος αποδέχεται αυτή την ανάλυση είναι ενταγμένοι στον πατριωτικό χώρο ανεξαρτήτως πολιτικής πεποίθησης πχ. ΝΔ, ΠΑΣΟΚ κτλ. Ανεξαρτ ήτως πολιτικού χώρου, αν αποδέχεται τη μήτρα της γέννησης, εμείς τον δεχόμαστε. Είναι αποδεκτός'.

34. Original: 'Οι ψηφοφόροι του ΛΑ.Ο.Σ. προέρχονται απ'όλα τα πολιτικά ρεύματα'.

35. Original: 'σε πολιτικό επίπεδο, έχει κατορθώσει η ατζέντα του να συμπίπτει με την πραγματική αντζέντα της κοινωνίας'.

36. Original: 'Και στην Ευρώπη πηγαίνουμε με στόχους'.

37. Original: 'Πιστεύουμε ότι η χώρα μας πρέπει να έχει μία υπερκομματική εθνική Εξωτερική πολιτική, με συνέχεια, με δυναμική, με συνέπεια και, κυρίως, με διαχρονική στρατηγική που θα διαμορφώνεται με αποκλειστικό κριτήριο το Συμφέρον της χώρας μας και του Ελληνικού Έθνους'.

38. Original: 'Αυτή η φωνή θα υψωθεί και θα συγκλονίσει τους Ευρωπαίους μέσα στο Ευρωκοινοβούλιο από τους βουλευτάς του Λαϊκού Ορθόδοξου Συναγερμού

που εσείς με την ψήφο σας θα στείλετε στις Βρυξέλλες και το Στρασβούργο. Μια φωνή που θα ξαναφωνάζει όχι στην αδικία, όχι στον ενδοτισμό. Μία φωνή που θα ακούσουν όχι μόνο οι Ευρωπαίοι αλλά και οι Έλληνες υπεύθυνοι που με την υποχωρητικότητα και τον ενδοτισμό τους κινδυνεύουν να γράψουν την πιο μαύρη σελίδα της Ελληνικής ιστορίας. Γενιές Ελλήνων με θυσίες μεγάλωσαν και κράτησαν όρθια την Ελλάδα. Της χάρισαν αξιοπρέπεια, αναγνώριση, σεβασμό και γόητρο. Ιδιότητες που δυστυχώς σήμερα θυσιάζονται στο βωμό ιδιοτελών σκοπιμοτήτων. Στόχος όλων μας πρέπει να είναι η απομόνωση των συμβιβασμών και υποχωρητικών συνειδήσεων. Εδώ και στη Ευρώπη! Πρώτα η Ελλάδα.Μ' αυτό το σύνθημα εμείς θα δώσουμε την μάχη μας στην Ευρώπη'.

39. Original: 'Μνημείο υποχωρητικότητας, ύμνο εις την ποδολειχία και έπαινο εις την εθνική μειοδοσία, αποτελεί η ψήφος μεγάλου μέρους των εθνικών κομματικών αντιπροσώπων μας στο Ευρωπαϊκό Κοινοβούλιο. [...] Ψήφοι Ελλήνων Ευρωβουλευτών μεταβλήθηκαν σε βέλη κατά της πατρίδας. Δεν τους κατηγορούμε για αργυροφρενίτιδα. Δεν τους κατηγορούμε για εγγενή ολιγοφρένεια. Τους καλούμε όμως να εξηγήσουν με ποίου την εντολή και έναντι ποίου ανταλλάγματος με την ψήφο τους ελάκτισαν ή εσύλησαν το ιερό σώμα της Μακεδονίας'.

40. Original: 'Μου λένε, γιατί επιμένεις και λες να μην μπει η Τουρκία στην Ευρώπη; Γιατί ακούω, αφουγκράζομαι την καρδιά, την ψυχή και τη συνείδηση του Έλληνα, που σε δημοσκόπηση σε μεγάλη εφημερίδα είπε, το 78%, δεν θέλουμε την Τουρκία στην Ευρώπη'.

41. Original: 'Είμαστε το μόνο κόμμα που δίνει μάχη στην ΕΕ'.

42. Original: 'Ο «ΛΑ.Ο.Σ.» σήμερα εκφράζει πειστικά τις πολιτικές εκείνες θέσεις που ικανοποιούν το κοινό αίσθημα'.

43. Original: 'Ποιοί Ευρωβουλευτές χωρίς αιδώ αποκάλυπτα και χωρίς αναστολές προασπίζοντα τα συμφέροντα Τούρκων και Σκοπιανών!'.

44. The party did not issue an official manifesto for the 2014 EP elections.

CHAPTER 6

1. *In Fini* (2003), 47–48.

2. Original: 'Un popolo senza coscienza nazionale non solo è dimentico del proprio passato, ma è disgregato nel presente e privo di avvenire'.

3. Original: 'un sano sentimento di nazionalità non va confuso con il nazionalismo'.

4. Original: 'L'Italia è il luogo che ha sintetizzato meglio di altri la filosofia greca, inverata dal cristianesimo, la tradizione giuridica e politica romana, l'articolazione sociale medievale, le migliori intuizioni dell'Umanesimo, in un insieme organico e non confuso di lingua e di religione'.

5. Original: 'il genio italiano ha contribuito a diffondere il genio europeo nel mondo, dando forma politica e sostanza culturale ad altri territori'.

6. Original: 'L'idea dell' "Europa delle Patrie", propria del gollismo degli anni '60, può garantire, attraverso un intelligente adeguamento, quell'unità storica degli Stati Nazionali che è peculiare caratteristica della civiltà del continente'.

7. Original: 'L'Europa costituisce, per Alleanza Nazionale, un riferimento culturale e spirituale frutto della storia e delle specificità di suoi popoli, dall'antica Grecia alla romanità, alla Cristianità'.

8. Original: 'qualcosa di più profondo, una certa forma di civiltà quale si è stratificata in secoli di storia'.

9. Original: 'La Patria europea'.

10. Original: 'Quando parliamo di valori, quali la dignità della persona umana, lo Stato di diritto, la solidarietà, il valore della famiglia, il rispetto della vita, senza accorgercene facciamo un riferimento ai quei principi che le radici giudaico-cristiane hanno donato all'Europa'.

11. Original: 'l'inserimento di un riferimento alle radici giudaico-cristiane diventa un riconoscimento dell'unità secolare'.

12. Original: 'Auspichiamo che la Conferenza intergovernativa, per quanto riguarda il preambolo, trovi un accordo per il riconoscimento delle radici dalle quali ha preso vita l'Unione. La storia greco-romana, la tradizione giudaico-cristiana, i valori laici e liberali che si sono via via definiti, non possono essere ignorati perché da essi il futuro dell'Europa trae forza culturale e morale'.

13. Original: 'bisogno però di difendere anche le nostre identità e le nostre tradizioni'.

14. Original: 'Il modello ideale è quello della Confederazione, nella quale gli Stati hanno un loro spazio di autonomia, ma decidono di delegare parte della loro sovranità alle istituzioni centrali per la gestione di determinati settori'.

15. Original: 'l'Europa non può nascere contro gli Stati e contro gli interessi nazionali'.

16. Original: 'non annullando gli Stati nazionali bensì costituendo una Confederazione di Statinazione; in questo senso gli Stati e gli interessi nazionali contribuiscono e non sono di ostacolo alla formazione dell'interesse e delle priorità europei'.

17. Original: 'È attraverso gli Stati e i governi nazionali, quindi, […] che la Confederazione di Stati può acquisire "personalità politica" […] gli Stati ritrovano la loro centralità'.

18. Original: 'Ci siamo ispirati in tanti nostri documenti e prese di posizioni al modello gollista'.

19. Original: 'Preciso subito che siamo favorevoli a delegare alcune competenze dello Stato, ma non ad abbandonare la sovranità nazionale, perche l'Europa unita dovrà essere l'"Europa delle Nazioni", dove ogni membro dovrà mantenere la propria identità in un assetto non centralistico'.

20. Original: 'Ma la Destra ha anche sempre affermano il valore di un'Europa delle nazioni, ricchezza plurima di identità e culture, che vanno alimentate e rispettate e non possono essere annullate in un super Stato informe'.

21. Wording in Italian: 'Ci opponiamo ad una integrazione europea che rappresenti l'omologazione ad un modello unico. Siamo per un'Europa che rispetti le diversità e le culture che la arricchiscono'.

22. Original: 'il modo migliore per far parte a pieno titolo del club europeo è quello di non rinunciare alle proprie prerogative nazionale, alla propria identità storico-culturale. Essere buoni europei presuppone essere e sentirsi buoni italiani'.

23. Original: 'dobbiamo costruire l'unità politica europea, salvaguardando le identità e le specificità nazionali'.

24. Original: 'Integrazione ove necessario, decentramento ove possibile'.

25. Original: 'L'Italia Paese [...] deve poter trovare nell'Europa unita la possibilità di sviluppare e affermare le sue caratteristiche'.

26. Original: 'Europeisti a parole, non abbiamo mai preso troppo sul serio le istituzioni europee, non ci siamo battuti [...] per inserire nostri tecnici e funzionari all'interno della struttura burocratica della Comunità'.

27. Original: 'Solo in anni molto recenti, grazie all'azione culturale della Destra, si è tornato a parlare di "riscoperta dell'interesse nazionale"'.

28. Original: 'Siamo contrari a regolamentazioni di alcuni settori che valgano da Capo Nord all'isola di Lampedusa'.

29. Original: 'ad oggi ancora troppe decisioni dell'Unione, lungi dall'essere prese in sede parlamentare scaturiscono dalle riunioni del Consiglio e sono attuate dagli organi della Commissione. Il primo decide in segreto, la seconda attua in maniera politicamente "non responsabile". Questi due evidenti paradossi, in chiara contraddizione con lo spirito democratico di cui l'Europa è stata nei secoli portatrice'.

30. Original: 'incapace di affermare finanche le radice della propria identità'.

31. Original: 'Fissare la curvatura delle banane o il diametro dei piselli o la lunghezza dei contraccettivi e crede di regolare, in questo modo, il mercato, significa essere lontani mille miglia dalla realtà quotidiana dei cittadini'.

32. Original: 'il futuro d'Europa non può essere segnato dall'uniformità nel centralismo ma dall'unità nella diversità'.

33. Original: 'la Costituzione non venga strumentalizzata a fini partitici contro governi regolarmente eletti dai propri cittadini. L'Unione europea non deve rischiare di divenire il luogo in cui maggioranze ideologiche si scontrano per contrastare libere scelte nazionali'.

34. Original: 'approfondire per allargare, dando vita a cooperazioni rafforzate su temi strategici per l'Unione'.

35. Original: 'Il futuro dell'Europa, a questo punto, è quello di essere niente più che un vasto mercato [...] un mercato retto da una logica meramente economistica'.

36. Original: 'Vogliamo creare una grande Alleanza per l'Italia che agisca nell'immediato ma guardi al futuro, per ridare speranza, per uscire dalla sindrome di chi pensa ad una Italia priva di prospettive e relegata ai margini della Storia'.

37. Original: 'Un progetto politico culturale che passa attraverso la riaffermazione del Modello Italiano che deriva dalla nostra storia, dalla nostra cultura e dalla nostra identità'.

38. Original: 'Dissi al presidente Berlusconi: "Io sono disponibile a farlo"'.

39. Original: 'desiderio di cimentarmi con un tema come quello della politica comunitaria che sempre di più determina anche le scelte della politica nazionale'.

40. Original: 'Fatto sta che alla fine il rappresentante del governo italiano è stato considerato uno dei protagonisti del buon esito della Convenzione'.

41. Original: 'La Destra italiana appartiene ad una delle grandi famiglie della tradizione politica europea, che ha già dato un forte contributo alla causa europeista e che continuerà a darlo'.

42. Original: 'Per usare una formula ad effetto: centrali ma non centristi'.

43. Original: 'I due anni in cui mi sono occupato della Costituzione europea e il mandato alla Farnesina hanno dimostrato con i fatti che An ha valori affini a quelli del Ppe'.

44. Original: 'Alleanza Nazionale ha il diritto - dovere di coltivare l'ambizione di diventare, stabilmente, la forza centrale dell'alleanza attraverso [...] il suo progetto politico - culturale [...] nell'ottica di un grande partito nazionale e popolare di ispirazione e respiro europeo'.

45. Original: 'Non escludo di candidarmi premier'.

46. Original: 'Ma un sistema di alleanze alternative di Pd è possibile, con o senza il demolitore' and 'Rifaccio io il centrodestra. Anche da solo'.

47. Original: 'Lontana dall'Europa, l'Italia diventerebbe sempre più eccentrica rispetto ai processi della modernizzazione e della globalizzazione'.

48. Original: 'Ritiene che l'Italia e l'Europa debbano svolgere un ruolo propulsivo nelle relazioni internazionali; poiché esistono ancora aree importanti del globo nelle quali si realizza la quotidiana e sistematica violazione delle dignità della persona'.

49. Original: 'Vogliamo un'Europa politica capace di ispirare la voglia di democrazia laddove nel mondo milioni di donne e uomini ancora subiscono la mancanza di libertà e di legalità'.

50. Original: 'l'Europa non potrà svolgere nel mondo un ruolo corrispondente al suo peso economico e commerciale e potrebbe essere costretto ad accettare scelte fatte da altri'.

51. Original: 'Dobbiamo immaginare gli scenari futuri e non, come nel caso del Kosovo, trovarci impreparati e divisi di fronte a uno scenario quanto mai delicato'.

52. Orignal: 'un'Unione di Stati sovrani è capace d'agire efficacemente attraverso l'espressione di una volontà comune'.

53. Original: 'Infatti, in questa fase delicata per l'Unione europea, mentre ci si avvia all'ampliamento ad Est, mentre sono già in atto tutte le trasformazioni economiche e finanziarie legate alla realizzazione della moneta unica, non dobbiamo dimenticare il valore "cultura", le specificità e le diversità della cultura europea, la sua valorizzazione e la sua diffusione. La cultura, che vuol dire anche storia, lingue, tradizioni, deve rimanere per i cittadini europei un legame fondamentale ed irrinunciabile'.

54. Original: 'La famiglia prevede da sempre un padre e una madre, un maschio e una femmina, e non credo che l'UE, con la promozione di campagne contro ipotetiche discriminazioni, possa arrogarsi il diritto di scavalcare i governi nazionali, solamente per assecondare i desideri di alcune lobby non proprio nobili. In tema di valori, cultura e famiglia, l'Unione europea non può agire come in materia di mercato unico, invitando gli Stati membri a legalizzare unioni omosessuali all'insegna dell'uniformità e di un falso garantismo, rischiando di minare, al contrario, il sistema di valori alla base della nostra società millenaria'.

55. Original: 'il Mediterraneo come porta non soltanto verso il Medio Oriente ma anche verso l'Atlantico, realtà culturale, non solo economica, per rinsaldare il dialogo Sud-Sud, ma anche Nord-Sud, Est-Sud, nel momento nel quale il vicino allargamento richiama tutti noi a precise responsabilità'.

References

A1 (2009a) *Επικός και συναισθηματικός ο λόγος του προέδρου* (7 June). LAOS official newspaper, (no author cited).
———. (2009b) *We are here to stay!* (June 14). LAOS official newspaper (no author cited).

Adams, J., Clark, M., Ezrow, L. and Glasgow, G. (2006) 'Are Niche Parties Fundamentally Different from Mainstream Parties? The Causes and the Electoral Consequences of Western European Parties' Policy Shifts, 1976–1998', *American Journal of Political Science*, 50(3): 513–529.

Aivaliotis, C. (2009) [LAOS MP] *Interview with the author* [13 April].

Akkerman, T. (2012) 'Comparing radical right parties in government: immigration and integration policies in nine countries (1996–2010)', *West European Politics*, 35(3): 511–529.

Altemeyer, B. (1981) *Right-wing authoritarianism*, Winnipeg, Canada: University of Manitoba Press.

Anders, H. (1998) *Mass communication research methods*, New York: New York University Press.

Angelilli, R. (2001) *European Parliament Speech* [17 December], http://www.europarl.europa.eu/.
———. (2007) *European Parliament Speech* [22 May], http://www.europarl.europa.eu/.

Art, D. (2011) *Inside the radical right: The development of anti-immigrant parties in Western Europe*, Cambridge: Cambridge University Press.

Arzheimer, K. (2015) 'The AfD: Finally a Successful Right-Wing Populist Eurosceptic Party for Germany?', *West European Politics*, 38: 535–556.

Aspinwall, M. (2002) 'Preferring Europe: Ideology and national preferences on European integration', *European Union Politics*, 3(1): 81–111.

Attack (2009). *Програмна схема* (National Elections Manifesto), http://www.ataka.bg/index.php?option=com_content&task=view&id=14&Itemid=ast (accessed 13 February 2009).

————. (2013) *Electoral manifesto for the 2013 elections* (National Elections Manifesto).

Au Front (2008) *Bulletin de liaison du Front National* (December), http://www.front-national.com/?page_id=909 (accessed 9 April 2010).

Austrian Freedom Party (2004) *Türkei in die EU?* (EP Elections manifesto).

————. (2005) *Das Parteiprogramm der Freiheitlichen Partei Österreichs Mit Berück-sichtigung der beschlossenen Änderungen vom 27. Ordentlichen Bundesparteitag der FPÖ am 23. April 2005 in Salzburg* [Party Congress Document], http://www.fpoe-bildungsinstitut.at/documents/10180/20998/Parteiprogramm+der+FP%C3%96%20 1997+mit+den+2005+beschlossenen+%C3%84nderungen.pdf/abf304e8-3871-4dfc-80d3-6ee60259bf93 (accessed 10 August 2016).

————. (2008) *FPO: Die Soziale heimatpartei. Österreich im Wort. Wie für euch* (National Elections Manifesto).

————. (2009) *Unser Kurs ist Klar: Echte Volksvertreter Statt EU-Verräter. Tag der Abrechnung am 7 Juni 2009 FPŐ* (EP Elections manifesto).

————. (2013) *Handbuch freiheitlicher Politik* (National Elections manifesto), http://www.fpoe.at/fileadmin/user_upload/www.fpoe.at/dokumente/2015/Handbuch_freiheitlicher_Politik_WEB.pdf (accessed 7 November 2016).

BBC (2017) *Donald Trump says UK 'doing great' after Brexit vote* [16 January], http://www.bbc.co.uk/news/uk-politics-38631832 (accessed 8 April 2017).

Bakke, E. and Sitter, N. (2005) 'Patterns of stability: Party competition and strategy in Central Europe since 1989', *Party Politics,* 11(2): 243–363.

Bakker, R., de Vries, C., Edwards, E., Hooghe, L., Jolly, S., Marks, G., Polk, J., Rovny, J., Steenbergen, M. and Vachudova, M. (2015) 'Measuring Party Positions in Europe: The Chapel Hill Expert Survey Trend File, 1999–2010', *Party Politics,* 21(1): 143–152.

Baldini, G. and Vignati, R. (1996) 'Dal MSI ad AN: una nuova cultura politica?', *Poils,* 1(10): 81–101.

Bartolini, S., Chiaramonte, A. and D'Alimonte, R. (2004) 'The Italian Party System between Parties and Coalitions', *West European Politics,* 27(1):1–19.

Bartolini, S. (2005) *Restructuring Europe. Centre formation, system building and political structuring between the nation state and the EU,* Oxford: Oxford University Press.

Bastow, S. (1997) 'Front national economic policy: from neo-liberalism to protectionism', *Modern & Contemporary France,* 5(1): 61–72.

Batory, A. and Sitter, N. (2004) 'Cleavages, competition and coalition-building: Agrarian parties and the European question in Western and East Central Europe', *European Journal of Political Research,* 43: 523–546.

Benedetto, G. and Quaglia, L. (2007) 'The comparative politics of Communist Euroscepticism in France, Italy and Spain', *Party Politics,* 13(4): 478–499.

Benoit, B. (1998) *Social-nationalism: an anatomy of French Euroscepticism,* Brookfield, VT: Ashgate.

Betz, H. G. and Immerfall, S. (1998) *The new politics of the Right: neo-Populist parties and movements in established democracies,* New York: St. Martin's Press.

Bianchi, S. (2007) *La destra nell'epoca del leaderismo: movimento di massa, leader e cultura in AN,* Rimini: Il cerchio.

Blais, A. and Loewen, P. J. (2009) 'The French electoral system and its effects', *West European Politics*, 32(2): 345–359.

Bochel, J. and Denver, D. (1983) 'Candidate Selection in the Labour Party: What the Selectors Seek', *British Journal of Political Science*, 13(1): 45–69.

Bollen, K. (1993) 'Liberal Democracy: Validity and Method Factors in Cross-National Measures', *American Journal of Political Science*, 37(4): 1207–1230.

Bornschier, S. (2009) 'Cleavage Politics in Old and New Democracies', *Living Reviews in Democracy*, 1: 1–13.

Bornschier, S. and Lachat,R. (2009) 'The evolution of the French political space and party system', *West European Politics*, 32(2): 360–383.

Braun, D., Hutter, S. and Kerscher, A. (2016) 'What type of Europe? The salience of polity and policy issues in European Parliament elections', *European Union Politics*, 17(4): 570–592.

British National Party (1999) *Taking back our freedom!* (European Elections Manifesto).

———. (2001) *What we stand for* (National Elections Manifesto).

———. (2005) *Rebuilding British Democracy* (National Elections Manifesto).

———. (2009) *Manifesto for the European Elections* (European Elections Manifesto).

———. (2010) *Democracy, freedom, culture and identity* (National Elections Manifesto).

———. (2014) *Out of the EU* (European Elections Manifesto).

———. (2015) *Securing our British future* (National Elections Manifesto).

Bruter, M. (2005) *Citizens of Europe?: The emergence of a mass European identity*, New York: Palgrave Macmillan.

Bruter, M. and Harrison, S. (2011) *Mapping extreme right ideology: An empirical geography of the European extreme right*, Basingstoke: Palgrave Macmillan.

Bull, M. (2004) 'Parliamentary democracy in Italy', *Parliamentary Affairs*, 57(3): 550–567.

Cole, A. (2005) 'Old right or new right? The ideological positioning of parties of the far right', *European Journal of Political Research*, 44: 203–230.

Caiani, M. and Conti, N. (2014) 'In the Name of the People: The Euroscepticism of the Italian Radical Right', *Perspectives on European Politics and Society*, 15(2): 183–197.

Campi, A. (2006) *La destra di Fini: i dieci anni di Alleanza Nazionale, 1995–2005*, Lungro di Cosenza (Cosenza): Marco.

Capoccia, G. (2002) 'Anti-System Parties: A Conceptual Reassessment', *Journal of Theoretical Politics*, 14(9): 9–35.

Carter, E. L. (2005) *The extreme right in Western Europe: Success or failure?* Manchester: Manchester University Press.

Cheles, L. (2010) 'Back to the future. The visual propaganda of Alleanza Nazionale (1994–2009)', *Journal of Modern Italian Studies*, 15(2): 232–311.

Chrisanthakopoulos, A. (2008) *Ευρωπαϊκή συνομοσπονδία κυρίαρχων κρατών ή κοινοπολιτεία αυτόνομων περιφερειών;* http://www.metharros.gr/modules/article/view.article.php/31/c8 (accessed 25 November 2009).

———. (2009) [LAOS Party Official] *Interview with the author* [8 April].

Clogg, R. (1987) *Parties and elections in Greece: The search for legitimacy*, Durham: Duke University Press.

Conti, N. (2003) *Party attitudes to European integration: A longitudinal analysis of the Italian Case*, SEI Working Paper No. 70, EPERN Working Paper No. 13, Sussex European Institute.

———. (2009) 'Tied hands? Italian political parties and Europe', *Modern Italy*, 14(2): 203–216.

Cramme, O. and Hobolt, S. (2015) 'A European Union under stress', in Cramme, O. and Hobolt, S. (eds.) *Democratic Politics in a European Union under stress*, Oxford: Oxford University Press, pp: 1–15.

Dahl, R. (1989) *Democracy and its Critics*, New Haven: Yale University Press.

Danish People's Party (1999) *EP elections manifesto* (European Elections Manifesto).

———. (2002) Princip Program "The Party Program of the Danish People's Party as established in 2002, http://www.danskfolkeparti.dk/pictures_org/DF_Princip-ProgramA5.pdf (accessed 8 November 2016).

———. (2004) *Den Europæiske Union* (European Elections Manifesto).

———. (2007) *2007 Programme* (National Elections Manifesto).

———. (2009) *Arbejdsprogram* http://www.danskfolkeparti.dk/pictures_org/arbejdesprog-net(3).pdf (accessed 8 November 2016).

———. (2011) *Slaget om Danmark* (National Elections Manifesto).

Davies, P. (1999) *The National Front in France: Ideology, discourse, and power*, London: Routledge.

Davis, T. C. (1998) 'The Iberian peninsula and Greece: Retreat from the radical right?', in Betz, H. G. and Immerfall, S. (eds.) *The new politics of the Right: Neo-Populist parties and movements in established democracies*, New York: St. Martin's Press, pp. 157–172.

de Danne, L. (2010) [Front National European Parliamentary Consultant] *Interview with the author* [5 March]. In English.

de Saint-Just, W. (2010) [Member of Front National's executive bureau/Treasurer] *Interview with the author* [4 February].

de la Tocnaye, T. (2010) [Member of Front National's political bureau] *Interview with the author* [3 February].

De Lange, S. and Guerrra, S. (2009) 'The League of Polish Families between East and, West, past and present', *Communist and Post-Communist Studies,* 42: 527–549.

De Sio, L. (2007) 'For a few votes more: The Italian general elections of April 2006', *South European Society and Politics* 12(1): 95–109.

De Vries, C. and Edwards, E. (2009) 'Taking Europe to Its Extremes: Extremist Parties and Public Euroscepticism', *Party Politics,* (15)1: 5–28.

De Vries, C. and Hobolt, S. (2012) 'When dimensions collide: The electoral success of issue entrepreneurs', *European Union Politics*, 13(2): 246–268.

De Wilde, P., Laupold, A. and Schmidtke, H. (2016) 'Introduction: the differentiated politicisation of European governance', *West European Politics*, 39 (1): 3–22.

DeClair, E. G. (1999) *Politics on the fringe: The people, policies, and organization of the French National Front*, Durham, NC: Duke University Press.

Dehousse, R. and Tacea, A. (2015) 'Europe in the 2012 French presidential election', in G. Goodliffe and R. Brizzi (eds.) *France after 2012*, New York: Berghahn pp.152–166.

Di Quirico, R. (2003) 'Italy, Europe and the European Presidency of 2003', *Notre Europe* (27).

Dimitras, P. E. (1992) 'Greece: The Virtual Absence of an Extreme Right', in Hainsworth, P. (ed.) *The Extreme Right in Europe and the USA,* London: Pinter, pp. 246–268.

Dinas, E. (2008) 'The Greek General Election of 2007: You Cannot Lose If Your Opponent Cannot Win', *West European Politics*, 31(3): 600–607.

Downs, A. (1957) *An economic theory of democracy*, New York: Harper & Row.

Druckman, N., and Nelson, K. (2003) 'Framing and Deliberation: How Citizens' Conversations Limit Elite Influence', *American Journal of Political Science*, 47(4): 729–745.

Dunn, K. (2015) 'Preference for radical right-wing populist parties among exclusive-nationalists and authoritarians', *Party Politics*, 21(3): 367–380.

Duverger, M. (1954) *Political parties: Their organization and activity in the modern state*, Methuen: Wiley.

Easton, D. (1965) *A framework for political analysis,* Englewood Cliffs, NJ: Prentice Hall.

Eatwell R. (2000) 'The rebirth of the extreme right in Western Europe?', *Parliamentary Affairs*, 53(3): 407–25.

———. (2002) 'The Rebirth of Right-Wing Charisma? The Cases of Jean-Marie Le Pen and Vladimir Zhirinovsky', *Totalitarian Movements and Political Religions*, 3(3): 1–23.

Economides, S. (2005) 'The Europeanisation of Greek foreign policy', *West European Politics*, 28(2): 471–491.

Economist, The. (2001a) *Fit to run Italy?* [26 April], http://www.economist.com/node/593654 (accessed 13 April 2010).

Economist, The. (2001b) *So, Mr Berlusconi . . . A triumph for Silvio Berlusconi, but not for Italy* [17 May], http://www.economist.com/node/626457 (accessed 13 April 2010).

Egmond, M., Van der Brug, W., Hobolt, S., Franklin, M. and Eliyahu V. (2013) *European Parliament Election Study 2009, Voter Study*. GESIS Data Archive, Cologne. ZA5055 Data file Version 1.1.0, doi:10.4232/1.11760.

Eleftherotypia (2006) *Το Τριώδιο της ακροδεξιάς* [16 February], http://www.iospress.gr/ios2006/ios20060226.htm (accessed 8 December 2016).

Ellinas, A. (2010) *The Media and the Far Right in Western Europe: Playing the Nationalist Card,* New York: Cambridge University Press.

Elo, S. and Kyngs, H. (2008) 'The qualitative content analysis process', *Journal of Advanced Nursing*, 62(1): 107–115.

Entman, R. M. (1993) 'Framing: Toward clarification of a fractured paradigm', *Journal of Communication,* 43(4): 51–58.

Erk, Jan (2005) 'From Vlaams Blok to Vlaams Belang: The Belgian Far-Right Renames Itself', *West European Politics*, 28(3): 493–502.

Eurobarometer (2016) *Standard Eurobarometer 86, Autumn 2016*, http://ec.europa.eu/ COMMFrontOffice/publicopinion/index.cfm/General/index (accessed 27 March 2017).

European Union (2002) *Consolidated version of the Treaty on European Union 1992*. Official Journal of the European Communities, http://eur-lex.europa.eu/ legal-content/EN/TXT/PDF/?uri=CELEX:12002E/TXT&from=EN (accessed 30 August 2016).

————. (2012) *Consolidated version of the treaty on the functioning of the European Union. Official Journal of the European Union,* http://eur-lex.europa.eu/legal-content/ EN/TXT/PDF/?uri=CELEX:12012E/TXT&from=EN (accessed 30 August 2016).

————. (2017) *The Rome Declaration* [25 March], http://www.consilium.europa. eu/en/press/press-releases/2017/03/25-rome-declaration/ (accessed 8 April 2017).

Fabbrini, S. (2006) 'The Italian case of a transition within democracy', *Journal of Balkan and Near Eastern Studies*, 8(2): 145–161.

————. (2009) 'The Transformation of Italian Democracy', *Bulletin of Italian Politics*, 1(1): 29–47.

Featherstone, K. (1988) *Socialist Parties and European Integration: A Comparative History*, Manchester: Manchester University Press.

————. (1990) 'Political parties and democratic consolidation in Greece'," , in Pridham, G. (ed.) *Political Parties and Democratic Consolidation in Southern Europe*, London: Routledge, pp. 179–202.

————. (1994a) 'Political Parties', in Kazakos, P. and Ioakimidis, P (eds.) *Greece and EC Membership Evaluated*, London: Pinter pp. 140–154.

————. (1994b) 'The challenge of liberalisation: Parties and the state in Greece after the 1993 elections', *Democratisation,* 1(2): 280–294.

————. (2006) 'From Fiuggi to the Farnesina: Gianfranco Fini's remarkable journey', *Journal of Contemporary European Studies*, 14(1): 11–23.

Fella, S. and Ruzza, C. (2006) 'Changing political opportunities and the re-invention of the Italian right', *Journal of Balkan and Near Eastern Studies*, 8(2): 179–200.

Fieschi, C., Shields, J. and Woods, R. (1996) 'Extreme Right-Wing Parties and the European Union,' in Gaffney, J. (ed.) *Political Parties and the European Union*, London: Routledge, pp. 235–253.

Fini, G. (2003) *L'Europa che verrà: il destino del continente e il ruolo dell'Italia*, Roma: Fazi.

————. (2007a) *Interview with Maurizio Battista in Arena* [15 December].

————. (2007b) *Interview with Vittorio Feltri in Libero* [16 December].

————. (2008) *Interview with Fabrizio de Feo at Il Giornale* [01 February].

————. (2009) *Il Futuro della Libertà*, Milano: Rizzoli.

————. (1999) *Un'Italia civile*, Milano: Ponte alle Grazie.

Flanagan, S. and Lee, A. (2003) 'The New Politics, Culture Wars, and the Authoritarian-Libertarian Value Change in Advanced Industrial Democracies', *Comparative Political Studies*, 36(3): 235–270.

Flemish Interest (2004) *Vlaamse Staat, Europese Natie Verkiezingsprogramma 2004 Europees Parlement* (European Elections Manifesto).

————. (2009a) Het *programma van het Vlaams Belang*, http://www.vlaamsbelangeuropa.eu/ (accessed June 2009).

————. (2009b) *What we stand for*, http://www.vlaamsbelangeuropa.eu/ (accessed June 2009).

————. (2009c) *Dit is ons land. Programma Europese verkiezingen 7 juni 2009* (European Elections Manifesto).

————. (2010) *Programma Federale Verkiezingen 2010 Vlamingen Eerst!* (National Elections Manifesto).

————. (2014) *Uw stok achter de deur. Verkiezingen 25 Mei 2014* (European Elections Manifesto).

Flood, C. (1997) 'National Populism', in C. Flood and L. Bell. (eds.) *Political ideologies in contemporary France*, London: Pinter.

————. (2002) 'Euroscepticism: A problematic concept', UACES 32nd Annual Conference and 7th Research Conference, Queen's University Belfast.

For Fatherland and Freedom (2004) *Apvienība "Tēvzemei un Brīvībai"/LNNK priekšvēlēšanu programma 2004.gada Eiropas Parlamenta vēlēšanām* (European Elections Manifesto).

————. (2009) *Apvienība "Tēvzemei un Brīvībai"/LNNK priekšvēlēšanu programma 2009.gada Eiropas Parlamenta vēlēšanām* (European Elections Manifesto).

————. (2006) *Tēvzemei un Brīvībai / LNNK programma* (National Elections Manifesto) http://www.tb.lv/page.php?pgID=1d7f7abc18fcb43975065399b0d1e48e&lang=est (accessed 15 January 2009).

————. (2012) *National association "All for Latvia!" – "For Fatherland and Freedom / LNNK" PROGRAMME* (Version 4.1. 03.12.2012.), http://www.nacionalaapvieniba.lv/wp-content/uploads/2016/03/Nacionalas_apvienibas_VL_TB-LNNK_programma_v4.1.pdf (accessed 5 December 2016).

Ford, R. and Goodwin, M. (2014) *Revolt on the Right: Explaining Support for the Radical Right in Britain*, Abingdon: Routledge.

France24 (2012) *Far-right candidate attacks 'deadly' globalisation, immigration,* http://www.france24.com/en/20120219-france-far-right-candidate-french-presidential-election-marine-le-pen-lille-convention-sarkozy (accessed 4 April 2017).

French Communist Party (2004) *Programme électoral du PCF en vue des élections européennes 2004 (Parti Communiste Français).* http://discours.vie-publique.fr/notices/043001732.html (accessed on 8 April 2010).

Gallagher, M. and Mitchell, P. (2005) *The Politics of Electoral Systems*, Oxford: Oxford University Press.

Gallagher, M., Laver, M. and P. Mair (2011) *Representative government in modern Europe*, Berkshire: McGraw Hill Education.

Gazi, E. (2013) ''Fatherland, Religion, Family': Exploring the History of a Slogan in Greece, 1880–1930', *Gender & History*, 25(3): 700–710.

Gellner, E. (1983) *Nations and nationalism*, Oxford: Blackwell.

Gemenis, K. and Dinas, E. (2010) 'Confrontation still? Examining parties' policy positions in Greece', *Comparative European Politics,* 8(2): 179–201.

Gemenis, K., Katsanidou, A. and Vasilopoulou, S. (2012) 'The politics of anti-environmentalism: positional issue framing by the European radical right' (presented at the 2012 MPSA meeting).

George, S. (2000) 'Britain: Anatomy of a Eurosceptic state', *Journal of European Integration*, 22: 15–33.

Georgiadis, S. A. (2009) [LAOS MP] *Interview with the author* [12 June].

Georgiadou, V. (2008). 'Ψηφίζοντας την άκρα δεξιά. Η εκλογική επιλογή του ΛΑ.Ο.Σ.', *Epistimi kai Koinonia* 19 (Spring).

Georgiou, G. (2009) [LAOS MEP] *Interview with the author* [13 April].

———. (2014) [LAOS MEP] *Interview with the author* [2 April].

Germani, G. (1978) *Authoritarianism, Fascism, and National Populism*, New Brunswick: Transaction.

Gerring, J. (2012) *Social Science methodology: A unified framework,* 2nd edition, Cambridge: Cambridge University Press.

Glencross, A. (2013) 'The EU Response to the Eurozone Crisis: Democratic Contestation and the New Fault Lines in European Integration', Discussion Paper Europa-Kolleg Hamburg, 13:3.

Golden Dawn (2012) *Οι θέσεις μας: Προτάσεις για μια νέα εθνική πολιτική* (National Elections Manifesto).

———. (2015). *Πολιτικό πρόγραμμα 2015: Οι κλέφτες στη φυλακή, οι Έλληνες στην Εξουσία* (National Elections Manifesto).

Gollnisch, B. (2006a) *European Parliament Speech* [17 January], http://www.europarl.europa.eu/.

———. (2006b) *European Parliament Speech* [13 December], http://www.europarl.europa.eu/.

———. (2007) *European Parliament Speech* [13 February], http://www.europarl.europa.eu/.

———. (2009a) [Front National MEP/Executive vice-President] *Interview with the author* [18 February].

———. (2009b) *European Parliament Speech* [2 April], http://www.europarl.europa.eu/.

Goodliffe, G. (2015) 'Europe's salience and 'owning' Euroscepticism: Explaining the Front National's victory in the 2014 European elections in France', *French Politics* 13(4): 324–345.

Griffin, R. (1994) 'Europe for the Europeans: The fascist vision of the new Europe', Humanities Research Centre Occasional Paper, No. 1, 1994.

———. (1996) 'The Post-fascism of the Alleanza nazionale: A case-study in Ideological Morphology', *Journal of Political Ideologies*, 1(2): 123–146.

———. (2011) 'Alien influence? The international context of BNP's modernisation', in Copsey, N. and Maclin, G. (eds.) *British National Party: Contemporary Perspectives*, Abingdon: Routledge, pp. 190–206.

Grunberga, G. and Schweisguth, E. (2003) 'French Political Space: Two, Three or Four Blocs?', *French Politics*, 1(3): 331–347.

Guinaudeau, I. and Persico, S. (2014) 'What Is Issue Competition? Conflict, Consensus and Issue Ownership in Party Competition', *Journal of Elections, Public Opinion and Parties,* 24(3): 312–333.

Gunther, R., Montero, J.R. and Linz, J. (eds.) (2002) *Political Parties: Old Concepts and New Challenges*, Oxford: Oxford University Press.

Gunther, R. and Diamond, L. (2003) 'Species of Political Parties: A New Typology', *Party Politics,* 9(2): 167–199.

Hainsworth, P. (ed.) (2000a) *The politics of the extreme right: From the margins to the mainstream*, New York: Pinter.

———. (2000b) 'The Front National: from ascendancy to fragmentation on the French extreme right', in Hainsworth, P. (ed.) *The politics of the extreme right: from the margins to the mainstream*, New York: Pinter, pp. 18–32.

———. (2008) *The extreme right in Western Europe*, Abingdon: Routledge.

Hainsworth, P., O'Brien, C. and Mitchell, P. (2004) 'Defending the nation: The politics of Euroscepticism on the French right', in Harmsen, R. and Spiering, M. (eds.) *Euroscepticism: Party Politics, National Identity and European Integration*, Amsterdam: Rodopi, pp. 37–58.

Halikiopoulou, D, Mock, S and Vasilopoulou, S. (2013) 'The civic Zeitgeist: nationalism and liberal values in the European radical right', *Nations and Nationalism*, 19(1): 107–127.

Halikiopoulou, D., Nanou, K. and Vasilopoulou, S. (2016) *Changing the policy agenda?: The impact of the Golden Dawn on Greek party politics*, Greece: Hellenic Observatory Papers on Greece and Southeast Europe, London: LSE.

Halikiopoulou, D., Nanou, K. and Vasilopoulou, S. (2012) 'The Paradox of Nationalism: The Common Denominator of Radical Right and Radical Left Euroscepticis', *European Journal of Political Research*, 51(4): 504–539.

Halikiopoulou, D. and Vasilopoulou, S. (2014) 'Support for the Far Right in the 2014 European Parliament Elections: A Comparative Perspective', *Political Quarterly*, 85(3): 285–288.

Hancké, B. (2009) *Intelligent research design: A guide for beginning researchers in the social sciences*, Oxford and New York: Oxford University Press.

Hanley, D. (2001) 'French political parties, globalisation and Europe', *Modern & Contemporary France,* 9(3): 301–312.

Harmsen, R. and Spiering, M. (2004) 'Introduction: Euroscepticism and the Evolution of European Political Debate', in Harmsen, R. and Spiering, M. (eds.) *Euroscepticism: Party Politics, National Identity and European Integration*, Amsterdam: Rodopi, pp. 13–35.

Helbling, M., Hoeglinger, D. and Wüest, B. (2010) 'How Political Parties Frame European Integration', *European Journal of Political Research*, 49(4): 496–521.

Hix, S. (1999) 'Dimensions and alignments in European Union Politics: Cognitive constraints and partisan responses', *European Journal of Political Research*, 35: 69–106.

———. (2015) 'Democratizing a Macroeconomic Union in Europe', in Cramme, O. and Hobolt, S. (eds.) *Democratic Politics in a European Union under stress*, Oxford: Oxford University Press, pp. 180–198.

Hix, S. and Lord, C. J. (1997) *Political parties in the European union*, Basingstoke: Macmillan.

Hobolt, S. and Tilley, J. (2016) 'Fleeing the centre: The rise of challenger parties in the aftermath of the Euro crisis', *West European Politics*, 39 (5): 971–991.

Hooghe, L. (2001) *The European Commission and the integration of Europe: Images of governance.* Cambridge: Cambridge University Press.

Hooghe, L. and Marks, G. (2009) 'A Postfunctionalist Theory of European Integration: From Permissive Consensus to Constraining Dissensus', *British Journal of Political Science,* 39: 1–23.

———. (2016) 'Europe's crises and political contestation', Paper presented at the Conference, "Theory Meets Crisis," Robert Schuman Centre, EUI, June 30–July 1, 2016, available at: http://www.euengage.eu/wp-content/uploads/2016/05/Hooghe-Marks-Europes-Crises-and-Political-Contestation.pdf.

Hooghe, L., Marks, G. and Wilson, C. (2002) 'Does Left/Right Structure Party Positions on European Integration?', *Comparative Political Studies*, 35(8): 965–989.

Horobin, W. (2017) 'Marine Le Pen Centers Presidential Run on Getting France Out of Eurozone' [18 January], Available at http://www.wsj.com/articles/marine-le-pen-centers-presidential-run-on-getting-france-out-of-eurozone-1484735580 (accessed on 23 January 2017).

Hutter, S., Grande, E. and Kriesi, H. (2016) *Politicising Europe: Integration and Mass Politics*, Cambridge: Cambridge University Press.

Ignazi, P. (1994) *Postfascisti?: dal Movimento sociale italiano ad Alleanza nazionale*, Bologna: Il Mulino.

———. (2003) *Extreme right parties in Western Europe.* Oxford: Oxford University Press.

———. (2005) 'Legitimation and Evolution on the Italian Right Wing: Social and Ideological Repositioning of Alleanza Nazionale and the Lega Nord', *South European Society and Politics*, 10(2): 333–349.

Ignazi, P., Bardi, L. and Massari, O. (2010) 'Party organisational change in Italy (1991–2006)', *Modern Italy,* 15(2): 197–216.

Immerzeel, T., Coffé, H. and van der Lippe, T. (2015) 'Explaining the Gender Gap in Radical Right Voting: A Cross-National Investigation in 12 Western European countries', *Comparative European Politics*, 13(2): 263–286.

In.gr (2000) *Η «Σαλώμη» αποκεφαλίζει τον Καρατζαφέρη*, http://archive.in.gr/news/2000/greece/g_may03.htm (accessed 8 December 2016).

Ivaldi, G. (2015) 'Towards the median economic crisis voter? The new leftist economic agenda of the Front National in France', *French Politics*, 13(4): 346–369.

Jagers, J. and Walgrave, S. (2007) 'Populism as Political Communication Style: An Empirical Study of Political Parties' Discourse in Belgium', *European Journal of Political Research*, 46(3): 319–345.

Jobbik (2010) *Radikális változás A Jobbik országgyűlési választási programja a nemzeti önrendelkezésért és a társadalmi igazságosságért* (National Elections Manifesto).

———. (2014) *Kimondjuk. Megoldjuk. A Jobbik országgyűlési választási programja. A nemzet felemelkedéséért* (National Elections Manifesto).

Johansson, K. and Raunio, T. (2001) 'Partisan responses to Europe: Comparing Finnish and Swedish political parties', *European Journal of Political Research*, 39(2): 225–249.

Karatzaferis, G. (2005) *Speech in Luxemburg* [11 January].

―――. (2006) *Δεν γυρίζω στην Ν.Δ.* Interview of George Karatzaferis in the newspaper Metro, http://www.e-grammes.gr/article.php?id=1979 (accessed 22 April 2010).

―――. (2008) *Parliamentary speech on the ratification of the Lisbon Treaty* [11 June], www.laos.gr (accessed 10 July 2009).

―――. (2009) Speech during the 4th Party Congress (Ομιλία Του Προέδρου του Λα.Ο.Σ κ. Γ. Καρατζαφέρη στην Εναρξη του 4ου Τακτικού Συνεδρίου του ΛΑ.Ο.Σ), http://www.karatzaferis.gr/index.asp?epilogi=CenPage\mainleft /ΣΥΝΕΔΡΙΟ040709.txt (accessed 7 July 2009).

Kathimerini (2012) *Profile of parties running in May 6 Greek elections* [03 May], http://www.ekathimerini.com/141278/article/ekathimerini/comment/profile-of-parties-running-in-may-6-greek-elections (accessed 8 December 2016).

Katz, R. and Mair, P. (1995) 'Changing Models of Party Organization and Party Democracy: The Emergence of the Cartel Party', *Party Politics*, 1(1): 5–28.

Ker-lindsay, J. (2007) 'The policies of Greece and Cyprus towards Turkey's EU accession' *Turkish Studies*, 8(1): 71–83.

Kerr, H. (1973) 'Changing attitudes through international participation: European Parliamentarians and integration', *International Organization*, 27(1): 45–83.

King, G., Keohane, R. O. and Verba, S. (1994) *Designing social inquiry: Scientific inference in qualitative research*, Princeton NJ: Princeton University Press.

Kirchheimer, O. (1966) 'The Transformation of West European Party Systems', in LaPalombara, J. and Weiner, M. (eds.) *Political Parties and Political Development*, Princeton, NJ: Princeton University Press, pp. 177–200.

Kitschelt, H. and McGann, A. J. (1995) *The radical right in Western Europe: A comparative analysis*, Ann Arbor: University of Michigan Press.

Kopecky, P. and Mudde, C. (2002) 'The two sides of Euroscepticism', *European Union Politics*, 3(3): 297–326.

Kriesi, H., Grande, E., Lachat, R., Dolezal, M., Bornschier, S. and Frey, R. (2006). 'Globalization and the Transformation of the National Political Space: Six European Countries Compared', *European Journal of Political Research*, 45(6): 921–957.

―――. (2008) *West European Politics in the Age of Globalization*, Cambridge: Cambridge University Press.

Krippendorff, K. (2004) *Content analysis: an introduction to its methodology*, Thousand Oaks, CA: Sage.

Kritzinger, S., Cavatorta, F. and Chari, R. (2004) 'Continuity and change in party positions towards Europe in Italian parties: An examination of parties' manifestos', *Journal of European Public Policy*, 11(6): 954–974.

Kroet, C. (2016) *Hungary's far-right Jobbik says leaving EU no longer on the agenda*, [3 June] http://www.politico.eu/article/hungarys-far-right-jobbik-leader-gabor-vonasays-leaving-eu-no-longer-on-the-agenda/ (accessed 1 September 2016).

Krouwel, A. (2003) 'Otto Kirchheimer and the catch-all party', *West European Politics*, 26(2): 23–40.

LAOS (2003) *Ιδεολογική Προγραμματική Πλατφόρμα*. Athens, LAOS.

———. (2004) *Ευρωεκλογές 2004 Ο ΛΑ.Ο.Σ δυνατός δυνατή Ελλάδα* (European Elections Manifesto).

———. (2005) *Διακήρυξη της 11ης Αυγούστου*. http://www.laos.gr/D-11.August.pdf (accessed 10 August 2008).

———. (2007) *Πλαίσιο Θέσεων* (National Elections Manifesto).

———. (2008) *Ψήφοι – Μαχαιριές στο Ευρωκοινοβούλιο: Τα ντοκουμέντα της ντροπής*, www.laos.gr (accessed on 10 August 2008).

———. (2009) *Ευρωεκλογές 2009* (European Elections Manifesto).

———. (2012) *Βασικές θέσεις και βασικές προγραμματικές κατευθύνσεις* (National Elections Manifesto).

La Russa, R. M. (2005) European Parliament Speech [27 September], http://www.europarl.europa.eu/.

Laakso, M. and Taagapera, R. (1979) 'Effective number of parties: A measure with application to West Europe', *Comparative Political Studies*, 12(1): 3–27.

Lang, C. (2001) European Parliament Speech [4 September], http://www.europarl.europa.eu/.

Le Pen, J-M. (1984) *Les Français d'abord Paris*, Carrère: Michel Lafon.

———. (2005a) *La lettre européenne de Jean Marie Le Pen August/September 2005 N 5*, http://www.europnat.com/lettreseuropeennes/jmlp5.pdf (accessed 4 August 2009).

———. (2005b) *La lettre européenne de Jean Marie Le Pen November 2005 N 7*, http://www.europnat.com/lettreseuropeennes/jmlp5.pdf (accessed 4 August 2009).

———. (2006) *La lettre européenne de Jean Marie Le Pen March 2006 N 8*, http://www.europnat.com/lettreseuropeennes/jmlp5.pdf (accessed 4 August 2009).

———. (2007) *European Parliament Speech* [9 May], http://www.europarl.europa.eu/.

———. (2014) *Marine Le Pen declaration prior to the 2014 EP elections published on the party's website*, www.fn-europeennes.fr/ (accessed 15 October 2017).

———. (2005) *European Parliament Speech* [12 May], http://www.europarl.europa.eu/.

Le Pen, M. (2009) Sauvons la France de l'arnaque européenne, http://www.marinelepen.com/images/stories/docs/tract_marine_20.pdf (accessed 3 August 2009).

———. (2016a) Franc*e's Marine Le Pen on Brexit: 'This Is the Beginning of the End of the European Union* [29 June], http://time.com/4386695/brexit-france-q-and-a-marine-le-pen-national-front/ (accessed 29 January 2016).

———. (2016b) *Marine Le Pen: la victoire de Trump marque «l'émergence d'un nouveau monde»* [13 November], http://www.lefigaro.fr/politique/le-scan/citations/2016/11/13/25002-20161113ARTFIG00062-marine-le-pen-espere-une-victoire-a-la-donald-trump-en-2017.php (accessed 29 January 2017).

———. (2017) Personal Twitter account [28 January] (accessed 29 January 2017).

League of Polish Families (2004) *My wybieramy Polskę!* (European Elections Manifesto).

———. (2005) *Skrót Programu Gospodarczego. Dla Niepodleglej Polski oraz Suwerennego Narodu Polskiego* (National Elections Manifesto).

————. (2007) *Dbamy o Polske, Dbamy o Polaków. Program 2007 Prawa I Sprawiedliwosci* (National Elections Manifesto).

Lee, M. (2000) *The beast reawakens: Fascism's resurgence from Hitler's spymasters to today's neo-Nazi groups and right-wing extremists*, New York: Routledge.

Lefevere, J., Tresch, A. and Walgrave, S. (2015) 'Introduction: Issue Ownership', *West European Politics*, 38:4, 755–760

Legg, K. R. and Roberts, J. M. (1997) *Modern Greece: A civilization on the periphery*, Boulder, CO: Westview Press.

Lindberg, L. N. and Scheingold, S. A. (1970) *Europe's would-be polity: Patterns of change in the European community*, Englewood Cliffs, NJ: Prentice Hall.

Lipset, S. M. and Rokkan, S. (1967) 'Cleavage structures, party systems, and voter alignments: An introduction', in Lipset, S. M. and Rokkan, S. (eds.) *Party systems and voter alignments: Cross-national perspectives*, London: Collier Macmillan, pp. 1–64.

Locatelli, G. and Martini, D. (1994) *Duce addio: la biografia di Gianfranco Fini*, Milano: Longanesi.

Lyrintzis, C. (2005) 'The Changing Party System: Stable Democracy, Contested "Modernisation"', *West European Politics*, 28(2): 242–259.

Lyris, A. (2014) *Προς την Ευρώπη των Εθνών* (Towards a Europe of Nations) published in the Golden Dawn's weekly printed newspaper 'Golden Dawn' [14 May], number 876, p. 18.

Mair, P. (2007) 'Political Opposition and the European Union', *Government and Opposition*, 42(1): 1–17.

March, L. (2008) *Contemporary Far Left Parties in Europe. From Marxism to the Mainstream?*, Berlin: Friedrich-Ebert-Stiftung, International Policy Analysis.

————. (2011) *Radical Left Parties in Contemporary Europe*, Abingdon: Routledge.

Marks, G. and Steenbergen, M. (2004) *European integration and political conflict*, Cambridge: Cambridge University Press.

Marks, G. and Wilson, C. J. (2000) 'The past in the present: A cleavage theory of party response to European integration', *British Journal of Political Science* 30(2): 433–459.

Marsiglia, S. (2005) *Fini: una storia near*, Roma: Malatempora.

Martin, D. (2010). [Member of Front National's political bureau] *Interview with the author* [18 February].

Martinez, J-C. (2006a) *European Parliament Speech* [18 January], http://www.europarl.europa.eu/

————. (2006b) *European Parliament Speech* [4 July], http://www.europarl.europa.eu/

————. (2006c) *European Parliament Speech* [5 September], http://www.europarl.europa.eu/

Mavrogordatos, G. T. (1984). 'The Greek party system: A case of 'limited but polarised pluralism?', *West European Politics* 7(4): 156–169.

Mayer, N. (1998) 'The French National Front', in Immerfall, S. and Betz, H. G. (eds.) *The new politics of the Right: Neo-Populist parties and movements in established democracies*, New York: St. Martin's Press, pp. 11–26.

————. (2002a) *Ces Français qui votent Le Pen*, Paris: Flammarion.

————. (2002b) 'Les hauts et les bas du vote Le Pen 2002', *Revue Française de Science Politique,* 52(5–6): 505–520.

————. (2007) 'Comment Nicolas Sarkozy a rétréci l'électorat Le Pen', *Revue Francaise de Science Politique,* 57(3–4): 429–445.

————. (2013a) 'From Jean-Marie to Marine Le Pen: Electoral Change on the Far Right', *Parliamentary Affairs,* 66(1): 160–178.

————. (2013b) *The de-demonisation of the Front National,* Policy Network, http://www.policy-network.net/pno_detail.aspx?ID=4358&title=The+de-demonisation+of+the+Front+National (accessed 20 January 2017).

————. (2015) *Le mythe de la dédiabolisation du FN,* La Vie des idées , 4 décembre 2015. ISSN : 2105–3030, http://www.laviedesidees.fr/Le-mythe-de-la-dediabolisation-du-FN.html (accessed 15 April 2017).

McCulloch, T. (2006) 'The Nouvelle Droite in the 1980s and 1990s: Ideology and entryism, the relationship with the Front National', *French Politics,* 4: 158–178.

Meguid, B. M. (2008) *Party competition between unequals: strategies and electoral fortunes in Western Europe,* Cambridge: Cambridge University Press.

Meyer, T. and Wagner, M. (2013) 'Mainstream or Niche? Vote-Seeking Incentives and the Programmatic Strategies of Political Parties', *Comparative Political Studies,* 46(10) 1246–1272.

Meyer, T. (2013) *Constraints on Party Policy Change,* Colchester: ECPR Press.

Millard, F. (2003) 'The parliamentary elections in Poland, September 2001', *Electoral Studies,* 22(2): 367–374.

Minkenberg, M. (2001) 'The Radical Right in Public Office: Agenda-Setting and Policy Effects', *West European Politics,* 24(4):1–21.

Mitsopoulos, M. and Pelagidis, T. (2011) *Understanding the Crisis in Greece: From Boom to Bust,* Basingstoke: Palgrave Macmillan.

Morini, M. (2007) 'Movimento Sociale Italiano - Alleanza Nazionale', in Bardi, L., Ignazi, P. and Massari, O. (eds.) *I partiti italiani: iscritti, dirigenti, eletti,* Milano, EGEA : Università Bocconi, pp. 149–197.

Mudde, C. (2000) *The ideology of the extreme right,* Manchester: Manchester University Press.

————. (2007) *Populist radical right parties in Europe,* Cambridge: Cambridge University Press.

————. (2010) 'The Populist Radical Right: A Pathological Normalcy', *West European Politics,* 33(6): 1167–1186.

————. (2011) *Sussex v. North Carolina The Comparative Study of Party-Based Euroscepticism,* SEI Working Paper No 121, EPERN Working Paper No. 23, Sussex European Institute.

————. (2014) 'Fighting the system? Populist radical right parties and party system change', *Party Politics,* 20(2): 217–226.

Muller, W. and Strom, K. (eds.) (1999) *Policy, office or votes? How political parties in Western Europe make hard decisions,* Cambridge: Cambridge University Press.

Muscardini, C. (2001) *European Parliament Speech,* [31 January], http://www.europarl.europa.eu/.

————. (2003) *European Parliament Speech* [2 July], http://www.europarl.europa.eu/.

————. (2005) *European Parliament Speech* [11 January], http://www.europarl.europa.eu/.

————. (2007a) *European Parliament Speech* [16 January], http://www.europarl.europa.eu/.

————. (2007b) *European Parliament Speech* [13 February], http://www.europarl.europa.eu/.

————. (2007c) *European Parliament Speech* [14 March], http://www.europarl.europa.eu/.

————. (2007d) *European Parliament Speech* [28 March], http://www.europarl.europa.eu/.

————. (2007f) *European Parliament Speech* [11 July], http://www.europarl.europa.eu/.

————. (2008) *European Parliament Speech* [19 February], http://www.europarl.europa.eu/.

————. (2009) [Alleanza Nazionale MEP] *Interview with the author* [18 November].

Mölzer, A. (2007) *The FPO and Europe*, http://www.andreas-moelzer.at/index.php?id=62 (accessed 10 August 2008).

Naftemporiki (2012) *Πρωτοβουλία της Βουλής για την κατάσταση στην ευρωζώνη, ζητεί ο Γ. Καρατζαφέρης* [16 February], http://www.naftemporiki.gr/story/393464/protoboulia-tis-boulis-gia-tin-katastasi-stin-eurozoni-zitei-o-g-karatzaferis (accessed 11 December 2016).

National Alliance (1995) *Pensiamo l'Italia. Il domani c'è già: Valori, idee e progetti per l'National Alliance*. Fiuggi Congress.

————. (1998) *Un progetto per l'Italia del Duemila*. Verona Congress.

————. (1999) *Elezioni Europee '99 Il programma politico: L'Unione Politica dell'Europa* (European Elections Manifesto).

————. (2000) *Carta dei Valori di National Alliance*, http://www.alleanzanazionale.it/ (accessed on 5 March 2008).

————. (2001) *Libero, forte, giusto: Il governo che vogliamo*. 2nd Programmatic Conference, Naples.

————. (2002) *Vince la Patria, nasce l'Europa*. 2nd National Congress, Bologna.

————. (2004) *Elezioni del Parlamento Europeo 12/13 Giugno 2004 Programma*. (European Elections Manifesto).

————. (2006a) *Ripensare il centrodestra nella prospettiva europea* [18 July], http://www.alleanzanazionale.it/ (accessed 5 March 2008).

————. (2006b) *Le Proposte di AN (Onorevole Maurizio Gasparri)*. 3rd Programmatic Conference.

————. (2008a) *Alleanza per l'Italia, la sfida del future* http://www.alleanzanazionale.it/ (accessed on 5 March 2008).

————. (2008b). *La sicurezza in Italia: I fatti del Centrodestra, i danni del Centrosinistra*.

————. (2009). *Dalla Destra al Popolo della Libertà: Il partito degli Italiani*. Mozione coongressuale, 3rd National Congress, Rome.

National Front (2002a) *Programme du Front National pour les élections législatives de 2002* (National Elections Manifesto).

———. (2002b) *La France: L'universalité, la mémoire, le sacré*, http://frontnational. com/questions/index.php?title=Europe (accessed 12 January 2008).

———. (2004) *Programme du Front National* (European Elections Manifesto).

———. (2007) *Programme de Gouvernement de Jean-Marie Le Pen* (National Elections Manifesto).

———. (2008) *Europe: Sommaire*, http://frontnational.com/questions/index. php?title=Europe (accessed 12 October 2008).

———. (2009) *Programme Europe du Front National: Leur Europe n'est pas la nôtre! Voilà l'Europe que nous voulons* (European Elections Manifesto).

———. (2012a) *Notre projet programme politique du front national* (National Elections Manifesto).

———. (2012b) *Mon project pour la France et les français. Marine Le Pen, la voix du people, l'esprit de la France* (National Elections Manifesto).

———. (2017) *144 Engagements presidentiels, Marine 2017* (National Elections Manifesto).

Neumann, S. (1956) 'Toward a Comparative Study of Political Parties', in S. Neumann (ed.), *Modern Political Parties: Approaches to Comparative Politics,* Chicago: University of Chicago Press.

Newell, J. (2000) 'Italy: The extreme right comes in from the cold', *Parliamentary Affairs,* 53(3): 469–485.

Newell, J. and Bull, M. (2002) 'Italian politics after the 2001 General Election: Plus ça change, plus c'est la même chose?', *Parliamentary Affairs,* 55(4): 626–642.

Newsbomb (2015) *Δεν κατεβαίνει στις εκλογές ο ΛΑΟΣ του Καρατζαφέρη* [3 September], http://www.newsbomb.gr/politikh/news/story/620737/den-katevainei-stis-ekloges-o-laos-toy-karatzaferi (accessed 8 December 2016).

Norris, P. (2005) *Radical right: Voters and parties in the electoral market.* Cambridge: Cambridge University Press.

Northern League (1999) *Elezioni Europee 1999 Per una Padania libera in una libera Europa* (European Elections Manifesto).

———. (2004) *Programma per le elezioni europee 2004* (European Elections Manifesto).

———. (2006) *Errori ed orrori del programma Prodi e dell'Unione*, http://www.leg-anord.org/specialeelezioni/politiche/unione_critica.pdf (accessed 10 August 2008).

———. (2013) *Programma elezioni politiche* (National Elections Manifesto).

Novinite (2016) *Bulgaria Nationalist Leader Calls for EU In/Out Referendum after Brexit*[25 June], http://www.novinite.com/articles/175127/Bulgaria+Nationalist+Leader+Calls+for+%3Cb%3EEU%3C/b%3E+In+Out+%3Cb%3EReferendum%3C/b%3E+after+%3Cb%3EBrexit%3C/b%3E (accessed 15 August 2016).

Panebianco, A. (1988) *Political parties: Organization and power*, Cambridge: Cambridge University Press.

Papadopoulos, V. (2009) *Μοναδικός νικητής* A1 - LAOS official newspaper. Athens: LAOS.

Pappas, T. (2003) 'The Transformation of the Greek Party System Since 1951', *West European Politics,* 26(2): 90–114.

Pasquino, G. (2008) 'The 2008 Italian national elections: Berlusconi's third victory', *South European Society and Politics*, 13(3): 345–362.

Pedahzur, A. and Brichta, A. (2002) 'The institutionalization of extreme right-wing charismatic parties: A paradox?', *Party Politics*, 8(1): 31–49.

Pelinka, A. (2004) 'Austrian Euroscepticism: The shift from the left to the right' in Harmsen, R. and Spiering, M. (eds.) *Euroscepticism: Party Politics, National Identity and European Integration,* Amsterdam: Rodopi, pp. 207–224.

Pirro, A. (2014) 'Digging into the breeding ground: insights into the electoral performance of populist radical right parties in Central and Eastern Europe', *East European Politics*, 30(2): 246–270.

Poguntke, T. and Webb, P. (2005) *The Presidentialization of Politics: A Comparative Study of Modern Democracies,* Oxford: Oxford University Press.

Polatides, E. (2009) [LAOS MP] Interview with the author [8 April].

Poli Bortone, A. (1999) *European Parliament Speech* [16 November], http://www.europarl.europa.eu/.

———. (2005) *European Parliament Speech* [23 February], http://www.europarl.europa.eu/.

Popper, K. R. (1968) *The logic of scientific discovery*, London: Hutchinson.

Psarras, D. (2001) *Το ΠΑΣΟΚ στην κυβέρνηση και ο ΛΑΟΣ στην εξουσία* [13 November], http://www.enet.gr/?i=news.el.article&id=325464 (accessed 8 December 2016).

Public Issue (2007) *Greek public opinion on the heroic 'no' of 28 October 1940* [22–24 October], http://www.publicissue.gr/158/28oct/ (accessed 2 February 2017).

———. (2008) *Greek public opinion on foreign policy* [25–27 February], http://www.publicissue.gr/122/foreign-affairs/ (accessed 2 February 2017).

———. (2009a) *EP Elections public opinion survey* [18 June], http://www.publicissue.gr/1171/euro-index-2009-2/#3 (accessed 15 August 2015).

———. (2009b) *Opinion poll*, http://www.publicissue.gr/category/pi/analysis/polls/ (accessed 15 August 2015).

Quaglia, L. (2005) 'The right and Europe in Italy: An ambivalent relationship', *South European Society and Politics,* 10(2): 281–295.

Ray, L. (1999) 'Measuring party orientations towards European integration: Results from an expert survey', *European Journal of Political Research,* 36(6): 283–306.

Renwick, A., Hanretty, C. and Hine, D. (2009) 'Partisan self-interest and electoral reform: The new Italian electoral law of 2005', *Electoral Studies*, 28(3): 437–447.

Reveau, J. P. (2010) [Member of Front National's political bureau] *Interview with the author* [5 February].

Revolutionary Communist League (2006) *Tous ensemble, nous pouvons changer le monde* (Ligue Communiste Révolutionnaire), http://www.lcr-rouge.org/IMG/pdf/manifeste_32p.pdf (accessed 8 April 2010).

Riker, W. (1982) *Liberalism against populism: A confrontation between the theory of democracy and the theory of social choice*, Long Grove, IL: Waveland Press.

Risse-Kappen, T. (1996) 'Exploring the Nature of the Beast: International Relations Theory and Comparative Policy Analysis Meet the European Union', *JCMS: Journal of Common Market Studies*, 34: 53–80.

Rontoulis, A. (2009) [LAOS MP] Interview with the author [8 April].

Roux, C. and Verzichelli, L. (2010) 'Italy: Still a pro-European, but not fully Europe-anised elite?', *South European Society and Politics*, 15(1): 11–33.

Ruzza, C. and Fella, S. (2009) *Reinventing the Italian right: Territorial politics, populism and "post-fascism"*, New York: Routledge.

Rydgren, J. (2007) 'The Sociology of the radical right', *Annual Review of Sociology*, (33): 241–262.

Salagnac, C. (2010) [Member of Front National's political bureau] Interview with the author [5 February].

Sartori, G. (2005) *Parties and Party Systems: A Framework for Analysis*, Colchester: ECPR Press.

Scarrow, S. (1996) 'Politicians against parties: Anti-party arguments as weapons for change in Germany', *European Journal of Political Research*, 29(3): 297–317.

Schmitt, H., Bartolini, S., van der Brug, W., van der Eijk, C., Franklin, M., Fuchs, D., Toka, G., Marsh, M. and Thomassen, J. (2009) *European Election Study 2004* (2nd edition), GESIS Data Archive, Cologne. ZA4566 Data file Version 2.0.0, doi:10.4232/1.10086

Schumpeter, Joseph A. (1950) *Capitalism, Socialism, and Democracy*, New York: Harper & Row. 3rd edition.

Schénardi, L. (2009) [Front National former MEP] Interview with the author [29 October].

Seferiades, S. (1986) 'Polarization and Nonproportionality: The Greek Party System in the Postwar Era', *Comparative Politics*, 19(1): 69–93.

Seliger, M. (1976) *Ideology and politics*, London: Allen & Unwin.

Shields, J. (2007) *The Extreme Right in France: From Pétain to Le Pen*, Abingdon: Routledge.

———. (2013) 'Marine Le Pen and the 'New' FN: A change of style or of substance? ' *Parliamentary affairs*, 66(1): 179–196.

Sitter, N. (2001) 'The politics of opposition and European integration in Scandinavia: Is Euro-scepticism a Government - Opposition dynamic?', *West European Politics*, 24(4): 22–39.

Slater, D. and Ziblatt, D. (2013) 'The Enduring Indispensability of the Controlled Comparison', *Comparative Political Studies*, 46(10): 1301–1327.

Slothus, R. and De Vreese, C. (2010) 'Political Parties, Motivated Reasoning, and Issue Framing Effects', *The Journal of Politics*, 72(3): 630–645.

Smith, A. D. (1991) *National Identity*, London: Penguin.

Spiegel (2014) *Interview with Marine Le Pen: 'I Don't Want this European Soviet Union* [3 June], http://www.spiegel.de/international/europe/interview-with-french-front-national-leader-marine-le-pen-a-972925.html (accessed 27 March 2017).

Spiering, M. (2004) 'British Euroscepticism. Euroscepticism: Party politics, national identity and European integration', in Harmsen, R. and Spiering, M. (eds.) *Euroscepticism: Party Politics, National Identity and European Integration*, Amsterdam: Rodopi, pp. 127–149.

Spruce, D. (2007) 'Empire and counter empire in the Italian far right: Conflicting nationalisms and the split between the Lega Nord and Alleanza Nazionale on immigration' *Theory, Culture and Society*, 24(5): 99–126.

Startin, N. (2008) 'The French rejection of the 2005 EU Constitution in a global context: A public opinion perspective', in Maclean, M. and Szarka, J. (eds.) *France on the world stage: Nation state strategies in the global era,* Basingstoke: Palgrave Macmillan, pp. 91–110.

———. (2010) 'Where to for the Radical Right in the European Parliament? The Rise and Fall of Transnational Political Cooperation', *Perspectives on European Politics and Society,* 11(4): 429–449.

Stemler, S. (2001) 'An overview of content analysis', *Practical Assessment, Research & Evaluation,* 7(17).

Stockemer, D. (2015) 'Introduction to the special issue: Explaining the spike in electoral support for the Front National in France', *French Politics,* 13(4): 319–323.

Stockemer, D. and Amengay, A. (2015) 'The voters of the FN under Jean-Marie Le Pen and Marine Le Pen: Continuity or change?', *French Politics,* 13(4): 370–390.

Strom, K. (1990) 'A behavioural theory of competitive political parties', *American Journal of Political Science,* 34(2): 565–598.

Swyngedouw, M. and Ivaldi, G. (2001) 'The extreme right utopia in Belgium and France: The ideology of the Flemish Vlaams Blok and the French front national', *West European Politics,* 24(3): 1–22.

Szczerbiak, A. and P. Taggart (2000) *Opposing Europe: Party Systems and Opposition to the Union, the Euro and Europeanisation,* SEI Working Paper No. 36 Opposing Europe Research Network Working Paper No. 1, Sussex European Institute.

———. (2003) *Theorising Party-Based Euroscepticism: Problems of Definition, Measurement and Causality,* SEI Working Paper No. 69 EPRN Working Paper No. 12, Sussex European Institute.

———. (eds.) (2008a) *Opposing Europe? The comparative party politics of Euroscepticism Volume 1 Case studies and country surveys,* Oxford: Oxford University Press.

———. (eds.) (2008b) *Opposing Europe? The comparative party politics of Euroscepticism Volume 2 Comparative and theoretical perspectives,* Oxford: Oxford University Press.

———. (2008c) 'Introduction: Researching Euroscepticism in European party systems: A comparative and theoretical agenda', in Szczerbiak, A, and Taggart, P. (eds.) *Opposing Europe? The comparative party politics of Euroscepticism Volume 2 Comparative and theoretical perspectives,* Oxford: Oxford University Press, pp. 1–27.

Sørensen, C. (2008) *Love Me, Love Me Not: A Typology of Public Euroscepticism,* SEI Working Paper No. 101, EPERN Working Paper No. 19, Sussex European Institute.

Ta Nea (2002) *Καλοί χριστιανοί οι ψηφοφόροι του Καρατζαφέρη* [15 October], http://www.tanea.gr/news/greece/article/4252793/?iid=2 (accessed 9 December 2016).

Taggart, P. (1998) 'A Touchstone of dissent: Euroscepticism in contemporary Western European party systems', *European Journal of Political Research,* 33(3): 363–388.

———. (2000) *Populism,* Philadelphia: Open University Press.

Taggart, P. and Szczerbiak, A. (2001) *Parties, positions and Europe: Euroscepticism in the EU candidate states of Central and Eastern Europe*, SEI Working Paper No. 46, Opposing Europe Research Network Working Paper No. 2, Sussex European Institute.

―――. (2004) 'Contemporary Euroscepticism in the party systems of the European Union candidate states of Central and Eastern Europe', *European Journal of Political Research*, 43: 1–27.

―――. (2013) 'Coming in from the cold? Euroscepticism and government participation and party positions on Europe', *JCMS: Journal of Common Market Studies*, 51(1): 17–37.

Tarchi, M. (2003) 'The political culture of Alleanza Nazionale: An analysis of the party's programmatic documents (1995–2002)', *Journal of Modern Italian Studies*, 8(2): 135–181.

Tatarella, S. (2008) *European Parliament Speech* [16 December], http://www.europarl.europa.eu/.

Terzis, G. (2016) *Εθνική Ενότητα, το νέο κόμμα Καρατζαφέρη, Μπαλτάκου* [9 April], http://www.kathimerini.gr/856007/article/epikairothta/politikh/e8nikh-enothta-to-neo-komma-karatzaferh-mpaltakoy (accessed 8 December 2016).

The Comparative Study of Electoral Systems (www.cses.org). CSES MODULE 2 (2001–2006) FULL RELEASE [dataset]. 15 December 2015 version. doi:10.7804/cses.module2.2015-12-15.

The Comparative Study of Electoral Systems (www.cses.org). CSES MODULE 3 (2006–2011) FULL RELEASE [dataset]. 15 December 2015 version. doi:10.7804/cses.module3.2015-12-15.

The Comparative Study of Electoral Systems (www.cses.org). CSES MODULE 4 (2011–2016) THIRD ADVANCE RELEASE [dataset]. 22 June 2016 version. doi:10.7804/cses.module4.2016-06-22.

The Guardian (2017) *Brexit is a failure and a tragedy, says EC chief Juncker* [24 March], https://www.theguardian.com/politics/2017/mar/24/brexit-a-failure-and-a-tragedy-says-ec-chief-jean-claude-juncker (accessed 8 April 2017).

Treschel, A. and Mair, P. (2009) *When parties (also) position themselves: An introduction to the EU profiler*, EUI Working Papers, Robert Schuman Centre for Advanced Studies, European Union Democracy Observatory 65.

Triandafyllidou, A., Calloni, M. and Mikrakis, A. (1997) 'New Greek Nationalism', *Sociological Research Online*, 2(1) www.socresonline.org.uk/2/1/7.html

Tricolour Flame (2006) *Programma Politico* (National Elections Manifesto).

―――. (2013) *Programma Politico* (National Elections Manifesto).

Tsatsanis, E. and Teperoglou, E. (2016) 'Realignment under Stress: The July 2015 Referendum and the September Parliamentary Election in Greece', *South European Society and Politics*, 21(4): 427–450.

Tsatsis, T. (2006) *Χέρι - χέρι με τον Καρατζαφέρη*, Ελευθεροτυπία [22 June].

Tsiras, S. (2012) *Εθνος και ΛΑΟΣ: Νέα άκρα δεξιά και λαϊκισμός*, Thessaloniki: Epikendro.

Tsoukalis, L. (2014) *The Unhappy State of the Union: Europe needs a new grand bargain*, London: Policy Network.

Usherwood, S. (2008) 'The dilemmas of a single-issue party: The UK Independence Party', *Representation*, 44 (3): 255–264.

Usherwood, S. and Startin, N. (2013) 'Euroscepticism as a Persistent Phenomenon', *JCMS: Journal of Common Market Studies*, 57(1): 1–16.

Van de Wardt, M., De Vries, C. and Hobolt, S. (2014) 'Exploiting the Cracks: Wedge Issues in Multiparty Competition', *The Journal of Politics*, 76(4): 986–999.

Van der Brug, W., Fennema, M., De Lange, S. and I. Baller, (2013 'Radical right parties: their voters and their electoral competitors', in Rydgren, J. (ed.) *Class politics and the radical right*, London: Routledge, pp. 52–74.

Vasilopoulou, S. (2011) 'European Integration and the Radical Right: Three Patterns of Opposition', *Government and Opposition*, 46(2): 223–244.

———. (2013) 'Continuity and change in the study of Euroscepticism: plus ça change?', *JCMS: Journal of Common Market Studies*, 51(1): 153–168.

———. (2018) 'The Radical Right and Euroscepticism', in Rydgren, J. (ed.) *The Oxford Handbook of the Radical Right*, New York: Oxford University Press.

Vasilopoulou, S. and Halikiopoulou, D. (2013) 'In the Shadow of Grexit: The Greek Election of 11 June 2012', *South European Society and Politics*, 18(4): 523–542.

———. (2015) *The Golden Dawn's 'nationalist solution': Explaining the rise of the far right in Greece*, New York: Palgrave Macmillan.

Vasilopoulou, S, Halikiopoulou, D. and Exadaktylos, T. (2014) 'Greece in crisis: austerity, populism and the politics of blame', *JCMS: Journal of Common Market Studies*, 52(2): 388–402.

Vernardakis, C. (2007) 'Ευρωπαϊσμός και ευρωσκεπτικισμός στην Ελλάδα: Ιδεολογικές διαστάσεις και πολιτικές εκπροσωπήσεις', in Vernardakis, C. (ed.) *Η κοινή γνώμη στην Ελλάδα 2005–2006: Πολιτικές και Κοινωνικές Εκπροσωπήσεις, Ευρωσκεπτικισμός, MKO*, Athens: Savvalas, Institute VPRC.

Verney, S. (2011) 'An Exceptional Case? Party and Popular Euroscepticism in Greece, 1959–2009', *South European Society and Politics*, 16(1): 51–79.

Vinocur, N. (2017) '*Marine Le Pen makes globalization the enemy*', available at http://www.politico.eu/article/marine-le-pen-globalization-campaign-launch-french-politics-news-lyon-islam/ (accessed 4 April 2017).

Voridis, M. (2009) [General Secretary of LAOS's Parliamentary Team and LAOS MP] *Interview with the author* [10 April].

Wagner, M. (2012) 'When do parties emphasise extreme positions? How strategic incentives for policy differentiation influence issue importance', *European Journal of Political Research*, 51: 64–88.

Webb, P. and Bale, T. (2014) 'Why Do Tories Defect to UKIP? Conservative Party Members and the Temptations of the Populist Radical Right', *Political Studies*, 62(4): 961–970.

Whitefield, S. and Rohrschneider, R. (2015) 'The Salience of European Integration to Party Competition: Western and Eastern Europe Compared', *East European Politics and Societies and Cultures*, 29(1): 12–39.

Wolinetz, S. (2002) 'Beyond the Catch-all Party: Approaches to the Study of Parties and Party Organization', in Gunther, R., Montero, J. R. and Linz, J. J. (eds.) *Political Parties: Old Concepts and New Challenges*, Oxford: Oxford University Press, pp. 136–165.

Workers' Struggle (2004) *Projet de Lutte ouvrière pour les élections européennes de juin 2004* (Lutte Ouvrière), http://discours.vie-publique.fr/notices/043001756.html (accessed 8 April 2010).

Zaslove, A. (2004) 'The Dark Side of European Politics: Unmasking the Radical Right', *Journal of European Integration*, 26(1): 61–81.

Zhirkov, K. (2014) 'Nativist but not alienated: A comparative perspective on the radical right vote in Western Europe', *Party Politics* 20(2): 286–296.

Zimmer, O. (2003) 'Boundary mechanisms and symbolic resources: Towards a process-oriented approach to national identity', *Nations and Nationalism*, 9(2): 173–193.

Index

Figures and tables noted with *italics*.

www.ingramcontent.com/pod-product-compliance
Lightning Source LLC
Chambersburg PA
CBHW021817270326
41932CB00007B/219